DEBT CLEANSE

STOP PAYING Settlement Wallet
identify deficiencies STOP PAYING
DISPUTE DEBTS Welcome Lawsuits
stop paying PATIENCE settlement wallet
Dispute Debts IGNORE CREDITORS
welcome lawsuits ignore creditors STOP PAYING
Identify Deficiencies assets
settlement wallet PROTECT ASSETS protect
patience DISPUTE DEBTS settlement wallet
PROTECT ASSETS patience STOP PAYING
Patience identify deficiencies
welcome
Ignore Creditors lawsuits ignore creditors

HOW TO SETTLE YOUR UNAFFORDABLE DEBTS FOR PENNIES ON THE DOLLAR

(AND NOT PAY SOME AT ALL)

JORGE P. NEWBERY

DEBT CLEANSE

*How to Settle Your Unaffordable Debts for
Pennies on the Dollar (And Not Pay Some at All)*

BY JORGE P. NEWBERY

Community
Books

ISBN 978-1-61961-322-5

CONTENTS

PROLOGUE

Behind on your debts?

Getting relentless collection calls and notices?

Being sued by creditors?

Bank account levied or wages garnished?

Working two jobs or foregoing basic needs in order to pay debts?

Constantly worrying that you are one car repair, medical need, or job cutback from being unable to keep up with your debts?

Staying in a negative relationship only because you don't believe you can afford your debts by yourself?

If any of these apply to you, you are not alone. You are one of the majority of Americans with unaffordable debts:

- 4 million American workers whose wages are being garnished to pay delinquent consumer debts.[1]
- 8 million Americans who use payday loans to pay ordinary living expenses.[2]
- 10 million American families who owe more on their mortgages than their homes are worth.[3]
- 16 million Americans who owe more than their vehicles are worth.[4]
- 22 million Americans with student loans who are not making payments.[5]
- 43 million Americans with unpaid medical bills.[6]
- 55 million Americans with credit cards who only make the minimum payments.[7]
- 77 million Americans with collection accounts.[8]

1   Arnold, C. "Millions of Americans' Wages Seized Over Credit Card and Medical Debt. NPR, http://www.npr.org/2014/09/15/347957729/when-consumer-debts-go-unpaid-paychecks-can-take-a-big-hit (September 15, 2014)

2   "Payday Lending in America: Who Borrows, Where They Borrow, and Why" The Pew Charitable Trusts, http://www.pewtrusts.org/~/media/legacy/uploadedfiles/pcs_assets/2012/PewPaydayLendingReportpdf.pdf

3   Hopkins, C., "The Nation's Most Affordable Homes Also the Most Likely to be Underwater", Zillow Blog, http://www.zillow.com/blog/q1-2014-negative-equity-report-152403/ (May 19, 2014).

4   "Equifax Reports Auto Loan Growth Continues, Subprime Bubble Not Occurring", Equifax National Consumer Trends Report, http://investor.equifax.com/releasedetail.cfm?ReleaseID=874692 (October 6, 2014) and Apicella, R. and Halloran, G., "The Rising Repossession Tide" Benchmark Consulting International, http://www.benchmarkinternational.com/Articles/TheRisingRepossessionTide.pdf (April 2008).

5   Druden, T. "The Fed's Startling Student Debt Numbers That Every Young Person Should See", Zero Hedge, http://www.zerohedge.com/news/2015-03-30/feds-startling-student-numbers-every-young-person-should-see

6   Boak, O., "Nearly 43 Million Americans Have Unpaid Medical Bills" The Associated Press, http://www.dailyfinance.com/2014/12/11/cfpb-us-medical-debt/ (December 11, 2014).

7   "Report on the Economic Well-Being of U.S. Households in 2013", The Federal Reserve, http://www.federalreserve.gov/econresdata/2013-report-economic-well-being-us-households-201407.pdf

8   Marte, J. "A Third of Consumers With Credit Files Had Debts in Collections Last Year", The Washington Post, http://www.washingtonpost.com/blogs/wonkblog/wp/2014/07/29/a-third-of-consumers-had-debts-in-collections-last-year/ (July 29, 2014).

There are more Americans than ever bloated with debt and America's economy cannot fully recover until this glut of debt is cleansed. We are not talking a spare tire around the tummy, but a whole set of tires weighing us down. This burden is one I know from my own experience. I also know how difficult it can be to find helpful advice and resources when you're already underwater in your debt.

Before I started writing Debt Cleanse, I researched several "how to get out of debt" books. Although many preach budgeting and teach their readers about compound interest and how to pay off debt faster, there is little practical information about what to do if you are already in over your head with debt. Telling someone who is already overburdened with debt to be mindful of compound interest is the equivalent of telling a lung cancer patient to stop smoking. It might have been good advice at some point, but it's a bit late for that now. The same goes for teaching budgeting to a family that is buried by their unaffordable mortgage, with a car threatened with repo, and payday loan payments overdrawing their bank account. The struggling family needs a viable solution to get them out of a jam, and that's what I am here to share.

Don't worry. There won't be any condescending lectures about what you should have done differently years ago. Instead, I will take you step-by-step through the process of settling your debts for much less than you owe (or make them go away entirely). Better still, you can do most or all of this on your own. If you do need help, stay away from debt settlement companies and nonprofit credit counseling agencies. Both of them often act as agents of the creditors as much as agents of debtors. Instead, if needed, I will also show you how to carefully select an attorney who can really help. In some cases, you can get your legal fees paid by the creditor and, if your circumstances are just right, get the creditor to forgive your debt and maybe even pay you a settlement.

Debt Cleanse is not an easy process, nor is it a quick one. In fact, it may take years to wipe away your debt. Your time and effort will be worth it, though. Imagine your life without debt.

Debt Cleanse is…

Choosing yourself over creditors

Living a fulfilling life, not just paying bills

Spending time with family and friends

Replacing worry and stress with hope and happiness

Leading a life in which dreams are not financed

INTRODUCTION

Like a bad hangover that will not go away, America is still debt-drunk eight years after the financial crisis began. 60% of the 38 million Americans with student loans are not making payments,[9] and 53% of the 105 million Americans with credit cards only make the minimum payments.[10] 43% of Americans spend more than they make,[11] and 76% live paycheck to paycheck.[12] 50% of women earning around $100,000 fear that they are going to lose everything and end up as bag ladies.[13] 60% of women report that their greatest

9   http://www.zerohedge.com/news/2015-03-30/
    feds-startling-student-numbers-every-young-person-should-see

10 "Report on the Economic Well-Being of U.S. Households in 2013", The Federal Reserve, http://
    www.federalreserve.gov/econresdata/2013-report-economic-well-being-us-households-201407.
    pdf

11 Khan, K. "The Basics: How Does Your Debt Compare?" MSN Money, (2010)

12 "76% of Americans are living paycheck-to-paycheck" CNN Money www.money.cnn.com (June 24,
    2013).

13 The Female Affect, http://www.thefemaleaffect.com/consulting-services/ citing Employee
    Benefit Research Institute.

financial priority is "just getting by" or paying off debt.[14] The median liquid wealth for Latino families is $340 and for African American families it is $200,[15] less than a week's worth of groceries for many families. The U.S. National Debt of $18,265,538,166,155 equates to $56,891 each for every American man, woman and child, and $154,298 for every taxpayer.[16] Debt intoxication is a silent addiction killing America. How do we sober up?

Debt Cleanse is my solution to this staggering challenge facing America. It is a series of strategies for families who cannot afford their debts to simply stop paying, settle their debts at steep discounts, or not pay them at all, and go on to live debt-free lives. Debt Cleanse can be utilized for mortgages, car loans, student loans, credit cards, business loans, medical bills, equipment loans and other debts—even payday loans!

Debt is a reality I have known all too well. An entrepreneur to the core, I have been running my own businesses since I was a kid. I became a paperboy when I was seven years old and started my first business at 11. I then dropped out of high school at 16, too eager to learn in the real world to stay in a classroom. I built a record company, raced bicycles alongside some of the best in the world, and embarked on a real estate crusade to fix the unfixable. I took on our country's most troubled buildings and transformed them into assets to benefit residents and communities.

Despite the financial success that came as my real estate empire

14   "Scary Stats" citing 11th Annual TransAmerica Retirement 2010 Survey, by TransAmerica Center for Retirement Studies

15   Figueroa, A. "5 Alarming Facts About the Racial Wealth Gap" AlterNet, www.alternet.org (May 23, 2014)

16   http://www.usdebtclock.org/

grew, I eschewed any trappings of luxury, instead living a Spartan lifestyle. The majority of my meals emerged from a Crockpot into which brown rice and beans were mixed with whatever vegetables were on sale that week. I took pride in driving any car to 200,000 miles before casting it away. I even clipped coupons, recognizing that the dollar you save is more important than the dollar you earn (after all, the earned dollar is taxed). I lived with my parents until I was 29, though this would not be considered uncommon in my father's homeland of Argentina. Further, my parents seemed to enjoy having one of their five children stay in the nest so long. It was a sparse existence to be sure, but my thrifty lifestyle maximized the dollars I had available to play with in my real-life game of Monopoly.

Between 1992 and 2004, I amassed over 4,000 apartment units across the United States, paid for by the cash I had earned and saved, resulting in a net worth in the tens of millions. I repeatedly took risks and worked tirelessly to turn my visions into reality. But, I took one risk too many.

One natural disaster erased everything. An ice storm devastated my largest holding, the 1,100-unit Woodland Meadows apartment complex in Columbus, Ohio. The aftermath of the storm triggered an implausible series of events which plunged me into a battle with the elite, those much more powerful than me. In my struggle to survive, I was maligned, publicly shamed, and financially gutted: I lost everything and emerged over $26 million in debt.

I was too proud to file bankruptcy. Instead I simply did not pay the debts, whether it was $5,600,000 to KeyBank or $200 to Sears. Creditors began to call me incessantly, mail letters, and negatively report to credit bureaus. The strain made me grind my teeth at night. However, what I found time and time again was that after I survived each onslaught, the original creditors would write off the debts and often sell to debt buyers, typically at huge discounts. Collection activity, like a migraine, would come and go as the debts were sold again and again for progressively lower and lower amounts.

I learned what to expect and developed strategies to withstand the offenses. I discovered that proactive planning, patience and, when necessary, offensive attacks could often compromise creditors' positions. As a result, over time, I could settle many of the debts for pennies on the dollar, or simply not pay some at all.

For a minority of debts, the creditors would sue to try to obtain a judgment. In these cases, I found that creditors' attorneys were often "foreclosure mills" or "collection mills" frequently handling thousands of cases. As a result, paralegals often prepared filings that were inaccurate or missing key documents. In many cases, debt buyers receive incomplete files from the banks in the first place. I realized that if I could identify and exploit deficiencies, creditors would typically settle for a fraction of the amount owed in order to spare the expense and risk of continued litigation.

In an extreme example, I fought a creditor all the way to the Missouri Court of Appeals, which ultimately sided with me. In a unanimous ruling, the judges wrote, "We sympathetically recognize, of course, that the potential financial consequences to Vestin [the creditor] probably range from substantial to disastrous." The court ruling went on to state "the entire debt was inadvertently extinguished"[17] by sloppy legal work. The debt was over $5,800,000.

---

17   *Vestin Realty Mortgage, Inc v. Pickwick Partners*, 279 SW 3d 536, 542 (MO 2009).

I wanted to help others facing overwhelming debt and put my newfound expertise to positive use. In 2008, I founded American Homeowner Preservation, a debt buyer that purchases pools of non-paying mortgages from banks at huge discounts. AHP often buys "litigation loans," in which families fighting foreclosure are in court trying to save their homes. Once acquired, AHP utilizes strategies based on my challenges as a debtor and offers sustainable solutions to borrowers so they can keep their homes with reduced payments and discounted principal balances. Since its inception, AHP has helped hundreds of families keep their homes, eliminating over $64 million in negative equity and reducing borrowers' payments by more than $3 million annually.

All the challenges I have bled through, my destroyed finances, wrecked credit, and ground down teeth, will have been worthwhile. I had to go through all that to write this book. My mistakes, my failures, my reckoning can all be put to good use. I can share what I learned with others in a time of turmoil in America.

Debt Cleanse is not intended to show you how to go out, buy stuff, and then not pay. Instead, I want to show you how to rid yourself of the unaffordable debts you have today and go on to live fulfilling debt-free lives forever more, never again taking on debt. Struggling families across America can collectively utilize Debt Cleanse strategies to clear their debts so that they can live satisfying lives without constant worry, working two jobs, or foregoing basic needs in order to pay creditors. The solution to unaffordable debt is not government handouts, nonprofit counseling programs, bailouts, subsidies, or even protests.

The answer is to simply not pay.

CHAPTER 1

CREDITORS & CHICKENS

"This isn't just a problem for the people caught up in rising debts. It's a potential problem for everyone. An economy built on borrowed money is an economy built on borrowed time."

– GEORGE OSBORNE, BRITISH POLITICIAN

There are 17 billion chickens in the world, 7 billion humans and 1,826 billionaires.[18] The 85 richest people in the world have as much wealth as the poorest 3.5 billion people.[19] 400 American billionaires have as much wealth as the entire African American

---

18 Dolan, K., "Inside the 2015 Forbes Billionaires List: Facts and Figures", Forbes, http://www.forbes.com/sites/kerryadolan/2015/03/02/inside-the-2015-forbes-billionaires-list-facts-and-figures/ (March, 2, 2015), citing "The World's Billionaires" Forbes, http://www.forbes.com/billionaires/list/.

19 Shin, L., "The 85 Richest People in the World Have as Much Wealth as the 3.5 Billion Poorest, Forbes, http://www.forbes.com/sites/laurashin/2014/01/23/the-85-richest-people-in-the-world-have-as-much-wealth-as-the-3-5-billion-poorest/ (January 23, 2014).

population of the United States, 41 Million people.[20] The average net worth of America's 400 richest rose by $800 million in 2013,[21] while the median net worth of African American families sunk to $4,955,[22] poorer than the average household in India. At the same time, the median net worth for single African American women dropped to $5,[23] less than the cost of a Big Mac with a small order of fries. Half the collective wealth of African American families was stripped away during the Great Recession.[24] Where did all this money go? To the elite. Since 2009, 95% of U.S. economic gains have gone to the richest 1%,[25] who control more wealth than the bottom 99%. We need to stop being chickens.

What do I mean by that? Chickens allow humans to take all of their lifelong output, their eggs, and eventually their bodies for meat. Humans are the chickens' creditors: we give them food and a place to stay and, in return, they give us eggs and McNuggets. Chickens outnumber humans more than 2 to 1, so they could turn on us, but

20 Collins, C., "Wealth of Forbes 400 Billionaires Equals Wealth of All 41 Million African-Americans", Huffington Post, http://www.huffingtonpost.com/chuck-collins/wealth-of-forbes-400-bill_b_4617743.html (January 21, 2014) citing, Lord, B., "Dr. King's Nightmare The Wealth Possessed by Our Nation's 400 Richest Billionaires is Equal to the Collective Net Worth of All African-American Households" Other Words Blog, http://otherwords.org/dr-kings-nightmare-racial-wealth-gap-forbes400/

21 Kroll, L., "Inside the 2013 Forbes 400: Facts and Figures on America's Richest" www.forbes.com (September 16, 2013).

22 Williamson, K., "A Shocking Number" National Review Online, www.nationalreview.com, (October 26, 2013).

23 Grant, T. "Study Finds Median Wealth for Single Black Women at $5" The Pittsburgh Post-Gazette, http://www.post-gazette.com/business/businessnews/2010/03/09/Study-finds-median-wealth-for-single-black-women-at-5/stories/201003090163 (March 9, 2010).

24 Shapiro, T., Meschede, T., and Osoro, S., "The Roots of the Widening Racial Wealth Gap: Explaining the Black-White Economic Divide", The Institute of Assets and Social Policy, http://iasp.brandeis.edu/pdfs/Author/shapiro-thomas-m/racialwealthgapbrief.pdf (February 2013).

25 "95% of Income Gains Since 2009 Went to the Top 1%: Here's What That Really Means" Business Insider, www.businessinsider.com (September 12, 2013).

they are comfortable enough that they don't. Similarly, Americans labor a lifetime and the bulk of our output goes to creditors. The majority of Americans are simply McNuggets for the elite. We outnumber the elite 99 to 1 and we could turn on them, but we are typically comfortable enough that we don't.

DEBT SLAVERY

"Those in debt are slaves," said Andrew Jackson, the seventh president of the United States. Debt and slavery have been intertwined since before currency existed. In ancient Rome, those in need of goods or services would agree to Nexum, a debt bondage contract in which a free man pledged himself as a bond slave as collateral for a loan. If additional collateral was needed, a son was often pledged. Rome's elite discovered that they could profit more from a motivated contract worker than a slave, as an indebted worker will toil away inspired by dreams of a better life.

America, the purported "land of opportunity," is a country of optimists. We often anticipate that a raise or job is just around the corner, or we will meet a wealthy Mr. or Ms. Right, that Mark Cuban will fund our great business idea on the next season of *Shark Tank*, or our teenager will win *American Idol*, or get a fat pro sports contract. The reality is that something bad happens just as often as something good happens. We are just as likely to move further away from what we want as we are to move toward it.

Nevertheless, spurred by the prosperous futures we envision, millions of Americans are taught from an early age to aspire to pledge big chunks of their income to creditors. Buying the most house we can by committing a third of our income for the majority of our working years is considered wise. Taking out huge student loans to go to college may make us the pride of the family, yet they often mire us in lifetimes of debt. We freely use credit cards; yet if we are over the age of 43 and live the average American lifespan of 78 years, just paying the minimum payment on $5,000 at 18.9% will not pay off the cards in our lifetimes. How about allocating 34% of our income to a mortgage, 14% to credit cards, 11% to vehicle loans, and 7% to student loan debt? These are common percentages and, when combined with the typical 23% subtracted from paychecks for taxes and other deductions, result in 89% of many Americans' paychecks being pledged to the elite in the form of debts and taxes. The other 11% goes to pay for food and necessities to actually live on. If we have an unexpected expense, maybe a medical emergency or a car repair, then we join the 43% of Americans whose income is less than expenses, an unsustainable situation. *Bawk-bawk!* The majority of us truly are chickens for the elite.

BEYOND BROKE

Creditors are not our friends. Families challenged by debt are often counseled to contact their creditors and explain the situation. Most creditors then go through a tedious and time-consuming review process in which they determine the most that they can squeeze out of you and still keep you motivated and paying. If you are over-whelmed with an impossible payment, then you lose motivation. However, if your lender gives you a payment that you can just barely afford, then they will take advantage of every penny they can get from your income and leave you with just enough to survive.

Lenders fantasize that you can get Netflix instead of cable, access the Internet at the local library instead of at home, eat all your meals off the dollar menus at McDonalds and Taco Bell instead of Panera and Chipotle, use Cricket instead of Verizon, walk instead of drive, and go to Wal-Mart instead of Whole Foods. Depending on your lifestyle, some of these choices may be wise (and the $1

Triple Layer Nachos at Taco Bell may be tasty) but you should not be forced into these choices as your lenders guzzle up ungodly chunks of your income. You are the one earning your living and you should have the freedom to decide how to use it best for you and your family.

BREAK UP YOUR BAD DEBT RELATIONSHIP

Debt Cleanse is not an overthrow of the 1%, but rather a disruption to improve the lives of the 99%. Think of Debt Cleansing like breaking up a bad relationship, getting away from an abusive mate who may be tough to shake. Breaking up with a creditor does not demand the usual awkward in-person "I quit you" along with some explanation as to why. Instead, you can take the easy way out with your creditors. Just stop taking their calls and install a free app on your mobile phone to block their numbers. When they send you letters, dispute the debts. "Ours wasn't that kind of relationship. I don't know what this fool is talking about," is the essence of your retort.

Tuck away all the correspondence that goes back and forth as you would love letters. They'll try to tempt you back, but stand your ground. You don't need all that emotional push and pull. Make a clean cut and be determined to look forward, not backward. When you are having a weak moment, call another friend to chat: no hooking up with debt for clandestine trysts, like one last credit card purchase. Your relationship with debt is over and done. There are better relationships out there for you.

Chances are you were playing the field, so you have several creditors and not just one. Hey—no judging here. We're cool. The breakup process works the same way no matter how many debts you have. Most creditors will get the message, write the debt off, and move on. Their recourse will be to give you a bad grade and mess up your credit score.

We're so over credit scores—we need to make low scores cool. Some people put credit scores in their dating profiles, like on match.com. That is, if they have a high one. That so screams to the world: "I'm a conformist, I bow to The Man." Let's usher in a new era in which a low credit score is sexy. That bad mark on your credit report may prevent you from getting into new relationships with other creditors, but that is what you want: no more creditors in your life, ever. So, welcome the bad marks and plunging credit score as they put you in vogue.

Some creditors just can't move on. Some may get desperate, saying they can't live without you. At this point, they may take matters to an extreme, like getting an attorney to try to get back at you. If that's the case, you have to bring out all the dirt you have on the creditor. They should have stayed quiet. You were ready to move on. So, put together whatever documents you have from when you first met plus all those love letters you've been stashing, and the lawsuit they served.

Then, ask your creditors for their records, some proof of your relationship. If you had a handful of relationships, or even dozens, chances are your creditors had thousands or even millions. "But you were special…" they might say. "Prove it, show me evidence, show me where I signed on the dotted line," you will respond. "Give me a reconciliation of all our time together. Prove I meant something." I am sorry to break this to you, but you were just another number. They didn't care enough about you to even keep the records straight.

I'll teach you to find your creditors' weaknesses and exploit them. I'll show you how to dish it right back at them. You will get a jab in for every time they disappointed you, threatened you mercilessly when you were late, and made staying together so unbearable that you didn't have time for your family, your friends, and even yourself. For every moment of worry, every sleepless night, every speck of enamel grinded off your teeth, every watt of energy wasted by stress over losing your home, your car, even your life: Now is your time to stop being a chicken. Now is your time to Debt Cleanse.

CHAPTER 2

PRE-CLEANSE

Over $12 trillion in consumer debt is originated each year.[26] Of this, $317 billion goes unpaid and is charged off,[27] meaning that the creditor gives up on collecting, writes off the debt, and typically assigns it to a collection agency or sells to a debt buyer. Many other debts go delinquent, but debtors struggle to make some payments and keep the debt from being charged off. The reality is that these debtors would better their situations by not paying anything and letting the creditors charge off their debts.

The charged-off debts are concentrated in five asset classes: auto ($8.5 billion), healthcare ($11.6 billion), credit card ($21 billion), mortgage ($30 billion) and student loans ($143 billion).[28] $150 billion to $200 billion of these charge-offs end up in the hands

---

26 Flock, M. "Debt Buyers—Shrinking Opportunities Amid Regulatory Reform" ABF Journal www.abfjournal.com (September 2014)

27 Id.

28 Id.

of collectors, which typically recover between 20% and 25% of what is due.[29] You want your debts to be in the 75% to 80% that are never collected.

Before we get started, let's get warmed up with some preparatory steps:

STEP ONE: LEARN KEY TERMS
The first set of terms you need to know are the four primary players in Debt Cleanse:

Debtor: You, the one who owes the money.

Creditor: The entity to whom you owe money. Also known as the Lender.

Debt Buyer: The entity that will hopefully buy your delinquent debt at a big discount from your Creditor.

Debt Collector: The entity that the Creditor or Debt Buyer may contract with to collect the debt from you. Sometimes, Debt Collectors receive a contingency fee, earning a percentage of what is recovered. May also be known as a Loan Servicer or Collection Agency.

You also need to be aware of the FDCPA:

Fair Debt Collection Practices Act: a consumer protection amendment to the Consumer Credit Protection Act, which establishes legal protection from abusive debt collection practices. The Act also provides consumers with an avenue for disputing and

---

29 Id.

obtaining validation of debt information in order to ensure the information's accuracy.[30]

The terms Creditor, Debt Buyer, and Debt Collector are often used interchangeably and can also be simply known as **Debt Holder**. There is no need to get too caught up in the differences. However, the FDCPA generally only applies to Debt Buyers and Debt Collectors, as opposed to what the FDCPA identifies as Creditors, which are the entities that originally provided the financing (sometimes referred to **Originators**, a term which also includes third-party brokers or dealers which work with borrowers to complete financing transactions).

For example, I once had a Southwest Airlines Rapid Rewards credit card issued by Chase Bank. Chase was the Creditor and was not bound by FDCPA. In 2006, when I stopped paying the credit card, Chase assigned the debt to a collection agency, which was bound by FDCPA. The debt was later sold several times to different debt buyers, all of which were bound by FDCPA. It's now 2015 and I never paid anything on the debt.

That said, many Creditors abide by the FDCPA as this is considered a prudent practice to limit litigation from consumers. Additionally, many states have enacted consumer protection laws that may overlap and be even more stringent than FDCPA. These often govern Creditors in addition to Debt Buyers and Debt Collectors. When you gather information and documentation using the strategies in this book, your attorney (should you end up in a lawsuit) can review your records for FDCPA violations and other deficiencies that might create leverage in negotiating a settlement.

---

30 Fair Debt Collection Practices Act (FDCPA), Pub. L. 95-109; 91 Stat. 874, codified as 15 U.S.C. §
     1692 –1692 (1977)

In addition to the four players and the FDCPA, there a few other key terms you need to know as you make your way through Debt Cleanse:

Deficiencies: These are errors made by Creditors, Debt Buyers, and Debt Collectors. These can include faulty and missing documentation, incomplete and lost records, defective and inaccurate legal pleadings, improper and illegal collection efforts (including FDCPA violations), and many other boo-boos. Deficiencies are common amongst all types of debt.

Discount: The difference between the amount you owe and the amount your Creditor sells to a Debt Buyer for; and from debt buyer to debt buyer, and so on.

Time: This is always the debtor's friend and creditor's enemy. In almost all situations, delaying debt resolutions will benefit debtors.

Here are some document-specific terms:

Allonge: An attachment to a Promissory Note, which transfers, or purports to transfer, ownership of the Note. This can also be accomplished by an **Endorsement** directly on the Note, similar to signing over a check. For instance, an Allonge or Endorsement or similar document transferred my unpaid credit card obligation from Chase to a debt buyer.

Assignment: Document that transfers ownership, often of a Security Instrument or other evidence of a debt.

Note: The document in which one party promises to pay another party on specific terms. Also known as Promissory Note.

Security Instrument: Document that evidences the pledging of an asset as security for a loan. This includes a Mortgage and Deed of Trust.

STEP TWO: REGISTER & CREATE DEBT HIT LIST AT DEBTCLEANSE.COM

Register at debtcleanse.com to access tools to streamline your Debt Cleanse, including creating a Debt Hit List. If getting online is a challenge, then use the manual list below.

A Debt Hit List is an inventory of every debt you have. Confessing every debt problem may be nerve-wracking. Go ahead, though, and pull out all your statements, or go online, to get the exact balances. Don't worry about writing down the monthly payment amounts—you aren't going to be paying any of these. You can also get details on your debts by obtaining free copies of your credit reports at annualcreditreport.com. For "type", insert "mortgage", "auto loan", or other descriptor.

DEBT HIT LIST

DEBT	ACCOUNT #	BALANCE	TYPE

Your Debt Hit List needs to be a complete inventory, so do not leave anything out, no matter how small or seemingly insignificant, such as the "four easy payments" for that dull knife set you bought off TV.

There, all your debts are contained in one place. Expect that some of your debts will be sold or assigned to collection agencies, so plan to update debt contact names as needed. There may be multiple transfers, which is good. Presumably, every time your debts are sold, they are sold for smaller and smaller amounts. Time is on your side. Over time, as you knock off your debts, whether you settle or they die, cross them off your Debt Hit List.

STEP THREE: ASSET PROTECTION

Asset protection is ideally done before you start to Debt Cleanse. The goal is to get assets out of your name. For instance, my name is Jorge Newbery and I do not want anything in my name: real estate, vehicles, bank accounts, ownership in a company, beneficial interests in a trust or estate, jewelry, furniture—nothing. Think of Asset Protection like going through TSA at the airport. If you have water, drink it up. If you have a pocketknife, mail it to a family member. Whatever you hang on to, you will likely have to give up to the TSA screeners.

50% of Americans have no net worth[31]—that is, the value of whatever assets they own equals (or is less than) whatever they owe. In fact, 25% of Americans have a negative net worth,[32] owing more than the value of what they own. Thus, for at least half of

---

31 King, N. "About Half of America has Zero Net Wealth" www.marketplace.org (April 21, 2014).

32 Tompor, S. "Many Households Have Negative Net Worth, Study Finds" USA Today Online www. usatoday.com (May 12, 2012).

the readers of this book, there are really no substantial assets to protect. This is good—great, even—as this will make your Debt Cleanse easier.

What we are trying to avoid is leaving any asset vulnerable to seizure by a creditor who is able to obtain a judgment. As you go through the book, I will teach you how to avoid getting a judgment. However, these judgment-prevention strategies do not work 100% of the time. So, just in case, I also teach you how to thwart collection of a judgment. This is much easier if you have no assets in your name.

YOUR GOAL: OWN NOTHING

If you have no real estate and modest assets, you can transfer your stuff to a friend or family member. In community property states such as California, transferring to a spouse will leave you with an ownership interest, so a parent or adult child might be best. For instance, I live in Illinois (not a community property state) and my wife owns all of our furniture, our TV, our food, even our dog. She lets me use these, of course. I don't much like the dog though, so sometimes I am tempted to license him in my name in hopes that one of my judgment creditors will take him.

You can transfer all these to a family member by letter, maybe notarizing to show the date. However, creditors have little interest in items worth under a couple of thousand as the cost to have the sheriff sell will likely exceed what the sale would generate. Thus, I have no documentation that my wife owns everything in our apartment: I just told my wife that all the stuff in our apartment is hers. (Except the avocado wrap in the fridge. I might get hungry later.)

If you have real estate, a car or boat, a business or business equipment, jewelry, or a watch, or any single items worth more than a couple of thousand, ask this question for each item: Do you have a loan (or loans) secured by this item that exceeds the value of the asset? If so, there is no equity, so nothing for a creditor to take.

If you have no loan, or the loan(s) is less than the asset value minus selling costs (such as real estate commissions), then you need to get the asset out of your name. You can do this a few ways:

a. Sell the item and keep the cash.

b. Transfer ownership to a friend or family member. Remember, if you are in a community property state, do not transfer to a spouse.

c. Transfer ownership to an entity such as a Limited Liability Company, Corporation, or similar structure. The law treats these entities like separate people. Note that the asset may need to have a business purpose, which could be to rent the asset to you.

For instance, I, Jorge Newbery, have virtually no assets. However, I exercise some control over several LLCs that do have assets. As an example, this book is published by Community Books LLC, an LLC that I control which earns a couple of bucks from every book sold. There is a debt buyer holding a purported $8 million judgment against me. The judgment holder can ask a court to grant a charging order, entitling the judgment holder to any monies paid by the LLC to me. However, the creditor does not have any management rights to make decisions for the LLC. Thus, even as Community Books LLC earns money, pays expenses, and accumulates cash, the judgment holder cannot force the LLC to pay me. Thus, there is nothing for the judgment holder to intercept. All the judgment holder would get from a charging order is some bills from their attorney.

HOW TO CREATE AN ENTITY

If you have higher value assets with equity to protect and you want to keep them, create an entity. You can do this online at a modest cost (less than a thousand for most states) through services such as Legal Zoom or Biz Filings. LLCs generally have the most flexibility and require the least maintenance, so that's what I would suggest. For a few hundred dollars extra, you can hire an attorney to help set this up: check debtcleanse.com for attorneys that are adept at asset protection. If you have never set up an LLC, consider having an attorney assist.

A sharp attorney will likely counsel you to add a second member to the LLC, as single member LLCs may be easier for a creditor to attack. Courts in some states have found that charging order protection does not apply to single member LLCs and have allowed creditors remedies such as foreclosing on the member's interest or ordering the LLC dissolved. The second member can be a spouse (except in community property states: Arizona, California, Idaho, Louisiana, Nevada, New Mexico, Texas, Washington, Wisconsin and—only if spouses opted in—Alaska), a family member, friend, or business associate.

However, the second member should not already be a co-debtor with you on your personal debts. State laws that restrict creditors to charging orders as the exclusive remedy against personal debtors were put in place in part to protect the interests of an LLC's innocent members, those who do not owe on the debt. Thus, if an LLC is owned by a husband and wife who also are debtors on the same unpaid credit card debt that becomes a judgment, then a creditor could argue that there are no innocent members being harmed and, at least in theory, a judge could allow a creditor to sell LLC assets to pay the judgment. There is no reason to risk this, so go ahead and make sure that at least one member of the LLC is not also a co-debtor on any of your personal debts.

To ensure creditors do not argue that the second member's interest exists only to stunt collection efforts, the second member should pay a market price for their interest, receive financial statements, participate in management decisions, and receive a share of any distributions equal to their interest. For example, if you create an LLC and the organizational costs are $1,000 and your adult child is 10% owner, then your adult child should contribute $100 to the organizational costs. Later on, if the LLC distributes $5,000 in profits, then the adult child should receive $500.

An attorney may also counsel you to create the LLC in a different state, one in which laws are more favorable for debtors. For instance, in December 2010, Michigan passed Senate Bill 1455 which clearly states that charging orders are the sole remedy of creditors against LLCs and that this applies to both multi member and single member LLCs without distinction. Thus, no second member is necessary for maximum protection from creditors if you establish your LLC in Michigan.

Your attorney or an online service can create a deed to transfer your real estate, which you can have notarized and recorded at the local recorder. You need to go to your state's department of motor vehicles to transfer vehicle ownership. Close bank accounts in your name and open new accounts in the name of your entity. If you are self-employed, put all the business assets and income into the

LLC. Pretty soon, you'll have nothing in your name.

If you already have a judgment creditor chasing you, you can still sell and transfer. However, the creditor may allege that the transfer was a fraudulent conveyance, done solely to evade collection. They would need to go to court to do this, and you can assert that there were other reasons for the transfer. For instance, if you transferred real estate to an LLC, this could be done for liability reasons, such as to protect you if someone slipped and fell and then sued you.

Here is the reality: unless your debt is large, the judgment collection process will likely be driven by a paralegal in a big firm handling hundreds of cases. Unless the judgment holder has already recorded an Abstract of Judgment or similar documents to lien your real estate or vehicle, or levied your bank account, chances are the transfers will not be scrutinized.

STEP FOUR: EMBRACE BAD CREDIT
In ancient Rome, slaves were taken to the slave-markets where they were paraded naked with placards around their necks explaining their best and worst qualities. Think of credit scores as the modern-day slave placard. In today's America, if you are a good slave and earn a good credit score, you can buy the cool stuff that marketers tell you is needed in order to be happy. A good credit score will open doors to all your dreams, plus some airline miles. But if you are a bad slave and don't pay the slave master on time, then you get a bad credit score, which means you need to buy cool stuff with cash. If you pay cash, then you cannot buy as much cool stuff. That's bad because marketers tell us that without cool stuff we can't have happiness.

After my financial meltdown, my credit score fell so low that I became "unrated," without any score. Being unrated on your credit is like a movie getting a NC-17 rating. The movie might be cool, but it's best to just stay away. If the movie had only been a little more conformist, then the movie could have gotten an R or PG13, ratings more akin to a good credit score and a strong box office.

If you Debt Cleanse, you will wreck your credit. You might even become "unrated" like I was. You may never be able to buy on credit again and only buy with cash. This is great. Embrace bad credit and your improving finances.

STEP FIVE: ACTIVATE YOUR FRIENDS & FAMILY PLAN
Forewarn your friends and family that your creditors may reach out to them in order to get your contact information, or at least some clues. Advise them to say nothing except to ask the creditor to no longer call them. The FDCPA only permits creditors to call each third-party once in order to request contact information, unless the third-party authorizes additional calls. If a creditor calls more than once, have your associates start logging the calls and your friend or family member may be able to sue for harassment and other violations of the FDCPA. Generally, creditors cannot discuss your debts with unauthorized third parties, including friends and family members. Thus, the caller will say something like "I need to reach Jorge Newbery to discuss an important business matter." The easiest strategy is to hang up.

If your friend or family member is willing to be bolder, they could ask something like, "What is the important business matter? I really need to know what's going on. I'm his BFF, so you can tell me. Is this about his debts?" If the caller gets loose and shares something, have your friend or family member notate the conversation's contents in a log, as this is a likely a FDCPA violation.

STEP SIX: BUILD PROFILE AT DEBTCLEANSE.COM

I invite you to debtcleanse.com, a legal plan and technology platform featuring tools to help consumers and small businesses in their Debt Cleanse journeys. As part of each plan, members receive a monthly one-on-one call with an attorney trained in Debt Cleanse tactics, plus 25% off legal fees. We want to provide members the resources necessary to settle their debts at big discounts, and not pay some at all.

The discounts you may be able to achieve can be substantial. Picture this: if a thousand Bank of America credit card borrowers each owe $5,000 and stop paying, then Bank of America will likely eventually sell those debts for around 4 cents on the dollar, roughly $200 each. The debt buyer, typically, will then aggressively pursue those 1,000 borrowers, collecting the full $5,000 plus interest and charges on some, and getting zero on others. Average recovery is usually 20%, in this case, $1 million on the $5 million (1,000 x $5,000) in credit card debt. After deducting the $200,000 paid for the debt, the costs of aggressively collecting can eat up a decent chunk of the $800,000 difference.

As an alternative, non-paying credit card borrowers may offer to settle their $5,000 debts for $400. The debt buyer will make less, but get paid faster and with minimum expense.

Importantly, the debt buyer may recognize that if they want to start getting aggressive, you are prepared to fight back. A debt buyer that decides to book a modest profit by taking your $400 is making a better business decision than choosing to scuffle, resulting in increased costs and an uncertain outcome.

To help you prepare for eventual creditor battles, debtcleanse.com enables you to save all the documents, correspondence, and call notes for each debt in one location. You can also compare representations between holders of your debts over time and look for errors and deficiencies. You can opt to share access to your debt-cleanse.com debt files with your attorney(s) and, whether you or your lawyer are reviewing the documents, having everything in one place makes identifying deficiencies more convenient. This streamlining should help minimize the time your attorneys spend on your case, which should reduce legal costs.

To make your Debt Cleanse as easy to follow as possible, debt-cleanse.com offers template letters to dispute and validate, or prove the existence of, your debts. Every letter in this book will be available in fillable form. Check the appropriate boxes, print out, sign and mail. You can dispute a debt, prepare a Qualified Written Request (a long tedious request for information and documents on mortgages), request an administrative hearing and documents on a student loan, and more. These will be improved and refined over time as needed, and new documents added as they are developed. All users will be invited to share experiences, strategies, and tips.

As you go through your Debt Cleanse and you receive assistance from an attorney, we'll ask you to review the service you receive so that other users can readily identify the most effective allies to engage. It's important to ensure that participating attorneys are providing consistently superior service at affordable rates.

Creditors keep credit reports on us, detailing our performance in paying (or not paying) our debts. On debtcleanse.com, creditor reports will be maintained, detailing each creditor's performance in settling unpaid debts. Creditors' strengths and weaknesses will be identified (the Debt Cleanse tactics have proven most effective against all kinds of creditors), as well as which deficiencies were uncovered and may be particularly prevalent for certain creditors. All users, such as attorneys and debtors, can add deficiencies, legal pleadings, discovery requests, and other information by debt type and creditor type.

The site will also serve as a matchmaker for class action lawsuits, uniting debtors with attorneys willing to represent crowds against specific creditors. Debtors can connect with other local Debt Cleanse participants and arrange to meet, organize debt strikes, and otherwise support each other in person.

Debtors can expect to be bombarded by creditors as they undergo their Debt Cleanse. Debtcleanse.com provides tools for debtors to get ready for combat. The goal in arming oneself is to resolve the debts, avoid skirmishes, and be prepared if a confrontation occurs.

STEP SEVEN: PAY NO TAX ON FORGIVEN DEBT

Some creditors may furnish you a 1099-C on the amount of your debt that is cancelled. If you owe $5,000 on a credit card and you settle for $400, then you could receive a 1099-C for the $4,600 difference. In some circumstances, you could be required to pay tax on this $4,600. Thankfully, the Internal Revenue Service provides that "if you are insolvent when the debt is cancelled, some or all of the cancelled debt may not be taxable to you. You are insolvent when your total debts are more than the fair market value of your total assets."[33] If your liabilities exceed your assets—as is common for the majority of Americans—you will not be taxed on forgiven debt.

You can make the assessment yourself. There is even a handy little tool for this on debtcleanse.com where you can store the record in the event the IRS ever has a question. Each time you make a settlement, list all of your assets in one column and all your liabilities in another. Here is an example:

ASSETS	LIABILITIES
$75,000 Home	$150,000 Mortgage
$5,000 Auto	$10,000 Auto Loan
$20,000 Personal Property	$40,000 Credit Cards
$100,000 Total Assets	$200,000 Total Liabilities

Additional assets may include bank accounts, other types of personal property, retirement accounts, and any other real estate. Other liabilities could include personal loans, credit lines, personal property loans, and mortgages on any other real estate.

If you can document that you were insolvent when the debt was forgiven, then you likely do not need to pay taxes on the forgiven debt, even if you receive a 1099-C.

STEP EIGHT: STOP DREAMING OF DEBT FREEDOM AND TAKE ACTION
Are you hungry to get started? Can you almost taste debt freedom? Ready to dig in? I hear you, but let's go through a few more

---

33   IRS Publication 4681, "Canceled Debts, Foreclosures, Repossessions and Abandonments (for individuals) (2014).

preparatory steps before we get into the step-by-step debt-cleansing recipe for each common debt type. If you are ready for a life freed of debt, let's proceed to Chapter 3: Quick Start, and get started settling your debts for pennies on the dollar.

CHAPTER 3

QUICK START

Did you come to this page first, before reading anything else in the book? Are you the type that likes to cut to the chase? Well, if you did, then you are just like me. I always want to get to the heart of a subject immediately, and then decide if I want to spend more time with it.

So here is the entirety of Debt Cleanse at its most elemental:

STOP PAYING

PROTECT ASSETS

IGNORE CREDITORS

SETTLEMENT WALLET

DISPUTE DEBTS

PATIENCE

IDENTIFY DEFICIENCIES

WELCOME LAWSUITS

These components form the foundation with which you will Debt

Cleanse. Now let's review each element.

STOP PAYING

This first step may appear to be the easiest and, out of necessity, you may have already stopped paying your bills. That's fine. For others, this may be the first time in your life you have not paid a bill on time. This may cause discomfort. However, as time passes, not paying will become easier. Realize that you will not be able to make deals to settle your unaffordable debts at big discounts until you are behind on your payments, so a little discomfort now will pay off in the long run.

And when I say stop paying, I mean stop paying every debt you have. *What if I can afford some and not others?* Stop paying every debt you have. *Shouldn't I keep one credit card for emergencies?* Stop paying every debt you have. The cash you save will be accessible for true emergencies, and you can keep a debit card tied to a bank account for convenience and travel.

Don't forget to shut off any automatic payments set up to debit from your bank accounts and/or debit cards. If you have payday loans, or recurring payments for which you have written post-dated checks or authorized automatic debits, close the bank account and withdraw your money.

If you owe money to the bank that holds your checking or savings accounts, close these accounts and move to another bank. Otherwise, they are likely to offset your unpaid payments from your accounts. If you are changing banks and/or accounts, make sure to switch any direct deposits such as paychecks or benefits to your new account.

PROTECT ASSETS

As we discussed in Chapter 2: Pre-Cleanse, in order to protect your assets you need to move them out of your name. Stick to the steps I laid out to transfer your valuables to a spouse, family member, friend, or even an LLC.

IGNORE CREDITORS

Once you stop paying, your creditors will start panicking, calling, and writing you like a spurned lover. Shut them down, tough-love style, and ignore them completely.

Phone Calls

When a creditor calls, hang up. Then, install a free call-blocking app such as Ultimate Call Blocker Free, Call Control, or Blacklist to block their numbers on your cell phone. If you have a home landline, now might be the time to get rid of it. If you want to keep it, buy Sentry Dual Mode Call Blocker or a similar device for about $50 on Amazon to block unwanted calls.

For the calls that do get through, start a communication log to record the date, time and content (i.e. "hung up") of any calls and voicemails you do receive. You can use a paper journal or the communication log tool at debtcleanse.com.

For an enhanced buffer, consider changing your phone number and give your new number only to those who you want to have it. However, be careful in using your new number to deal with your debt, lest the calls resume. If you call a creditor from your new number, they can capture your phone number using caller ID. If you share your number online during a purchase, complete a warranty card or survey, or give your new number to a bank or other company, the number may end up in a database such as

LexisNexis and be accessible to creditors. Nevertheless, changing your number is an advanced step to thwart your creditors' primary means of contact.

Written Correspondence
Learn to love letters. Ideally, all your correspondence with your creditors will be in writing and allow you to keep copies of everything. If and when you do respond to your creditors, only do so in writing. Send everything certified mail, return receipt requested. If you end up in litigation, having a trail of correspondence going back and forth can be very helpful. When you receive correspondence from your creditors, save it—even billing statements. Do not let the sometimes harsh language dampen your resolve. Ideally, scan and upload the document to debtcleanse.com.

Later on, if you need to litigate with a creditor, having the communication logs and all correspondence saved online in one place will prove to be advantageous. An attorney can readily review for violations of the Fair Debt Collection Practices Act, Telephone Consumer Protection Act,[34] Federal Trade Commission Act,[35] as well as state and local laws. Any violations may provide leverage when you settle your debts and, in some cases, you may actually have a debt extinguished and get the creditor to pay you a settlement payment.

Where to mail the letters? Most collection notices include a single address. However, early on in the process, you may receive billing statements with multiple addresses: mail letters to the addresses

[34] Telephone Consumer Protection Act 47 U.S.C. § 227

[35] Federal Trade Commission Act of 1914 15 U.S.C §§ 41-58,

identified for "correspondence", "send inquiries to", or some similar designation.

Almost every letter template in this book is topped with "**VIA CERTIFIED MAIL/RETURN RECEIPT REQUESTED/COPY RETAINED**." This is a reminder to you to mail certified, return receipt requested, and keep a copy. Further, this lets the recipient know that this is a serious matter to you—if any of your debts are ever litigated, you want to share a pile of letters demonstrating that you have been actively trying to resolve the debt. If this language is not on top of the letter, you still want to always keep a copy.

SETTLEMENT WALLET

Instead of paying your bills, stash the cash you would have otherwise paid into what I like to call your "settlement wallet." Keep the funds in a separate account, in cash at home, in a PayPal account or other online payment system, or with a trusted friend or family member. The goal is not to fritter away the extra money, but let it build up and utilize the funds to strategically settle your debts when doing so is in your best interests. In addition, these monies can be utilized to pay legal fees and related costs. The longer you don't pay, the fatter your settlement wallet will get and the more cash you will have to make lump sum settlements and, if needed, pay attorneys to fight on your behalf.

How much do you need to save up to settle your debts? Probably not as much as you think. A 2013 Federal Trade Commission study entitled *The Structures and Practices of the Debt Buying Industry* concluded that debt buyers paid an average of 4 cents per dollar of debt, with credit card debt being the most common type of debt purchased.[36] Thus, if you stop making payments on your $5,000 credit card debt, eventually your debt will likely be sold for around $200. As your minimum monthly payment is probably $100, the sale may be for the equivalent of two monthly payments.

Most debt buyers, however, will try to collect the full $5,000. But if you make collecting difficult, they may become open to a settlement of a few hundred dollars. They might even just give up and write off the debt, instead focusing their efforts on those debtors not pushing back. Mortgages and other secured debts will typically sell for more. AHP often pays 10 to 50 cents on mortgage debt, which leaves a lot of room for discounts to be shared with debtors.

DISPUTE DEBTS

As debts are sold and transferred, you may receive letters inviting you to dispute the debts. Historically, the vast majority of debtors ignore these invitations. Please, for heaven's sake, accept the invitations and dispute your debts *even if you owe them.* There is plenty of opportunity to find and challenge other inaccuracies, such as who owns the debt, whether the amounts demanded are correct, and whether any of the other "facts" alleged in the letters are disputable.

Your creditors need to have records and documents to prove what they are representing. However, creditors' records and documents are frequently lacking and they do not have the evidence necessary to validate debts. So send in your disputes.

The FTC study of the nine largest debt buyers in the U.S.,

36 https://www.ftc.gov/sites/default/files/documents/reports/structure-and-practices-debt-buying-industry/debtbuyingreport.pdf

representing more than 75% of the consumer debts sold in 2008, found that consumers dispute about a million debts per year, roughly 3.2% of the debt sold.[37] The same report revealed that debt buyers did not have the data and documents to verify almost half of the disputed debts. The debt buyers often could not verify the total due; breakdown what they demanded into principal, interest and charges; prove that they owned the debt; or even provide evidence that a debt existed.

If every consumer disputed the debts acquired by debt buyers in 2008 then, by extrapolating the FTC's findings, almost $70 billion of the $143 billion sold to debt buyers could not be verified.[38] Thus, the odds are about 50/50 that a debt buyer can verify your debt.

The Fair Debt Collection Practices Act prohibits debt collectors, including debt buyers, from seeking to recover on unverified disputed debt. Thus, your dispute letter may prove to be a death sentence for your debt, at least with the current holder.

Unfortunately, the debt buyers are not barred from reselling such debts to other purchasers, and subsequent purchasers are not barred from seeking to collect the debt. Still, even if disputed debt is verified, less than 5% of verified disputed debts are resold. If the debt buyer is unable to verify in response to dispute letters, then less than 1% of that debt is sold. If your unverified debt is sold, you can simply respond to the new debt buyer's invitation and dispute your debt as many times as needed until it's dead.

Most of the time, disputed debts are just written off. Although

37 Id.

38 Id.

you are unlikely to receive any notice that your debt is now dead, you will probably never hear about the debt again. All states have statute of limitations laws which recite that debtors cannot be sued after a certain time has passed, often three to six years, but sometimes 10 or even 15 years. However, if you go three years without paying, then you can generally relax. The odds of collecting from you are miserable and collectors will recognize this.

Although this may sound too easy, in many cases you will emerge without paying a dime on the unsecured debts you dispute, such as credit cards and payday loans. In each of the upcoming debt-specific chapters, I will share a dispute letter template. For many debt types, there is one common dispute letter template you can use. For others, there is a debt-specific form, such the Qualified Written Request for mortgages as a combination dispute/share-some-deficiencies-on-my-loan request.

Oftentimes, the invitations to dispute say they are good for 30 days. Ideally, dispute the debts within this period. However, if the 30 days have already passed, you can still dispute at any time.

PATIENCE

Delinquent debts, unlike wine, lose value with age. If debts get old enough, they become worthless and die. Any opportunity to delay collection efforts and buy time should be always be exercised.

Thus, learn the art of patience. "Inch by inch, everything's a cinch," I sometimes remind myself. Time is always the debtor's friend and the creditor's enemy, so get comfortable and realize that your Debt Cleanse may take quite a bit of time. This chapter may be called Quick Start, but I encourage you to approach your Debt Cleanse as a snow-melt. The passage of time and continued nonpayment will enhance your ability to settle your debts at big discounts. Furthermore, some debts will simply shrivel up and die as creditors realize that continued collection activity is not cost-effective.

Your journey may be slow, even tedious, and your progress may be only incremental and seemingly non-existent at times. But if you are patient, persistent, and strategic, you will settle your debts at big discounts, and not pay some at all.

IDENTIFY DEFICIENCIES

A deficiency is a flaw that you can exploit to gain leverage over whoever holds your debt. These can often be found in the documents from when you took out the debt, servicing records, correspondence and communication logs, and legal pleadings. Creditors' records are often riddled with inaccuracies. Documents are frequently deficient or missing altogether. Legal filings are typically rife with blunders, as these are often prepared by overworked paralegals. There are always cracks in debt transactions that can be exposed. No debt is crack-a-lacking. Deficiencies are the cracks you will exploit as you disintegrate your debts.

"I would say that roughly 90 percent of the credit card lawsuits are flawed and can't prove the person owes the debt," Noach Dear, a state civil court judge in Brooklyn, told the *New York Times*.[39] In my extensive experience as a debtor and creditor, I would expand Judge Dear's assessment to cover the majority of consumer creditor lawsuits. The creditor or debt buyer needs to prove ownership of the debt, that the amount due is accurate, and that they have all the documents to prove this. They also cannot make any mistakes

---

39 "Problems Riddle Moves to Collect Credit Card Debt" NY Times, www.nytimes.com (August 12, 2012).

in their collection or litigation procedures.

Creditors big and small make mistakes, documents get lost, and record keeping is infested with errors. Your goal is to find the blunders and exploit them. Even a small boo-boo can be parlayed into a big victory.

At the back of this book, in the Action Tools section, you will find a list of 134 Deficiencies. You can compare these to your debts to help identify deficiencies. Also, check out the perpetually updated deficiency list at debtcleanse.com (and contribute any new deficiencies you discover to the list). Deficiencies are the cornerstone of Debt Cleanse.

WELCOME LAWSUITS

Some of you will go through Debt Cleanse and constantly be threatened with litigation by your creditors, but never actually get sued. Do not be frightened by the prospect of lawsuits from your creditors. Recognize that the cost of litigation is a frequent deterrent for the creditor and many threats of legal action never result in actual lawsuits. Instead, if a creditor actually sues you, welcome the litigation. You, as a debtor, have rights just as a creditor does.

Creditors need to have a court awarded judgment in order to seize your property, levy your bank account, or garnish your wages. You will typically receive a summons and complaint as the initial step in the lawsuit process. You can then file an answer to dispute the creditor's claims. If you do not answer, the court will typically assume that everything the creditor alleges is correct and will award the judgment. If you simply answer the lawsuit, some creditors will dismiss your case and focus their efforts on the consumers who do not answer. Why waste time and money fighting a difficult debtor when there are plenty who are ready to give in without a fight?

If the litigation proceeds, this is probably because your debt is substantial and the creditor believes that they will be able to collect from you. They are wrong. There is an upside to litigation: you will finally get someone with authority involved in resolving your debt. Typically, up until this point, you would have only worked with collectors and customer service clerks. With litigation, you have the opportunity to really make a deal with a representative at the creditor who may have the authority to settle your debt.

Make It a Party
Bring into the litigation any other parties who may be responsible for creating your unaffordable debt. This could be the mortgage broker who fudged your income and, when you complained that the payments were unaffordable, promised you could refinance to a lower rate in two years. This could also be the student loan lead generation company that advertised that "Obama Wants You To Go Back To School," implying that the ad and school were government sanctioned or otherwise affiliated, which they likely were not.

If these types of sales pitches and chicanery contributed to you getting into debt, then those responsible need to contribute to getting you out of debt. In a student loan suit, you could end up suing the school, any marketers or lead generation companies, the debt holder, the original lender, or even the Board of Education. Think about it: did the President of the United States really want you to go back to school? Someone needs to prove that advertising was true or compensate you appropriately.

Get Sue Happy
For some debts, you may need to initiate the legal action: you

might need to sue a creditor, or even a few. This is most common for mortgages in non-judicial states, as well as government-backed student and business loans. You will learn more about these steps in the debt-specific chapters.

Jury Fury

With your answer or lawsuit, always request a jury trial. In addition, to support fellow Debt Cleanse participants, join a jury if called upon. You may end up on the jury of a traffic case, a carjacking, or some business dispute. Ideally, you may get called up to help decide a dispute between a debtor and creditor.

HIRE AN ATTORNEY

"Hey, I only owe $5,000," you might think. "Getting an attorney is going to eat up most of what I save."

Au contraire. If you need to litigate, don't go through the process cheapo or solo. Instead, get some help. Attorneys who are efficient and effective can save you money—and even get you paid. Some attorneys will represent you on contingency, meaning that you pay them nothing out of your pocket. Their goal is to not only help you settle your debt for little or nothing, but to get the creditor to pay your attorney's fees. As you identify and exploit the deficiencies that are commonplace in consumer credit transactions, you may even add a modest cash settlement (paid by the creditor *to* you) as a goal. The "free" attorneys will also typically want a share of the settlement as well. If an attorney finds your case strong enough to take on contingency, go with this arrangement.

Otherwise, attorneys can be expensive. I have spent over a million dollars on attorneys in my life; both in setting up deals correctly to keep me out of trouble, then later trying to get me out of debt trouble. Most debtors would only need to spend a fraction of what I spent, if they even have to spend anything. Nevertheless, cost is a big factor. This makes selecting the right attorney and utilizing the mindset that your selected attorney is working *with* you, not for you, essential.

Attorneys typically charge $100 – $600 an hour, with most in the $200 - $400 range. Thus, if they spend a day on your debt, your bill could be extraordinary. In fairness, most attorneys often have decent-sized overhead, including costly errors and omissions insurance. (Plus, many attorneys are still repaying big student loans of their own. Maybe once they start Debt Cleansing on their own debts, then they can drop their rates?)

At large firms, the focus is on generating billable hours. The more hours an attorney works, the more they bill, and the higher their pay or bonus. An attorney who is particularly efficient with his or her work may be liked by clients, but not by the firm. Nevertheless, a big firm can sometimes be helpful. In some egregious cases, the variety of talents at a larger firm may create an A-Team that can help win your case.

At the other end of the cost spectrum are student law clinics, which are offered through some law schools. You may be able to obtain quality representation at a substantially reduced fee, or even for free. Licensed attorneys supervise the students, and their efforts are often peppered with youthful "we're going to change the world" enthusiasm. You may be their opportunity to do just that.

I have had as much success with sole practitioners as I have with big firms. What matters most to me in selecting an attorney is that they have the willingness to employ tactics they may not have experience with, such as those in Debt Cleanse. When it comes down to it, I want an attorney who gets done what I need done.

Debtcleanse.com has a directory of attorneys trained to help you execute Debt Cleanse tactics in an efficient and affordable manner. Members receive a one-on-one call each month with an attorney licensed in their state, as well as 25% off legal fees. You can also readily share access to your debt files on debtcleanse.com with participating attorneys.

Some law firms operate as "bankruptcy mills" and will try to encourage you to file bankruptcy, which is a resolution they are more familiar with. Don't do it. Attorneys registered on debt-cleanse.com have agreed to not recommend bankruptcy as a solution unless your circumstances dictate that this is, in fact, the best option. You want an attorney with a broad view of the legal world, not a narrow one.

Find an attorney you feel comfortable with. Once you find the one you feel you can work with the best, request an engagement letter, but hold it and don't pay until you need them. In most situations, using the same attorney for all of your debts that require litigation is both efficient and economical.

If you get sued, then sign the engagement letter and pay the retainer using the funds in your settlement wallet.

DISCOVERY

Whether you are certain that the deficiencies you identified exist, or whether you simply speculate that they do, discovery is the process by which you engage in *the act or process of discovering* through *the usually pretrial disclosure of pertinent facts or documents by one or both parties to a legal action or proceeding.* If you suspect that your creditor does not have your original note, for instance, you get to demand that they produce this as part of the discovery process. Likewise, if you want the salesperson asked under oath whether he disclosed the terms of the financing to you, discovery is your opportunity. Whatever is uncovered in discovery can typically be utilized in the eventual trial. Most importantly, discovery can often accelerate settlement discussions if the creditor is unable to provide a certain crucial document, possesses a damaging piece of evidence they don't want to turn over, or their executive finds flying to wherever the deposition is being held inconvenient.

There are four primary discovery tools:

1. Document Requests, in which you can ask for whatever documents the creditor possesses. Your attorney will often be provided copies. If an original is needed, sometimes these are filed with the court or a time can be arranged for your side to inspect the document. There are 140 sample Document Requests in Action Tools.

2. Interrogatories, which are written questions required to be answered under direction of a court. Think of these as interrogations of your creditor on paper. You will find 208 sample Interrogatories in Action Tools.

3. Requests for Admissions, which are sets of statements sent from you to an opposing party for the purpose of having the adversary admit or deny the statements or allegations therein. 156 sample Requests for Admissions are in Action Tools.

4. Depositions, which are face-to-face interviews in which sworn

testimony is given. These are typically formal statements given by people who have facts pertinent to the lawsuit so that the statements can be used in court. A creditor-vexing 252 sample Deposition Questions are in Action Tools.

To create discovery pertinent to your case, your attorney will typically review the deficiencies identified (including those suspected) and then formally request the accompanying documents. The creditor may provide responses, or they may object to some of the requests with excuses such as "overly broad and burdensome." Neither side can use the discovery process to harass the other side—the requests must be reasonable and pertinent. Also, each party is only required to furnish documents or answers they actually have. In other words, the answering party generally is not required to create or go to third parties to obtain documents that they do not possess.

In some situations, a smart-aleck creditor may respond with a truckload of documents in response to your request. The documents you really want may be buried in with hundreds of others of marginal pertinence. Your side will then need to spend hours sifting through everything.

When a creditor possesses a document that is particularly damaging to their case, they may withhold documents. Your attorney may need to file a Motion to Compel with the court in order to force the creditor to turn over the document. On the other hand, a creditor may not be able to produce a document that is crucial to their case, and may ask the court for extensions of time to produce.

The creditor has the same discovery rights as you and can send discovery requests to your side. For instance, if you claim you made twelve payments, the creditor could ask you for cancelled checks to prove this. If you claim that the salesperson did not disclose the terms of the financing to you, you could be asked about this in a deposition. Your attorney will prepare you for this, if needed.

FIGHTING THE BIG ONE

The goal with litigation is to settle before trial, which can be costly for both sides. However, creditors can typically afford big litigation bills and use this as leverage to bully debtors. Thus, if a creditor insists on pushing your matter to trial, all the money in your settlement wallet may not be sufficient to pay legal costs. Thus, we all need to support you. You can use the Community Chest function on debtcleanse.com to crowdfund the legal fees needed. We all want to support those who go into big battles in order to remove the deep-pocket advantage that creditors typically have.

In return, you and your attorney will pledge to require that any positive resolution include reimbursement of your legal fees back to the Community Chest. This will repay your contributors, who can then use their funds to support others facing similar trials. We are all in this together and need to support each other.

Now, write down these key Debt Cleanse actions (or tweet them if you are on Twitter—the explanation is simple enough to cleanly fit within the 140-character limit) to reinforce the Debt Cleanse actions:

Stop Paying Protect Assets Ignore Creditors Settlement Wallet Dispute Debts Patience Identify Deficiencies Welcome Lawsuits #DEBTCLEANSE

If you came to this chapter first, I hope that you found this sufficiently intriguing that you decide to spend your time with this book. Read the chapters that came before this one—you will find them full of information that you will need as you move forward with your Debt Cleanse. In the next chapters, we'll go through each type of debt in depth to teach you how to settle for pennies on the dollar (or not pay at all). We'll start with the most difficult (judgments, mortgages, vehicle loans, student loans, business loans, secured personal loans) and progress to the easiest (credit cards, medical bills, payday loans, collection accounts). Ready, set... stop paying.

CHAPTER 4

JUDGMENTS

The goal of this book is to teach you *the ability to make good decisions about what should be done.* This is good judgment, at least in regards to your unaffordable debts. Although you are likely to succeed in settling most of your debts, you might not win every battle. As a result, you may also end up with a bad judgment: *an obligation (as a debt) created by the decree of a court.*

When a creditor sues and you lose, they are not awarded cash. Instead, courts award judgments to creditors. A judgment is just a piece of paper, kind of like toilet paper but less useful. Judgment holders can garnish wages, levy bank accounts, and record liens on property such as real estate. Nevertheless, some analysts estimate that 80% of court-ordered money judgments in America are never collected.[40] In this chapter, I will share some steps that you can implement to shut down your creditor's offense, and maybe even put them on defense. If all goes well, your judgment might

40 Forbes.com, http://www.forbes.com/byb/2008/byb08_the_judgment_group.html (2008)

get flushed and never be collected upon.

Years ago, I personally guaranteed a Key Bank loan of over $5 million. When my finances collapsed, I was unable to pay. They sued me and won a judgment in January 2011. Key Bank made some feeble collection efforts, which I easily thwarted with the techniques below. However, in November 2013, Key sold their judgment to a debt buyer, US Acquisition Property XXXVI. I took this as good news, as my educated guess is that they bought my debt for about $40,000, roughly half a penny on the $8 million the debt had purportedly ballooned to with interest and fees.

The first contact I had from US Acquisition was in late 2013 when I received a notification that one of their employees had viewed my LinkedIn profile. When they first called, I hung up, just like I tell everyone to do. However, given the size of the debt, I expected US Acquisition to put some muscle into collection.

A couple of months later, I was feeling great as I walked home after a productive day at AHP. However, as I approached my building, I saw a big guy who looked like Mr. T waiting outside my apartment. Neighbors later said he had been lurking there for hours. As I approached, he said "Jorge Newbery" in an inquisitive tone. I was a bit startled and said, "Yes?" He handed me a citation, which is a court document requiring me to appear in court and testify as to my income and assets. This is also referred to as a judgment debtor's exam. Even though I have been through this dozens of times before, the super-size of this debt troubled me and I didn't feel so good as I sat down in my apartment to analyze this invitation to my next debt battle.

The next day, I called US Acquisition and offered $25,000 as settlement in full. They countered at $2 million. I told them I could borrow money from a friend to pay close to six figures, maybe $100,000. They would have promptly made over 2.5 times what they likely paid for my debt. Fast, easy, no legal fees—that's the way win-win debt resolution works. Unfortunately, US Acquisition again countered at $2 million. *"This is going to be lose-lose,"* I determined, as we would both spend unnecessary funds on legal fees. *"But they're going to lose more."*

This is an effort I am still entrenched in. More than a year and a half later, US Acquisition has not collected a dime. They could have made a quick, fast return, and instead they have likely spent over $25,000 in legal fees trying to collect. My legal fees haven't been cheap, either. I have spent close to my original $25,000 settlement offer. Eventually, I hope to settle for $100,000, or even less.

In the meantime, here are the steps I am using, and which you can replicate to foil your judgment creditor:

STEP ONE: IGNORE COLLECTION EFFORTS
The judgment holder, their law firm, and/or their collection agency will likely reach out. "Let's make a payment plan," they might offer. Don't fall for it. You want a lump sum settlement at a big discount. Offer 5-10% of what is owed as payment in full, or even less if the judgment is particularly large.

STEP TWO: DEBTOR EXAMINATION OR CITATION
The judgment holder is likely to reject your offer. Instead, they will and send someone like Mr. T out to serve you with legal papers, which require you to appear in court on a set day and time. This is known as a debtor's exam or citation. You may be asked to bring documents such as paycheck stubs, tax returns, and keys and title

to any vehicles you own. You must attend and share whatever documents specifically answer their requests. If you are unsure if a document is pertinent, don't provide it. Your attorney can attend with you and help keep you calm through the process. The attorney may object to overly broad requests and generally keep the creditor's questions and your answers within the bounds of what is legally required.

Your answers should be brief and direct. Do not get conversational, as there is no benefit in saying too much. Simply answer questions truthfully and do not elaborate or explain. For instance, you may be asked how you arrived at court today. The ideal answer is that you walked or you were dropped off (those are the ideal modes of transportation on your way to court). If you drove a car, you may be asked who owns the car. If you took public transportation or a taxi, you may be asked how you paid.

You will be asked if you have a bank account. If you took the asset protection steps, your answer will be no. If the attorney acts incredulous, asking where you deposit your paycheck, just say you cash it, which is what you should be doing (it's what I do). If you are living with cash, this makes attaching your funds much more difficult. Likewise, the answers to whether you own real estate or a vehicle should be a truthful "no." No furniture, maybe you do own some clothes, but the cost to have the sheriff sell them will likely exceed what the creditor would recover. Besides, all states have designated certain types of property, typically basic items such as clothing and modest household furnishings, as "exempt" from seizure by judgment creditors.

As you can see, the ideal time for asset protection is before a hearing such as this. If you aren't hungry, though, you can volunteer to turn over the baloney and cheese sandwich that you packed for lunch. Since all turnovers besides cash generally need to go through the sheriff, your offer will likely be turned down as the sandwich is sure to spoil by the time the creditor finally gets their greedy hands on it.

You will be asked if you have a job and you are required to provide this information truthfully. If you receive a paycheck, then the creditor is likely to promptly attempt to garnish your wages. If you work for an LLC that you control, then provide the information on your LLC. If the LLC was set up properly in a debtor-friendly state, then the creditor can intercept any money the LLC pays you. However, the creditor cannot exert management control and force the LLC to pay you. Thus, there should be nothing for them to intercept.

STEP THREE: THIRD-PARTY DEBTOR OR CITATION EXAM
Once your creditor realizes that you have nothing, they may set their sights elsewhere. In May 2014, US Acquisition served third-party citations on my wife and the LLCs in which I had an interest. They wanted to know about any property my wife or the LLCs had that belonged to me personally.

I appeared in court on behalf of the LLCs twice in June 2014, and both times the citation examination interviews were continued, which postponed the proceedings. However, as a result of delays caused by my attempts to flush the judgment, US Acquisition forgot to renew the citations after six months and they expired. They could have easily asked the court to renew them, and their requests would surely have been granted. Once expired, citations are dead and US Acquisition cannot examine these LLCs again. Even if they did, they wouldn't be able to get anything. Still, their gaffes saved me some effort. Time is always the debtor's friend. The longer these collection efforts drag out, the more opportunities for creditors and their associates to misstep.

My wife has yet to be interviewed, but will likely be at some point. US Acquisition is trying to find a pain point, a vulnerability that will induce me to capitulate. Sure, this is inconvenient for my wife, and I wish she did not have to go through this. However, she has an attorney who will accompany her. She'll survive and the judgment will remain unpaid.

STEP FOUR: FIGHT WAGE GARNISHMENT

If your creditor finds your correct employer and begins garnishing your wages, you could quit your job and start working freelance, which generates income that is much harder to attach. Depending on the work you do, you could ask your employer to contract with your LLC to do your work. If you work construction or design or programming, particularly for a smaller firm, your employer may be receptive to a freelance arrangement. The employer will save their share of employment taxes as they pay the LLC's invoices.

However, to be classified as an independent contractor, the IRS dictates that your employer cannot set the hours you work. If you work at a big company like Burger King, this probably will not work. Nevertheless, there are benefits to working at a lower-wage job, as many states have laws that provide exemptions from garnishment if you make less than a certain amount. For instance, if you live in the state of Washington and earn less than $1,099.33 monthly, then no wages can be garnished.[41]

41   "Money That Cannot Be Taken From You ("Garnished") to Pay Off a Debt" *Northwest Justice Project,* January 2013. http://www.washingtonlawhelp.org/files/C9D2EA3F-0350-D9AF-ACAE-BF37E9BC9FFA/attachments/7B2D48E8-06A5-4C5A-B6EA-3ACD7D7561E1/0208en.pdf

State laws vary on wage garnishments. If you are in Texas, wage garnishments are generally disallowed. If you live in Ohio, you can request that the court appoint a trustee whom you pay and who then pays your creditors. As long as you are in trusteeship, no wage garnishment is allowed. If there are delays in appointing or setting up the trusteeship, this might buy you some time. In California, you can claim that you are exempt due to economic hardship, as the money is needed to support your family.

Ultimately, your creditor may win. If so, you can either quit your job or accept the garnishment. If you take a new job, the creditor has to figure out where you work and restart the garnishment process. You could work two or three months, or even more, before they catch up with you.

Furthermore, most states cap the amount garnished at a level designed to allow you to live, and federal law dictates that the cap cannot exceed 25% of your disposable income. In Illinois, 15% is the cap. Even if you have multiple creditors trying to garnish your wages, the cap covers all the garnishees (except those for child support and taxes), so an Illinois resident would still get to keep 85% of their paycheck even if multiple creditors were garnishing their wages at the same time.

If you have stunted collection on your judgment so far and completed asset protection and have nothing to collect, then you can skip the remaining steps, relax and let your creditor make fruitless efforts.

STEP FIVE: IDENTIFY DEFICIENCIES

If the judgment holder keeps pressing and you must remain an employee at the same company, then you could ask your attorney to fight the garnishment and the whole judgment collection proceeding. Filings for collection efforts such as garnishment orders are often sloppy and contain deficiencies. You and your attorney can go through the judgment, any assignments, and all other documents to find problems. Check out the 134 Deficiencies in Action Tools for some examples. Here are some blunders on my US Acquisition judgment:

1. The Assignment of Judgment was to US Acquisition Property XXXVI, a non-existent entity. Instead, US Acquisition Property XXXVI, LLC, a real entity but not the one that owned the judgment, was trying to collect from me.

2. The amount allegedly owed was inconsistent: My last letter from KeyBank, in February 2013, indicated that I owed $4,097,678.67 plus $1,745,694.13 in interest, for a total of $5,843,372.80. However, 15 months later, in April 2014, US Acquisition was demanding $8,239,064.60. Even after calculating the additional interest, that's a discrepancy of $1,535,700.85. The judgment creditor needs to prove you owe every penny of what they are trying to collect.

3. The judgment was signed by the judge on January 10, 2011, but was entered by the court clerk on January 12, 2011. In Ohio, the date of the clerk's entry is the date of the judgment. Both in the assignment and registration, US Acquisition referred to a judgment dated January 10, 2011, a judgment that did not exist.

4. On the registration of foreign judgment filing, which US Acquisition is attempting to utilize to enforce an Ohio judgment in Illinois, their attorney (or more likely some paralegal) entered the Ohio court case number in the place where the new Illinois case number was supposed to be inserted.

As a result, my attorney filed a Motion to Dismiss US Acquisition's registration of the judgment.

US Acquisition responded to the court that:

> Newbery's argument is the height of frivolousness...Newbery's Motion to Dismiss is yet another meritless filing designed to delay the regular and reasonable progression of this litigation and the lawful discovery of assets he possesses that may be attached to satisfy the judgment against him. Newbery's motion is a waste of this Court's and Plaintiff's time and resources...Newbery's Motion is plainly filed for the sole purpose of driving up litigation costs and delaying the process...

My counsel countered:

> Newbery's efforts to defend himself from the efforts of Plaintiff to recoup its investment in the judgment Plaintiff purchased from Key Bank are appropriate and within the rights afforded to persons to defend themselves under our legal system. Therefore, he should not be criticized for having thwarted Plaintiff's efforts to recover and profit from its investment.

> The Plaintiff has made a calculated decision to enter the business of purchasing judgments from judgment creditors and to seek to make a profit on its investment. The problems that Plaintiff has experienced herein in turning that profit are of Plaintiff's own doing. It has made numerous errors in the documents that purport to assign the ownership of the Key Bank judgment and in its filings herein. Unfortunately for the Plaintiff, our court system has been designed not only for the benefit of Plaintiffs, but also to allow parties being sued to defend themselves and

either avoid entirely, or in part, losses resulting from actions filed against them.

As of this writing, in August 2015, *US Acquisition Property XXXVI, LLC v. Jorge Newbery* continues to be litigated in Cook County, Illinois.[42]

STEP SIX: LET'S SETTLE OUR DIFFERENCES

Before doing any more work, ask your attorney to call the opposition and offer a settlement. The opposition already holds a judgment, so you have less leverage to force a resolution than non-judgment debts. Still, as time wears on, creditors tend to move on and focus their efforts on debtors more inclined to pay. You might be able to strike a deal.

STEP SEVEN: FILE SUIT AGAINST JUDGMENT HOLDER, COLLECTION AGENCY, AND/OR LAW FIRM

This is what may be coming next for US Acquisition: their team's missteps could create actionable offenses that may justify pursuing damages. They have registered a judgment in Illinois that is of a different amount than the judgment in Ohio. Anyone performing a background check on me will interpret these as two separate judgments due to their sloppy lawyering. They're also pursuing a judgment in which they claim that I owe more than the original creditor claims I do. Their filings are rife with errors.

Chat with your attorney and, once there is enough justification to file suit, go ahead and sue the judgment holder, collection agency, law firm, and any others who may have made boo-boos

---

42   US Acquisition Property XXXVI, LLC v. Jorge Newbery , Cook County Illinois Circuit Court Case # 2014-L-050109.

in attempting to collect the judgment. Your attorney will advise you if the new action will be part of the prior suit which created the judgment, or if you are filing a whole new matter. Regardless, this filing is likely to hasten a resolution.

STEP EIGHT: DISCOVERY

Whether you are in a new suit or fighting collection on the existing judgment, you are permitted discovery. See Action Tools for some samples. You can demand pertinent documents to explore and uncover new flubs, as well as get the judgment holder and their associates to answer questions to dig into any deficiencies.

STEP NINE: TRIAL

If a new trial is required, go to the Community Chest on debtcleanse.com to crowdfund your legal fees for preparation and representation. However, most judgment creditors would prefer to settle than go to trial, especially if this is to be heard in front of a jury.

STEP TEN: SETTLE OR DON'T PAY

At some point, you either settle or don't pay. Either way, post all the details at debtcleanse.com in order to share intel with others in similar battles. Feel good: you've applied all the leverage you could, so reckon with the result knowing you did your best. At worst, your creditor gets to collect some modest sum, maybe garnishing a small amount from your paychecks. This may be a positive trigger to get you to take a new job or step out on your own. US Acquisition's persistent collection efforts were one of the catalysts for this book, so good things often come from bad.

CHAPTER 5

MORTGAGES

A mortgage is the largest single debt for most families, an average of $155,192 per family in the U.S.[43] Of the $11.74 trillion in total U.S. consumer debt outstanding in December 2014, $8.14 trillion (almost 70%) was mortgage debt.[44] This is the biggest piece to most families' debt puzzle.

Luckily, lenders need to stringently follow several procedures in order to foreclose and get you out of your house. Each point in the process is an opportunity for your creditor to err, creating deficiencies for you to exploit. Below, I lay out the steps to Debt Cleanse a mortgage. Many borrowers will be able to resolve their mortgages by proceeding with just a portion of the steps. At some point, your lender will ideally recognize that a cooperative solution is better for all involved.

---

43 "Payment Systems, Consumer Credit, Mortgage Debt—The 2012 Statistical Abstract" US Census Bureau, www.census.gov.

44 Chen, T. "American Household Credit Card Debt Statistics 2015" Nerd Wallet, https://www.nerdwallet.com/blog/credit-card-data/average-credit-card-debt-household/ (June 2015)

Keeping your home is not assured, but following these steps maximizes your chances. Even if you don't get to keep your home, you can likely live for free for years, ideally saving enough in your settlement wallet to purchase a replacement home for cash. Let's get started.

STEP ONE: STOP PAYING MORTGAGE

Many mortgage companies will not seriously consider modifications or other solutions until you are at least 30 or 60 days delinquent. If you are current on your mortgage, lenders often assume that you can either afford your mortgage or you value your credit score so much that you will not let unpaid mortgage payments blemish your credit report. You will not receive a transformative solution until you are delinquent. So stop paying.

If you have a second mortgage, home equity line of credit, home improvement loan, or any other debt secured by your home, stop paying that as well. You can follow the same steps for all mortgages concurrently.

STEP TWO: STOP PAYING PROPERTY TAXES

Since you are not paying your mortgage, also stop paying your property taxes. This deteriorates the equity position of your mortgage holder and puts additional cash in your settlement wallet. Furthermore, your lender may pay your property taxes for you and may be required to send you notices to alert you of this. This is an opportunity for your lender or servicer to misstep (if the notice is not proper or timely), and may create a deficiency for you to exploit later.

STEP THREE: REQUEST MORTGAGE MODIFICATION PACKET

Expect a barrage of phone calls from your lender as soon as you stop paying. Go ahead and take one call and advise that you want to apply for a mortgage modification. Ignore any pressure to schedule a payment as well as requests for detail, such as "Why can't you pay?" or "When can you pay?" Just repeat your request for a mortgage modification. Eventually, the rep will either agree to mail you a mod application packet or transfer you to someone who can. After this one call, ignore all calls. There is no further benefit to you in talking to your mortgage company.

Follow up your telephone request with one in writing using the following template.

*   *   *

MORTGAGE MODIFICATION PACKET REQUEST

Your Name
Your Address
City, State Zip

**VIA CERTIFIED MAIL/RETURN RECEIPT REQUESTED/
COPY RETAINED**

Date

Mortgage Company Name
Address
City, State Zip

RE: Loan #_____, Property Address:_____

I cannot afford my mortgage. Thus, I want to apply for a mortgage modification in order to reduce my payments to an affordable level as well as discount the principal balance to an amount consistent with my property's current market value. Please forward me a mortgage modification application packet.

I look forward to receiving the package and getting on the road to making my home affordable.

In addition, please only contact me in writing regarding this purported mortgage obligation as well as my modification request. Please cease all telephonic communication, including contacting me at my place of work. My employer does not permit personal phone calls.

Sincerely,

Your Signature
Your Name

*   *   *

STEP FOUR: SUBMIT MORTGAGE MODIFICATION PACKET
Complete the mortgage modification packet. These are typically tedious, but reasonably straightforward. Don't try to make a bad situation look better, or a better situation look bad. Just be truthful and thorough. Then, hold the package.

Servicers generally do not start foreclosure until 120 days after you fall behind on payments, and typically will not proceed with foreclosure while a modification request is being reviewed. For example, if you did not make the payment due January 1, then hold the packet until April 20 (allowing ten days for delivery).

You will pick up four months of living free, which will fatten your settlement wallet. On the 110th day (or, if your lender initiates the foreclosure process earlier, 20-days after receipt of demand letter as identified in Step Nine), go ahead and submit your application with a cover letter such as the one below:

*   *   *

MORGTAGE MODIFICATION APPLICATION COVER LETTER

Your Name
Your Address
City, State Zip

VIA CERTIFIED MAIL/RETURN RECEIPT REQUESTED/ COPY RETAINED

Date

Mortgage Company Name
Address
City, State Zip

RE: Loan #_____, Property Address:_____

I am the borrower on the above-referenced loan. As a result of deteriorating economic conditions, I've been forced to dramatically alter my finances to avoid financial catastrophe. Accordingly, I am requesting a mortgage modification to lower my monthly payments and reduce my principal to an amount that more accurately reflects the actual value of my home. At that time, I'll be able to afford the payments and continue to work towards improving my financial situation without losing my home.

Enclosed with this letter is my application for mortgage modification and all supporting documentation I have available at this time.

As you know, time is of the essence so please contact me in writing as soon as possible to share available options and of course let me know if you need any additional information.

Thanks in advance for your anticipated cooperation.

Sincerely,

Your Signature
Your Name

*   *   *

STEP FIVE: WAIT FOR A RESPONSE, THEN REPLY AT LAST MINUTE

Most mortgage companies are terribly inefficient at processing modifications. They will often go back and forth dozens of times in a mind-numbing paper circus between you, the mortgage investor, and any government or private guarantee agencies that are involved. This can go on for months and even years. As your foreclosure is likely on hold, relish the delays as you gain value every day you stay in your home without paying, putting more and more payments in your settlement wallet.

You can help make your mortgage company process your modification even slower by always replying to everything they request near the end of the deadline. For example, they might ask that within 30 days you provide two updated paystubs not more than two months old. If you have them handy and could submit them immediately, don't. Instead, wait until day 25. You'll pick up 25 days of living for free. This may not seem like much, but if you answer every request near the end of the deadline, you can add a few extra months to the modification process. Whether your monthly mortgage payment, or rent elsewhere, would be $500 or $2,000, this can add up to a substantial amount.

At most banks and servicers, the modification review process is inherently robotic and time-insensitive. This is costly for mortgage servicers' investor clients, which are routinely losing millions due to servicer inefficiencies. With a little extra effort, you can make your loan among the costliest for them.

STEP SIX: IF YOU ARE DENIED FOR A MODIFICATION, APPEAL THE DECISION

If you are approved, skip to Step Eight.

You can generally appeal a modification denial within 14 days after your servicer denies your application. Use this letter:

*   *   *

APPEAL OF MORTGAGE MODIFICATION DENIAL

Your Name
Your Address
City, State Zip

VIA CERTIFIED MAIL/RETURN RECEIPT REQUESTED/ COPY RETAINED

Date

Mortgage Company Name
Address
City, State Zip

RE: Loan #_____, Property Address:_____

I just received the sad notice that my application for a loan modification has been denied. Please accept this letter as a formal appeal of the denial letter dated_____, _____. Although I appreciate all the time and consideration that likely went into the review process, I am dismayed at the result. I cannot pay the existing payments. Thus, I need a modification.

I am respectfully requesting that you reconsider my application for the following reasons:

- I am currently unable to afford the existing payment, however I am able to pay $_____ per month (insert "Reduced Payment" from Step Seven).
- Prior to my current financial hardship I was a customer in good standing on this mortgage for _____years.
- Despite my current financial hardship I would very much like to avoid losing my home to a foreclosure and I do have the financial resources to pay a reduced sum every month.
- [insert any other applicable reasons such as modification required under HAMP, modification previously agreed to or offered verbally, errors in the modification application, etc.]

I would like to thank you in advance for taking the time to review this letter and re-review my modification application. I truly hope that a modification will be possible. Please do not hesitate to contact me in writing for more information or any other matter regarding this appeal.

Sincerely,

Your Signature
Your Name

∗   ∗   ∗

The servicer has 30-days to respond to you. You will likely be denied again, but you will pick up another month or so without paying and likely without the foreclosure process having started.

STEP SEVEN: RESPOND TO APPEAL DECISION

If your appeal is denied, use the letter below to let your lender know what you want. Fill in the blanks with the following:

1. Reduced Payment: a payment that equals 1% of the value of your home or your lowest prior payment (for instance, the teaser payment when your loan first started), whichever is lower. If these options are unaffordable, name a payment that you can realistically afford, maybe 25% of your income.

2. Settlement of Your Delinquency: a lump sum equal to three of your new monthly payments in order to settle your delinquency. For instance, let's say you owe three years' worth of $1,500 payments, totaling $54,000. You are proposing a new payment of $1,000 (1% of your home value of $100,000), so you offer $3,000. The remaining back payments and charges need to be written off. This is what AHP typically accepts, but most lenders do not—at least, not yet.

3. Reduced Principal Balance: 95% of the current value of the home.

If you have a second mortgage, request that the payment is reduced to 15% of the existing payment, that the delinquency is settled for three of these new payments, and that the balance is reduced to the lesser of 15% of the existing balance or 5% of the value of the home. Although these requests may sound optimistic, these are plausible because debt buyers often acquire defaulted second mortgages for pennies on the dollar. There is typically no equity in the home, little leverage to apply in order to collect, and a high risk of recovering nothing in the event of a foreclosure by the first mortgage. If you reach an agreement with the second mortgage holder, do not sign and pay until you complete a resolution on your first mortgage.

* * *

NOTICE OF ACCEPTABLE MODIFICATION TERMS

Your Name
Your Address
City, State Zip

**VIA CERTIFIED MAIL/RETURN RECEIPT REQUESTED/
COPY RETAINED**

Date

Mortgage Company Name
Address
City, State Zip

RE: Loan #_____, Property Address:_____

Thank you for the time and effort your firm has expended in reviewing my modification application, including the appeal process. Nevertheless, I am disheartened and appalled that my modification request has been denied. As a final effort to resolve this matter, and in a demonstration of my good faith effort to achieve a successful loan modification, I am providing the terms to which I would agree. These figures have been carefully considered and are ones that are both reasonable and affordable:

   a. Reduce payment to _____.

   b. Settle the delinquent amount for _____.

   c. Reduce principal balance to _____.

These terms are an attempt to reach a loan modification now, or at any time in the future. Please take a few moments to carefully review these terms and my account and reconsider your unwillingness to enter into a loan modification. If these terms are agreeable, please forward the modification agreement promptly. If these terms are not agreeable, I would ask that you please respond with figures that would be agreeable to you. Furthermore, should we fail to reach a modification, I would ask that you re-review this request every 90 days in the event that the proposed terms become agreeable to you at some point in the future.

I look forward to an amicable resolution.

Sincerely,

Your Signature
Your Name

Expect to receive some generic, unhelpful answer to this. However, one day when the lender tires of fighting with you, they may find your letter in their file and agree to accept. This may happen when a bank VP is about to book a flight to attend a deposition to answer questions on your loan, or as the lender prepares for trial. Once your loan becomes inconvenient for someone individually at your lender, they will be searching for an answer to the question: "What does the debtor want?"

Move ahead to Step Nine.

STEP EIGHT: IF YOU GET APPROVED FOR A LOAN MODIFICATION, REJECT IT

Most loan modifications approved by banks and lenders are dismally unhelpful: payments reduced by token amounts, delinquencies added to the end of the loan, principal balances stay the same or even go up, and/or years are added to the loan. You can almost always do better than the first offer, so go ahead and counter. At worst, you will get more time in your home living for free. Tell them the terms you want using the letter below, filling in the blanks with the same amounts as in Step Seven.

If the initial modification offer meets all the requests above, which may become more commonplace as Debt Cleanse grows and creditors realize that early and amicable resolutions are best for everybody, then go ahead and advise your mortgage company that you accept. Congratulations, you are done.

*   *   *

COUNTER OFFER TO MODIFICATION APPROVAL

Your Name
Your Address
City, State Zip

**VIA CERTIFIED MAIL/RETURN RECEIPT REQUESTED/
COPY RETAINED**

Date

Mortgage Company Name
Address
City, State Zip

RE: Loan #_____, Property Address:_____

Thank you for the time and effort your firm has expended in reviewing my modification application. Furthermore, I appreciate the modification offer you have made. Nevertheless, after careful consideration, I have determined that the approved terms are not acceptable or reasonable when my current financial hardship is considered. I do not want to agree to a modification that puts me at risk of being unable to meet the terms. I do, however, sincerely wish to come to a mortgage modification agreement. In an effort to resolve this matter and as a demonstration of my good faith, I am providing you with the loan modification terms which I would agree to. These figures have been carefully considered and are ones that are both reasonable and affordable.

I am respectfully requesting a modification with the following terms:

1. Reduce payment to _____.

2. Settle the delinquent amount for _____.

3. Reduce principal balance to _____.

Please take a few moments to carefully review these terms and my account and reconsider your original proposed loan modification. If these terms are agreeable, or become so at some point in the future, please forward the modification agreement promptly. If these terms are not agreeable, I would ask that you please respond with figures that would be agreeable to you. Furthermore, should we fail to reach a modification, I would ask that you re-review this request every 90 days in the event that the proposed terms become agreeable to you at some point in the future.

I look forward to an amicable resolution.

Sincerely,

Your Signature
Your Name

*   *   *

Even if your counter is likely to get rejected at this time, this will likely become a part of your file and one day someone with authority may review your file trying to determine how to satisfy you. Once they find your counter in the file, you will have provided the answer for them.

STEP NINE: WAIT FOR LENDER TO SEND DEMAND LETTER, THEN SEND IN QUALIFIED WRITTEN REQUEST

Once the modification process has been exhausted, your lender is likely to send you a demand letter, also known as a breach letter or notice of acceleration. This notice typically gives you 30 days to bring your payments up-to-date. Depending on the laws of the state your property is in, additional pre-foreclosure notices may also need to be sent before the demand letter. For instance, New York first requires a 90-day notice to be sent to borrowers on owner-occupied properties to provide information on curing the default as well as a list of approved housing counseling agencies.

Once you receive the demand letter, submit a Qualified Written Request. See Letter D in Action Tools. The QWR wins the prize for the longest and most tedious letter in this book. Long-winded, overly detailed, annoying, nitpicky—the very essence of Debt Cleanse for creditors. You do not need to pay an attorney or anyone else to help with this. You only need to fill in the blanks on the first page, add in your attorney's contact information (if you have engaged one yet) on the third page under "Representative," and sign the last page. All the other responses need to be completed by your servicer and/or lender.

Submit the QWR at any time, although the timeframe between receipt of the demand letter and before the foreclosure action is commenced is typically most strategic—20 days after the demand letter is sent is probably ideal. Basically, you are responding to your servicer's demand for payment with a demand of your own, asking them to prove that you owe what they allege. Some servicers may put a hold on the foreclosure process while they complete the QWR.

Your servicer is required to acknowledge receipt of your QWR request or complete the requested action within five business days. Within 30 business days, the servicer is required to provide the information requested, make the correction you requested, let you know why it believes it cannot provide you with the information, or tell you that a mistake has not been made and that the information is correct. Your servicer may extend the response period another 15 days if, before the end of the 30-day period, your servicer notifies you of the extension and the reasons for the extension in writing.

The answers often help identify deficiencies that you can exploit. Speaking from experience as a debt buyer, QWRs are the stuff of nightmares. Many times, documents get lost and figures get fuzzy as files and data are transferred amongst lenders and servicers. Even at AHP, QWRs are a chore to respond to.

STEP TEN: IF NO RESPONSE TO YOUR QWR, SEND REMINDER LETTERS

If you have not received an acknowledgement of receipt 15 business days after mailing, send the following letter:

* * *

QUALIFIED WRITTEN REQUEST REMINDER TO SEND ACKNOWLEDGMENT

Your Name
Your Address
City, State Zip

VIA CERTIFIED MAIL/RETURN RECEIPT REQUESTED/ COPY RETAINED

Date

Mortgage Company Name
Address
City, State Zip

RE: Loan #_____, Property Address:_____

I mailed you a Qualified Written Request on _____, _____
that was received and signed for at your office on _____,
_____. This request was made pursuant to my rights under
RESPA and your compliance is required by law.

I have yet to receive an acknowledgement that my request has
been received. Federal law requires that servicers acknowledge
receipt of Qualified Written Requests within five business days of
receipt. This deadline appears to have passed. Please respond to
acknowledge receipt of my request.

Sincerely,

Your Signature
Your Name

*   *   *

If you have not received a response 40 business days after mailing
in the QWR, mail this:

*   *   *

QUALIFIED WRITTEN REQUEST REMINDER TO SEND
RESPONSE

Your Name
Your Address
City, State Zip

**VIA CERTIFIED MAIL/RETURN RECEIPT REQUESTED/
COPY RETAINED**

Date

Mortgage Company Name
Address
City, State Zip

RE: Loan #_____, Property Address:_____

I mailed you a Qualified Written Request on _____, _____
that was received and signed for at your office on _____,
_____. This request was made pursuant to my rights under
RESPA and your compliance is required by law.

I have yet to receive a response to my request. Federal law requires
that servicers respond to all Qualified Written Requests within
thirty (30) days of receipt. This deadline appears to have passed.
Please provide a full response to my request within ten (10) days
of the receipt of this letter. If I do not have a full response by that
time, I will pursue all remedies available to me under the law for
your failure to comply with RESPA.

Sincerely,

Your Signature
Your Name

Two reminders are sufficient. You are building a trail of correspondence demonstrating your reasonable, almost helpful, approach to resolving the situation. If your servicer and/or lender choose to not respond, or act unreasonably, this may aid you later if this debt is litigated.

STEP ELEVEN: CEASE COMMUNICATION WITH YOUR SERVICER
At this point, there is no further benefit in communicating with your servicer.

Once you receive the QWR response from your servicer, send in Letter C in Action Tools.

If your servicer does not respond to the QWR despite your reminder letters, then send it in 50 business days after you sent in your QWR request.

Once received, your servicer cannot contact you by phone or mail, except one time to tell you what they are going to do and to provide any notices required to pursue legal action. This may hasten the sale of your loan to a debt buyer at a big discount.

STEP TWELVE: HIRE AN ATTORNEY
See Chapter 3: Quick Start. Get the engagement letter, but don't pay yet.

STEP THIRTEEN: STOP TAKING CARE OF YOUR HOME
As a lender gears up for foreclosure, they will often order a drive-by Broker Price Opinion of your home. A local real estate agent will drive by your home and take photos, compare to other recent sales

in your neighborhood, then provide a report to your lender with an estimated value. There will often be multiple reports ordered during the period in which your loan is in default.

You want the report to indicate the lowest possible value. This may help a debt buyer buy your debt for a greater discount, which may translate to a better eventual settlement for you. To achieve this, you want the front of your home to look as bad as possible.

Stop taking care of your lawn, park cars on your front lawn if your neighbors don't get mad (or if you don't care if they get mad), and leave trashcans in the front of the home in a disheveled state. If you have kids, let them leave their toys strewn about the yard. Maybe let your dog (or a neighbor's) dig a few holes. You could even put up a sign "Dogs Welcome" and let owners know that cleanup is not required.

If you are comfortable, share your strategy with your neighbors and let them know this is a temporary effort. In fact, if they all stopped taking care of the fronts of their homes and started parking their cars on their lawns that might help as well. You want the report to come back to your lender with comments like, "poor condition, does not look kept-up, no pride of ownership," "worst house on the block," and "this street is the worst in the neighborhood." The latter one is if your neighbors join your effort. They may be unable to afford their mortgages either, so the makeshift deterioration of your block may help you all if they need to Debt Cleanse their mortgages as well. Sadly, in some neighborhoods, the deterioration has already occurred. If this is the case on your block, at least here you can use this to your advantage.

Back at your lender's headquarters, they'll be looking at the photos and may reason that the interior of the home is the same as the exterior. As a result, your home's value will likely be pegged at a lower price than if the home looked good. This may make your settlement offer appear more reasonable.

As the future is uncertain, if repair needs come up, make short-term fixes. Try to put off any significant repair costs as long as possible. This may prove advantageous later on.

STEP FOURTEEN: DETERMINE IF YOU ARE IN A JUDICIAL OR NON-JUDICIAL FORECLOSURE STATE
Your lender's next move is typically determined by whether your home is located in a judicial or non-judicial foreclosure state. Determine which you are in by consulting the lists below.

Judicial Foreclosure States:
Connecticut • Delaware • Florida • Illinois • Indiana • Kansas • Kentucky • Louisiana •Maine • Maryland • Massachusetts • Nebraska • New Jersey • New Mexico • New York • North Dakota • Ohio • Pennsylvania • South Carolina • Vermont • Wisconsin

Non-Judicial Foreclosure States:
Alabama • Alaska • Arizona • Arkansas • California • Colorado • Georgia • Hawaii • Idaho • Iowa • Michigan • Minnesota • Mississippi • Missouri • Montana • Nevada • New Hampshire • North Carolina • Oklahoma • Oregon • Rhode Island • South Dakota • Tennessee • Texas • Utah • Virginia • Washington • Washington D.C. • West Virginia • Wyoming

Judicial foreclosures are completed within the court system, offering borrowers protection and opportunities to assert their rights. Lenders are required to file foreclosure lawsuits in court and borrowers have a prescribed period, often 28 days, to respond.

Non-Judicial foreclosures are conducted outside the court system and inherently provide borrowers less protection and few, if any, opportunities to assert their rights. Furthermore, non-judicial actions are generally faster and cheaper for lenders. As a result, lenders prefer non-judicial foreclosures, but judicial foreclosures are better for borrowers.

STEP FIFTEEN: WAIT FOR YOUR LENDER TO START FORECLOSURE
JUDICIAL

If you are in a judicial state, once the foreclosure starts, your lender will file a court action and you will be served with the court documents in person or by certified mail. The clock ticking down to your answer due date does not start until you are served. No need to go the post office to pick up certified mail or to be particularly available in answering your front door.

Court filings are public record. You will probably know that the lawsuit has been filed, as you will start receiving mailings from attorneys offering to represent you in the foreclosure or to file bankruptcy, real estate agents wanting to list and sell your home, and investors wanting to buy your home. Once you are served or otherwise become aware that a lawsuit has been filed, get your attorney involved and, if needed, pay the retainer from your settlement wallet.

If you cannot be served after a month or two, then your lender will eventually complete service by publication. This can take several additional weeks, while you are living in your home for free, adding juice to your settlement wallet.

You are unlikely to see the publication, as these are in the legal notices buried at the back of some local news rag, in a section that no one reads. Once you know that the lawsuit has been filed, you or your attorney should check with the court regularly to review status of service. Court clerks in many jurisdictions have case records available online, so you or your attorney can access case details conveniently.

Whether served in person, by mail, or by publication, log the date of service (and write it on any document you receive) as this day starts the countdown before your answer is due.

NON-JUDICIAL

If you are in a non-judicial state, then you can typically expect to receive notices, such as a Notice of Default or Notice of Trustee Sale, by certified and regular mail. The countdowns start when the Notices are recorded, so answer your door as you normally would. However, still no need to go out of your way to pick up certified mail, as you typically will receive the same notices by regular mail.

In either case, now is the time to engage your attorney and pay the retainer from your settlement wallet.

The games are about to begin.

STEP SIXTEEN: IDENTIFY DEFICIENCIES

Mortgages provide a myriad of potential deficiencies that can help you compromise your lender's position and maximize leverage to gain a favorable settlement. You and your attorney can review all the documents you have compiled, including the lawsuit or Notice, original loan documents, any responses to your QWR, plus your communication log, in order to identify any deficiencies that exist.

Take a look at 134 Deficiencies in Action Tools to help.

Deficiencies are rampant. "Deceptions and shortcuts in mortgage servicing will not be tolerated," Consumer Financial Protection Bureau Director Richard Cordray said in December 2013. "Ocwen took advantage of borrowers at every stage of the process."[45] Ocwen is the nation's largest non-bank mortgage servicer and, sadly, their practices are commonplace.

"Frankly, the notion that government intervention has been required to get the mortgage industry to perform basic functions correctly—like customer service and record keeping—is bizarre to me but, regrettably, necessary," Steve Antonakes, deputy director of the CFPB, said in February 2014. "There will be no more shell games when the first servicer says the transfer ended all of its responsibility to consumers and the second servicer says it got a data dump missing critical documents."[46]

Missing documents may include the original promissory note or similar evidence of the debt. Additionally, there typically needs to be an allonge or endorsement for every transfer of the note, and an assignment for every transfer of the security instrument. When lost, lenders will often patch together an "affidavit of lost note, allonge, or assignment". These affidavits typically work if no one disputes them. However, these are examples of deficiencies that you can exploit to great effect.

45 CFPB, "CFPB, State Authorities Order Ocwen to Provide $2Billion in Relief to Homeowners for Servicing Wrongs", Consumer Financial Protection Bureau, http://www.consumerfinance.gov/newsroom/cfpb-state-authorities-order-ocwen-to-provide-2-billion-in-relief-to-homeowners-for-servicing-wrongs/ (December 19, 2013).

46 CFPB, "Deputy Director Steven Antonakes Remarks at the Mortgage Bankers Association", Consumer Financial Protection Bureau, http://www.consumerfinance.gov/newsroom/deputy-director-steven-antonakes-remarks-at-the-mortgage-bankers-association/ (February 19, 2014).

Even if the documents can be produced by your lender, odds are high that at least some of the documents have been robo-signed. An investigation of mortgage documents in one Massachusetts county revealed more than 25,000 suspect signatures; in one North Carolina county, 74 percent of signatures inspected on mortgage documents were questionable; and in one Illinois county, a random sample of 60 documents revealed that all 60—100 percent—carried robo-signed signatures. [47]

Robo-signing occurs when a creditor, collection agency, or mortgage servicer employee signs a document (such as an affidavit or assignment) without reviewing it. Although robo-signing came to light in a deposition pertaining to mortgage collections, the practice is rampant across all debt types. In some cases, employees sit in a room all day signing their own names and, other times, forging someone else's. Sometimes they appear to be just doodling, as signatures are indecipherable. Despite the mortgage industry claiming to have cleaned up this practice, the reality is that robo-signing continues, just more discreetly. Even authorized mortgage executives can sometimes be guilty when they sign a stack of documents without taking the time to verify the information in each one. Further, although billions were paid in fines, no one ever went back and corrected the millions of robo-signed documents generated before the scandal broke.

Proving that your documents were robo-signed, or signed without verifying the contents, generally cannot be determined by simply reviewing the document. You can reference, and contribute to, the directory of robo-signers at debtcleanse.com. If you get a match

47   Kella McCaskill. "What You Need To Know About Robo-Signing" *Hope for Women Magazine*. October 10, 2011. http://hopeforwomenmag.com/featured/what-you-need-to-know-about-robo-signing

and determine that a robo-signer signed one of the documents related to your debt, then you and your attorney can argue that the robo-signer did not have proper authority to sign and/or did not review the underlying documents properly, and therefore that document is invalid. This is not fatal, as your lender can now go back and get a properly authorized person to sign the document. Nevertheless, this may require that your lender restart the legal action, re-serve you, and lose time and money. A favorable settlement may become an attractive alternative.

If a signer's name is not on the robo-signer list, go ahead and Google the signer name and "robo-signer" and see what comes up. For fun, try goggling "Linda Green robo-signer" and see the results you get. If you are still uncertain whether documents in your file were robo-signed or improperly signed, go ahead and allege this deficiency and try to prove it in discovery.

Other flaws in servicers' record keeping and processing were recently exposed in a July 2014 jury award of $16.2 million in damages[48] to a California homeowner due to a servicer's refusal to correct an error caused by $616. In 2011, Phillip Linza, a salesman from Plumas Lakes, Calif., received a loan modification from servicer PHH Corp. A $616 shortfall in Linza's escrow account, used to pay property taxes and insurance as part of the monthly payment, caused PHH's computer systems to automatically generate letters demanding different amounts each month.

When Linza called PHH to inquire about the inconsistent payment requests and ask for a simple letter verifying the correct

---

48 Berry, K., "How a $600 Servicing Error Snowballed into a $16M Jury Verdict, Mortgage Servicing News, http://www.nationalmortgagenews.com/news/servicing/how-a-600-servicing-error-snowballed-into-a-16m-jury-verdict-1042366-1.html (August 13, 2014).

amount due, PHH refused to assist. Eventually, even though the modification had reduced his monthly payment to $1,543, PHH sent him a letter demanding $7,056. Linza then threatened to sue PHH, whose response was to tell him to "go ahead, file a lawsuit, and get in line because they had deeper pockets than he had to litigate this," according to Linza's attorney, Andre Cherney.

"PHH wouldn't own up to their own mistake and find a reasonable solution, which was to do the decent act of writing a letter to clarify everything," said attorney Jon Oldenburg, who also represented Linza. "It's a pretty consistent theme that servicers in this context very rarely admit that they've done anything wrong," Oldenburg added. "You don't see many servicers own up to their part in the process. They think that because the borrower went into default, they don't have any legal claims."

Linza's experience is common and borrower abuse by big banks and servicers is well documented. A judge (likely a member or friend of the elite) later reduced Linza's award, asserting that he knew better than the jury (likely members of the 99%).

Nevertheless, note how at some point in this litigation, the pendulum swung: instead of how much Linza needed to pay PHH to settle his debt, the question morphed into how much PHH was going to pay Linza.

A strong defense becomes a powerful offense. Both are built on a fundamental component: deficiencies. Find them and exploit them.

STEP SEVENTEEN: TAKE LEGAL ACTION

JUDICIAL: ANSWER LENDER'S LAWSUIT AND FILE COUNTER CLAIM AGAINST LENDER AND ANY OTHER PARTIES WHO MAY HAVE CONTRIBUTED TO YOUR UNAFFORDABLE MORTGAGE

In judicial foreclosure states, your attorney must file an answer to the lender's lawsuit. Your answer could be a simple general denial of the claims against you, or a robust answer and counter-claim against the lender and third parties. Your attorney will advise as to what makes the most sense in your circumstances.

Simply filing an answer will typically add months or years to the time you can stay in your home without paying. As part of the filing, you can add a counter claim against your lender, servicer, and any other parties that may share responsibility for your unaffordable mortgage and any related challenges. Third-parties can include prior lenders and servicers, real estate brokers, mortgage brokers, property sellers, appraisers, title companies, escrow companies, and notaries. For instance, home flippers and their real estate agents sometimes conspire with appraisers and mortgage brokers to sell homes for inflated values to consumers who are set up to fail from the outset, to the enrichment of the conspiring parties.

The second mortgage lender will already likely be named in the suit, but sometimes will not answer as the costs of participating in the litigation may exceed what they expect to recover.

In the answer and counterclaim, include all the deficiencies you and your attorney have identified. To maximize the time before the court action proceeds, do not file until the last few days before the answer deadline. This will typically gain a week or two of time and extra money into your settlement wallet.

NON-JUDICIAL: FILE LAWSUIT AGAINST LENDER AND ANY OTHER PARTIES WHO MAY HAVE CONTRIBUTED TO YOUR UNAFFORDABLE MORTGAGE. REQUEST TEMPORARY RESTRAINING ORDER AND INJUNCTION TO STOP FORECLOSURE. RECORD LIS PENDIS

In non-judicial foreclosure states, your goal is to put your foreclosure into the court system where you can fully exert your rights and have a judge oversee the process. Effectively, you are turning a non-judicial foreclosure into a judicial one. To do this, your attorney can file a lawsuit against your lender and any other parties that may share responsibility for your unaffordable payments and any related challenges. This could include the servicer, prior lenders and servicers, real estate brokers, mortgage brokers, property sellers, appraisers, title companies, escrow companies, and notaries. In addition, sue any second mortgage lender, the foreclosing agent, typically a trustee, and add requests for a Temporary Restraining Order, Preliminary Injunction, and Permanent Injunction to prevent your lender from foreclosing on your home. In your lawsuit, include all the deficiencies you and your attorney have identified.

To justify the TRO and injunctions, your attorney will likely need to argue that the foreclosure sale would extinguish your interest in the home. As the home may be sold to a third-party bidder at the foreclosure sale, it could be altered or destroyed. If that were to occur, the very subject matter of the lawsuit would be lost before you have the opportunity to prove the merits of your case. If the foreclosure action is permitted to move forward, the ultimate effect would be to deprive you of a legitimate opportunity to proceed with your lawsuit, and you would be irreparably harmed.

Your attorney can assert that you can demonstrate a likelihood that you will succeed on the merits of the lawsuit. Therefore, issuance of the preliminary injunction is absolutely necessary for the protection of your rights during the course of the litigation. Finally, your attorney can argue that the lender will suffer no harm if an injunction is ordered.

In some cases, the court may require that you post a bond. However, you can request a waiver if any of the following apply:

1. Your income is low.

2. The delay will not cause unreasonable harm to your lender.

3. The validity of the security instrument, i.e. deed of trust or mortgage, is in question.

4. The lender's interest could be protected by other means besides foreclosure, such as requiring you to make reasonable monthly payments during the course of the litigation. As a result, the court may require that you make these payments to the court clerk.

Finally, you and your attorney should consider recording a Lis Pendis—a public notice of the pending litigation against the property. This will blemish the title of your home pending the outcome of your lawsuit. As a result, title insurance companies will likely refuse to insure any sale of your home until the litigation is fully resolved and the Lis Pendis released. You have made completing the foreclosure almost useless for your lender until your lawsuit is decided upon.

STEP EIGHTEEN: DISCOVERY

As part of your litigation, your attorney can conduct discovery and request documents from your lender and cross-defendants. Even if you have documents that you have compiled, such as those in response to your Qualified Written Request, ask for them again to make them part of the court proceeding. You may receive new documents and identify new deficiencies. Also, you may find inconsistencies amongst the provided documents that may reveal additional deficiencies.

Your attorney can also request that the opposition respond to interrogatories, requests for admissions, and depositions. Your attorney will advise which, if any, may be beneficial to your case. See Action Tools for more details; you will find more than 750 sample document requests, interrogatories, requests for admissions, and deposition requests. You and your attorney can decide which are pertinent, and add your own based on the specifics of your case. These are part of the court proceeding and both sides are required to respond to the other's reasonable requests.

For example, ask your lender for the Notice of Sale or Transfer of Mortgage. In 2009, the Helping Families Save Their Homes Act amended the Truth In Lending Act to establish a new requirement for notifying consumers of the sale or transfer of their mortgage loans. The purchaser or assignee that acquires the loan must provide the required disclosures no later than 30 days after the date on which it acquired the loan. You want to make sure that this was furnished in the required timeframe

Additionally, you might want to depose the notary on any assignments of your mortgage, to confirm any allegation of robo-notarizing. Assume that a Vice President at Bank of America needed to sign hundreds of documents a day, including an assignment on your loan. Many of these documents needed to be notarized, which required that the notary actually witness the VP signing the document as it happens. The notary would have needed to hover over the VP for much of the day. This is not likely to have occurred. Instead, the VP probably signed a bunch of documents and then handed them off to the notary, who went through the batch signing and stamping.

Was this a malicious conspiracy by the VP and the notary? No, probably not. Instead, they were just trying to get their work done in a more efficient manner (or a lazier one, depending on one's perspective). However, this "efficiency" is improper, illegal and, if the notary were to be deposed, he or she might feel uncomfortable testifying under oath that he or she actually witnessed the signature on your assignment.

In a 2011 lawsuit against Chase Bank filed in Los Angeles County,[49] a borrower presented an assignment into Chase signed by alleged robo-signer Christina Allen on February 21, 2009 but not notarized until April 6, 2009. The borrower argued that Chase did not own the loan on February 23, 2009 when the Notice of Default was recorded. A settlement was reached.

Certainly notarizing a high volume of documents is inconvenient and open to non-malicious shortcuts (as well as occasional malicious ones). Depose the notary in discovery. You can ask how many documents were signed that day in addition to what other work the employee completed. If 100 documents were notarized

49 *Bradley Gerszt v. JP Morgan Chase Bank*, Superior Court of the State of California, County of Los Angeles, Central District, Case No. BC 465280

and they also attended to other duties, following proper procedure may seem implausible over an eight-hour timeframe. How many minutes did they spend notarizing each one? How many minutes did they spend notarizing your assignment? The notary may break under oath.

QUESTION EVERYTHING

Even if your lender produces a document with a seemingly-legitimate date, question it and ask for some evidence of mailing. In late 2014, New York regulators announced that Ocwen Financial had backdated letters to potentially hundreds of thousands of troubled mortgagees.[50] These misdated letters deprived modifications to struggling homeowners and expedited the process of seizing homes. Ocwen blamed the misdeeds on "software problems."

A BENEFIT OF NOT BEING A WHITE MALE

If you are not a white male, probe for discrimination. In the United States, there are roughly 97 men for every 100 women. Although women represent a statistical majority, they qualify as a minority group because they tend to have less power and fewer privileges than men. To sociologists, minorities are "singled out for unequal treatment." The U.S. population is approximately 63% white, 16% Hispanic, 12% African American, 4% Asian, 1% Native American, and 4% other and multiracial. If you are not a white male, you may have received unequal treatment at origination.

Big banks routinely steered borrowers—disproportionately minorities—who qualified for conventional loans to immensely more profitable subprime mortgages, which carried terms that

---

50 Sterngold, J., "Ocwen Accused Anew of Improper Practices", The Wall Street Journal, http://www.wsj.com/articles/ocwen-backdated-thousands-of-letters-to-distressed-homeowners-ny-state-says-1413909346 (October 21, 2014).

set up borrowers to fail. Wells Fargo's loan agents allegedly even joked about peddling "ghetto loans" to "mud people,"[51] according to an affidavit from a Wells Fargo loan officer in lawsuit filed by the City of Baltimore against the bank. The City alleged that Wells Fargo systematically singled out blacks in Baltimore and suburban Maryland for high-interest subprime mortgages.

Discovery is your opportunity to expose and verify this type of bad behavior, creating leverage to hasten a favorable settlement.

STEP NINETEEN: REQUEST MEDIATION

If the court case continues to move ahead, your attorney can request mediation. In some states, mediation is a mandatory step in the foreclosure process. The following states have foreclosure mediation programs: California, Connecticut, District of Columbia, Delaware, Florida, Hawaii, Idaho, Illinois, Indiana, Kentucky, Maine, Maryland, Massachusetts, Michigan, Nevada, New Hampshire, New Jersey, New York, New Mexico, Ohio, Oregon, Pennsylvania, Rhode Island, Vermont, Washington, and Wisconsin.

If there is not a formal mediation program, you can still request it and this is often granted by the court. Mediation typically is perceived as a reasonable approach from your side, an effort to try to cooperatively work towards a resolution.

STEP TWENTY: ATTEND MEDIATION

In most cases, a junior attorney at a local law firm will show up to represent the lender at mediation. This attorney will get a representative at the lender or servicer on the phone and a mediator

---

51 Popken, B., "Affidavits on How Wells Fargo Gave "Ghetto Loans" To "Mud People"", Consumerist, http://consumerist.com/2009/06/08/affidavits-on-how-wells-fargo-gave-ghetto-loans-to-mud-people/ (June 8, 2009).

will attempt to broker a deal between the two sides. The lender is typically required to negotiate in good faith. Upon rare occasion, the lender is ready to make a deal at the mediation. If so, reiterate the terms you want, the same ones you asked for in Steps Seven and Eight.

More frequently, the lender will simply request documents such as tax returns, paycheck stubs, and the like in order to process a new modification request. As you likely will not have the requested documents handy at the mediation (in order to maximize delays, don't bring any, unless required), the mediator will likely reschedule a follow-up meeting by phone or in-person a few weeks later. In order to demonstrate your good faith, provide the documents as requested. As always, do not hand over until a few days before the prescribed deadline in order to gain more free time in your home, and extra dollars in your settlement wallet.

STEP TWENTY-ONE: ATTEND MEDIATION FOLLOW-UP

At the subsequent get-together, the mediator will want to make sure you have provided what the lender requested, and check in with the lender regarding progress of their review. Essentially, you are now back to the beginning of a new modification process. This is advantageous as the foreclosure is typically on hold until this often-prolonged mediation step is completed. There may be multiple mediation follow-ups over the subsequent months. That's fine; the longer the mediation phase drags on, the more free time you get in your home.

STEP TWENTY-TWO: RESPOND TO LENDER'S MEDIATION OFFER

If the lender agrees to your modification request based on the terms in Steps Seven and Eight, then accept. If the lender presents you with unhelpful modification terms, denies your mod, or comes back "approving" you for a short sale or deed in lieu requiring you to leave your home, then counter with what you want. Ideally, the mediator may prod a resolution. However, if the mediator cannot get your lender to approve a result that you are happy with, then the mediator will hand your file back to the court. Either outcome is fine.

STEP TWENTY-THREE: PREPARE FOR TRIAL

Ideally, your lender will have capitulated and agreed to your demands, or something reasonably close, by now. However, if your matter appears on track to go to trial, start a crowdfunding campaign utilizing the Community Chest on debtcleanse.com to raise money to fund your legal fees. As part of any settlement, your attorney should require that your lender pays your attorney fees to allow the crowdfunded monies to be returned to your supporters. Your attorney will efficiently be able to do this through debtcleanse. com, so contributors can recycle their funds and aid other debtors facing challenges.

Realize that the lender does not want to go trial, as the outcome is unpredictable. Cases are often settled in the weeks before trial, even on the eve or day of trial. Stay focused on the outcome you want. As this drags on further and gets closer to trial, the odds of a successful outcome increase. Juries are more apt to relate to a struggling homeowner than a bank or Wall Street firm. So, if your case is strong, the lender could well lose.

STEP TWENTY-FOUR: WIN OR LOSE, YOU WIN

Every matter ends eventually. You may take a few Debt Cleanse steps and your lender may agree to a favorable deal early on. On the other hand, they could push to trial and you could lose, or you could win. Even if you lose, you will likely have a good-sized settlement wallet to apply towards new housing.

If you win, enjoy your sustainable housing solution.

If you lose, you can appeal if your attorney believes that there are grounds. If your attorney recommends this, then by all means do so. Appeals often take several months, or even years, and the lender may hold off proceeding with the foreclosure in the interim. However, your lender may ask the court to require that you post a bond during this period. You may be able to argue that the bond will create an undue economic hardship. At a minimum, these arguments may buy more time. If the court requires a bond and you do not pay, then the lender may be able to proceed with the foreclosure. Whether you appeal or not, you can still stay in your home. The fight is not over.

If a lender wins a foreclosure matter, a sale of your home will be conducted in which the winning bidder (frequently the mortgage holder) obtains title to your home. However, you still have possession. You are now in a position similar to a non-paying tenant in a rental property. The new owner needs to go to court to evict you. Sometimes, the eviction is part of the foreclosure court case, whereas other times a separate eviction lawsuit needs to be filed. Either way, there are several legally prescribed steps which can often take months to complete.

Some states require you to be served with a Notice to Quit or similar document. Your attorney can provide you some insight into what the new owner will need to do to try to get you out of the house. In most cases, the new owner will attempt to entice you to leave voluntarily with a pittance of a payment. Don't take the cheese.

Note: The completed foreclosure will typically extinguish any second mortgage holder's security interest. You still owe the debt, but the lender no longer has collateral and is unsecured. Cleanse using the steps in Chapter 10: Credit Cards & Unsecured Personal Debt.

STEP TWENTY-FIVE: COUNTER CASH FOR KEYS

If a foreclosure sale occurs, the lender or other winning bidder will typically send out a local agent to offer you cash for keys. Act like you are interested and ask them to put the offer in writing so you can have a spouse, trusted friend, or family member review. This is to buy time. Do not permit an inspection of your home unless legally compelled to do so. If you have not done so already, stop cutting the lawn, taking care of the yard, and do not remove snow unless absolutely needed for access. Log any in-person interaction and phone calls you have.

Then, respond to the cash for keys offer in writing by requesting a higher amount and more time. Let's say that the initial offer is $750 to move in 30 days. You could counter at $5,000 to move out in 120 days—terms that are unlikely to get accepted. That's fine. You don't want them to be. The negotiation will take some time, and your lender or other new owner will typically hold off on eviction if you demonstrate interest as they try to save legal fees.

You can use the letter below and respond to whoever contacted you. This can be done by email so there is a record. Otherwise, you can send by regular mail. No need to send certified mail, as this would seem unusual and may cause the agent to be on their guard. You want to keep communication casual and loose.

* * *

COUNTER TO CASH FOR KEYS OFFER

Your Name
Your Address
Your City, State & Zip

Date

Local Real Estate Agent/Foreclosure Sale Buyer Representative Name
Address
City, State Zip

RE: Loan #_____, Property Address:_____

I would like to thank you for your offer of $_____ to move out within _____ days. Unfortunately, the amount of the payment is insufficient. Furthermore, the move out date does not give me sufficient opportunity to find other suitable living arrangements. In an effort to resolve this matter, and as a demonstration of good faith, I am proposing a payment of $_____ to move out within _____ days. This proposal is based upon careful consideration of my current situation and financial hardship. I am hopeful that you can work with me to come to an amicable resolution of this matter. If this proposal is unacceptable to you, please reconsider your previous offer and let me know if there are other terms that you would be agreeable to. Please respond to this inquiry in writing so that I have proper documentation of this request for my records.

I look forward to an amicable resolution.

Sincerely,

Your Signature
Your Name

*   *   *

STEP TWENTY-SIX: REQUEST CASH FOR KEYS AGREEMENT, BUT DON'T SIGN ANYTHING

Make the best cash for keys offer you can, then request a copy of the cash for keys agreement for you to review using the letter below. Again, email or regular mail is fine.

*   *   *

CASH FOR KEYS AGREEMENT REQUEST

Your Name
Your Address
Your City, State & Zip

Date

Local Real Estate Agent/Foreclosure Sale Buyer Representative Name
Address
City, State Zip

RE: Loan #_____, Property Address:_____

Your most recent cash for keys offer of $_____ to move in ____ days appears to be reasonable and something I can likely agree to. Before I make any final decision though, I would like to review the full agreement. Please forward the cash for keys agreement to me so that I can review all of the terms and conditions. If they are acceptable, I expect to sign and return the agreement immediately.

Thank you for the time and effort you have put into this matter.

Sincerely,

Your Signature
Your Name

*　*　*

This will buy some more time while the agreement is prepared and, again, the eviction will likely continue to remain on hold.

STEP TWENTY-SEVEN: REJECT CASH FOR KEYS AGREEMENT, MAKE OFFER TO REPURCHASE HOME

The lender (or whoever acquired your home at the foreclosure sale) will often request that you sign and return the Cash for Keys Agreement by a certain date, maybe a week after receipt. Instead of returning the agreement, wait until the deadline and then forward the letter below.

Realize that, if you end up evicted, the new owner is probably going to then sell your home. Why not sell it to you? Your home will likely be sold through the same agent you are now likely corresponding with. Make an offer to buy the home back for cash, using the funds in your settlement wallet. If the low-end value of your home is close to what you have in your settlement wallet, make an offer at maybe 90% of the low-end value. If you don't have enough in your settlement wallet for this much, just offer what you have.

If you have a modest home that is now worth $50,000, maybe you stashed your $1,000 monthly mortgage and tax payments into your settlement wallet for three years. At this point, you put away $36,000 but spent $9,000 on legal fees. Thus, you have $27,000. However, you can ask to close in 90-days, which would give you another $3,000, a total of $30,000. You can offer that, but the amount is likely to get rejected.

However, maybe you also set aside $650 monthly from your unpaid auto loan and credit card payments. That's $23,400 saved over three years. Even if you paid $10,000 of that in discounted settlements and legal fees, you could still have $13,400 extra. Add that to the $30,000, and you have $43,400. Your lender (or whoever purchased at foreclosure sale) should realize that that's a great deal for them. This would be a great deal for you as well: you'd own your home free and clear.

If you have a higher-value home, getting the owner to agree to this and coming up with the cash may be challenging. Let's assume your home is worth $150,000 and your set aside $2,500 monthly. After 36 months, you saved $90,000, but $9,000 went to legal fees, so you have $81,000. Let's say you stashed another $1,500 monthly from your other debt payments for an additional $54,000. If you spent $15,000 of this on legal fees and settlements, you'd have $39,000 to add to the $81,000, for a total of $120,000. If you have 90 days to close, the extra three months of saved payments will bring you close to $123,000. You are now within range of what might be acceptable.

Don't be afraid to ask for what you want, so send the following letter by email or mail.

For the purchase price, input what you have available (but not more than 90% of the as-is value of your home) including what you can realistically set aside in the next 90 days.

For the modification terms, reiterate the same figures as you did in Steps Seven and Eight.

*   *   *

REJECTION OF CASH FOR KEYS OFFER/COUNTER PROPOSAL

Your Name
Your Address
Your City, State & Zip

VIA CERTIFIED MAIL/RETURN RECEIPT REQUESTED/ COPY RETAINED

Date

Local Real Estate Agent/Foreclosure Sale Buyer Representative Name
Address
City, State Zip

RE: Loan #_____, Property Address:_____

I do appreciate the offer of $_____ to move out within _____ days. However, upon careful review and consideration, I am unable to accept your offer at this time. I do not believe a cash for keys arrangement meets my needs or is something that is in my best interest.

However, I would like to buy back my home for $_____ cash, without financing, to be paid in full within 90 days.

If my buy-back proposal is not agreeable, I would like to work with the lender to have the foreclosure sale rescinded and my old loan modified. I have carefully considered my financial situation. In an effort to resolve this matter, and as a demonstration of good faith, I have provided the loan modification terms that I would accept. These figures have been carefully considered and are ones that are both reasonable and affordable:

a. Reduce payment to _____.

b. Settle the delinquent amount for _____.

c. Reduce principal balance to _____.

These terms are an attempt to reach an agreement for a buy-back or loan modification now, or at any time in the future. Please take a few moments to carefully review these terms and my account. If these terms are agreeable, please forward either the purchase or modification agreement promptly. If these terms are not agreeable, I would ask that you please respond with figures that would be agreeable to you. Should we fail to reach a purchase or modification agreement, I would ask that you re-review this request every 90 days in the event that the proposed terms become agreeable to you at some point in the future.

Please provide me with a written response. I look forward to coming to an amicable resolution of this matter.

Sincerely,

Your Signature
Your Name

*   *   *

The real estate agent may become an advocate for your offer, as this represents a relatively easy commission. If this gains traction, make sure you create a Limited Liability Company or other entity to buy and take title to the home (see instructions in Chapter 2: Pre-Cleanse). You can then rent the home from the LLC. Otherwise, if you have other creditors, a free and clear home would be an easy target for judgments, liens, and other adverse actions.

Your offer may be perceived as too low and/or some lenders have policies preventing the sale of a foreclosed home back to the prior owner. In either case, keep up the fight. A lawsuit settlement may be the best means to get a lender to make a policy exception.

At this point, you may be asked to allow access for the agent to inspect the interior of the home to help determine the value. Allow this and schedule at your convenience. However, make sure your home displays no pride of ownership. Poor housekeeping helps make sure that the photos that go back to the owner's headquarters show your home in the worst possible—and least valuable—state. Empty toy baskets and hampers full of dirty clothes on the floor. Have dirty dishes in the sink, an unflushed toilet or two (with the seats up), and make the tub look stopped up by filling with water and mixing in some dirt and Drano: you want just enough murkiness so that the tub stopper is not visible (don't worry – the agent is not likely to reach their hand in to see if there's a stopper in there). Leave the partially used Drano bottle on the side of the tub to drive home the illusion. Create some darkness and the presumption of electrical issues by partially unscrewing light bulbs here and there throughout your home, and keeping window coverings closed. Maybe let your dog have an accident on some non-carpeted surface and don't clean it up. Feed Fido well the night before so that the deposit is voluminous, then act surprised when you are showing the agent around—"Naughty Fido!" You want your home to reflect a generally unkempt appearance in the interior and exterior, so use any ideas you come up with towards this goal (and share on debtcleanse.com for others to replicate). Finally, point out all those repairs you have been putting off to the agent. Their estimate of value should reflect the property's apparent shoddy condition and help justify your modest offer.

STEP TWENTY-EIGHT: REQUEST REPAIRS

Once foreclosed, the owner may be responsible for repairs and maintenance of the home. Since you have been performing just bare-minimum repairs throughout the foreclosure process, now is the time to ask that proper repairs are completed. The goal right now is to create pressure on the owner to accept your offers of resolution, and to strengthen your case to fight the eviction. Wait a week after you tender your Rejection/Counter Proposal to see if you receive approval. If not approved, or no response is received, ask for repairs to be completed with the following letter:

*　*　*

REQUEST FOR REPAIRS

Your Name
Your Address
Your City, State & Zip

VIA CERTIFIED MAIL/RETURN RECEIPT REQUESTED/ COPY RETAINED

Date

Local Real Estate Agent/Foreclosure Sale Buyer Representative Name
Address
City, State Zip

Foreclosure Sale Buyer Name
Address
City, State Zip

RE: Loan #_____, Property Address:_____

Please accept this letter as a formal request for repairs to the property located at the address listed above. Due to the recent foreclosure sale, the new owner is now responsible for all maintenance and repairs at the property. There are many repairs needed, and failure to make the necessary repairs threatens to make the property unsafe and uninhabitable. As I'm sure you are aware, as the party legally responsible for the property, you would bear the liability for any claims arising from the condition of the property, particularly now that you have been properly notified of the needed repairs.

The repairs that need to be addressed immediately are listed below. Please have these resolved promptly. Your failure to respond and/ or act accordingly will be considered as an assumption of the risk of liability for any incident that may occur arising from the conditions disclosed in this letter. The necessary repairs are:

1. _____

2. _____

3. _____

4. _____

5. _____

6. _____

7. _____

8. _____

9. _____

10. _____

Please contact me in writing to schedule these repairs as soon as possible. I stand ready to cooperate fully with any and all efforts to complete these repairs.

Sincerely,

Your Signature
Your Name

*   *   *

STEP TWENTY-NINE: COMPLAIN TO THE AUTHORITIES

If the owner does respond, be reasonable and promptly schedule access. Owners often hire a property preservation company or local contractor to inspect and make the repairs.

If the owner or their agent does not respond to a repair request within ten business days, and there is no apparent progress on your counter proposal, contact local health and building & safety departments to report your concerns. Inspectors will likely schedule a visit to the property, at which time you should point out all issues, large and small. Provide owner contact information, including the local representative (i.e. real estate agent), to the inspectors, who will then write reports and likely send orders to the owner to make repairs. Request copies of the orders.

Given that there is no formal landlord-tenant relationship, the owner may believe that they are not responsible for repairs. However, local municipalities want homes to be kept up to local code. As the occupant, you are responsible for housekeeping. However, municipalities generally hold the property owner accountable for property upkeep and repairs, including grass cutting and snow removal.

STEP THIRTY: EXPECT TO BE SERVED WITH NOTICE TO VACATE, THEN EVICTION OR EJECTMENT ACTION

Typically, if the owner wants to evict you, you will be served with a Notice to Vacate, or an Eviction or Ejectment action. Since you did not have a landlord-tenant relationship, the action may be termed an ejectment. The litigation could be part of the existing foreclosure case or a brand new matter. No need to be particularly available for service. Eventually, though, you will be considered served even if publication becomes necessary. During this time, you remain living in your home for free, putting more and more cash in your settlement wallet.

STEP THIRTY-ONE: DÉJÀ VU: TAKE THE NEW NOTICE, LAWSUIT, AND OTHER DOCUMENTS TO YOUR ATTORNEY

Forward all the new documents, including those pertaining to cash for keys and repairs, and any correspondence, as well as your communication log to your attorney.

STEP THIRTY-TWO: FIND DEFICIENCIES

Again, review Deficiencies in Action Tools on debtcleanse.com. Eviction and ejectment actions are often prepared in assembly-line fashion by paralegals and are frequently teeming with errors, creating deficiencies to exploit.

Although the real estate agent who made you the cash for keys offer may have been licensed to conduct real estate sales and management, the agent was likely not employed by the servicer and was unlicensed to collect debts. If the deed resulting from the foreclosure sale was not recorded at the time of contact, their efforts may be illegal attempts to collect a debt and violations of state and federal laws.

Further, the owner may have breached their duty to maintain the property in a habitable condition. Take photos of any repair issues, work completed, inadequate repairs, and recount the date work was requested and completion date(s), if any.

STEP THIRTY-THREE: FILE ANSWER AND COUNTER CLAIMS AGAINST ALL WHO MAY HAVE ERRED IN THE CASH FOR KEYS AND EVICTION PROCESS

This is not a rehash of the foreclosure case, but disputes the foreclosure sale buyer's actions after that matter was decided. You may have potential claims against the owner, real estate broker, real estate agent, property preservation company, and others. Exploit any deficiencies.

STEP THIRTY-FOUR: CONDUCT DISCOVERY

You've been here before. Just as during the foreclosure case, you can now request documents from the owner and any cross-complaint defendants. Ideally, these will reveal additional deficiencies. No Qualified Written Request applies this time. Instead, your attorney will ask for documents based on your circumstances. Take a look in Action Tools for some to start with.

You can also request answers through interrogatories, requests for admissions, and depositions. These, especially depositions, will be inconvenient and costly for all sides. The owner's attorney may reach out to your attorney asking, "What do you want?" The answer should remain the same: sell the home back at the price offered. Alternately, rescind the foreclosure sale and modify loan to the terms first laid out in Steps Seven and Eight.

STEP THIRTY-FIVE: REQUEST MEDIATION

If the matter remains unresolved, request mediation. Time will continue to tick away while you live for free, stuffing your settlement wallet. In fairness, cash is coming out of your settlement wallet to pay legal bills, but you should still be ahead. The longer you keep this going, the more likely that you will achieve a positive result.

STEP THIRTY-SIX: ATTEND MEDIATION, PUSH TO REPURCHASE OR MODIFY

At the mediation, share your buyback price as well as desired modification terms. Ideally, the mediator can nudge this to a satisfactory conclusion.

STEP THIRTY-SEVEN: IF MEDIATION FAILS, PREPARE FOR TRIAL

As needed, start a crowdfunding campaign using the Community Chest on debtcleanse.com to fund your defense at trial. An eviction trial in front of a jury is unpredictable for all sides. However, you have won by just getting here. There is a chance that, just before the trial, the owner may finally capitulate and give you what you want. The owner has legal fees as well. Trying to kick a family out of their home when they have money to pay a reasonable price to buy back the home seems like pure vindictiveness. If I were on the jury, I would want to see the family stay and the owner get a reasonable amount. I wouldn't want to be part of a decision in which either side is getting screwed, especially the struggling family. So, go to trial.

STEP THIRTY-EIGHT: YOU'RE AHEAD NO MATTER THE OUTCOME

If you win, enjoy your sustainable housing solution.

If you lose, you can appeal if your attorney believes that there are grounds. If not, you need to make arrangements to move. Ideally, the monies in your settlement wallet will help you move and maybe even buy a replacement home for cash so you will never have another mortgage again.

Either way, keep us posted on your progress at debtcleanse.com. We can all learn from your experience. Resolving your mortgage can be an ultra-marathon and take years. Be patient and recognize that the drawn-out timeframe is as trying on your lender as it is on you. Remind yourself that the delays benefit you. If you follow every step, you will win even if you lose. Best wishes for a rewarding journey.

CHAPTER 6

VEHICLE LOANS

I witnessed my first car repo in early 1993 in Compton, California. I was a loan officer in the dining room of the home of Henry and Gloria as they signed second mortgage documents to consolidate their bills.

"Wait, that's my car!" Henry screamed as he looked out the window. "I'm going to pay," he said as he got up in a panic.

"What?" I said.

"I'm going to pay," Henry screamed again as he bolted out the front door. Gloria looked out the window as well, but remained seated. She then bowed her head.

"What's happening?" I asked as I got up, feeling confused. I looked out the window. The family car, an AMC Pacer like the one in *Wayne's World,* was in the driveway. A tow truck had backed in and hooked the back wheels up.

"The car note. We're late. We were going to catch it up when this loan came through," Gloria said solemnly.

"Maybe I can help," I said. I walked outside. There were two burly repo guys, looking like henchmen, and Henry. One of the henchmen was flat on the ground, apparently checking the hook up. The bigger one, wearing an L.A. Dodgers cap, was standing with his arms crossed and an impatient look on his face.

"I will have the payments caught up in a few days," Henry pleaded.

"Once it's hooked up, we got to take it in," said the capped henchman.

"Yup, no choice. Sorry," said the smaller one, getting up. He looked like a walking tattoo museum, with colorful markings etched all over his exposed skin.

"We are signing final documents for a new second mortgage. He will be making your payments in a few days," I said, trying to be helpful.

"Can't you just drop the car back down? Please," begged Henry.

"We just can't do it," the capped henchman said. "We got to go."

"If your company wants the payments, we can give you the payments," I said to the capped henchman as I followed. "I'll pay them from my checkbook right now. It seems silly to take the car in, and then this family has to come in and pay the payments, repo fees, storage fees, and all that junk. Wouldn't it be easier to just take the payments?"

"Those fees, repo, storage, and 'all that junk,' as you put it," the capped henchman said, "That's how I get paid. I don't care about the payments."

"This is such a waste of time and money," I thought.

Over the last several years, as many Americans' credit scores deteriorated due to challenges experienced during the financial downturn, there has been an explosion in the issuance of subprime auto debt. Wall Street gets giddy whenever consumers pay high interest rates on predatory loans. For example, a 2014 $390 million bond issue backed by auto loans made to borrowers who had filed bankruptcy featured interest rates averaging 18.6%.[52] The bonds, issued by Prestige Financial Services, were oversubscribed four times over, meaning that investors would have bought up to $1.5 billion of this debt if available. Most stunningly, Standard & Poor's rating agency provided a triple A rating to these bonds (remember, all the borrowers had filed bankruptcy). It seems like the agency's name got transposed in some Scrabble-fest gone bad: "Standard & Poor's" should be "Poor Standards".

The good news is that the big behemoths on Wall Street are easy targets for consumers who have been saddled with oppressive loans. Thus, even though their minions in the form of repo men, dealers, and collection agencies will try to earn some scratch by bullying you into paying, ultimately Wall Street can absorb the hit when you don't pay. You are David to their Goliath. Be a nuisance and you can win.

---

52 "Here They Go Again! Sub-Prime Auto Loans Fueling Phony Surge on Dealer Lots" Zero Hedge, http://davidstockmanscontracorner.com/here-they-go-again-sub-prime-auto-loans-fueling-phony-surge-on-dealer-lots/ (July 21, 2014).

Winning is not like merging into the express lane. The road is more like a detour over a gravel passageway that has been washed out in places. In contrast to holders of most other debts, auto lenders can typically repossess without going to court first. This creates challenges when you stop paying. Most of us need our vehicles to go to work, school, shopping, transporting kids or other family members, and other stuff. The prospect of losing one's primary means of transportation can be nerve rattling. However, I'll share some strategies to keep your car even after you stop paying.

Just stay relaxed and focused and let Debt Cleanse be a GPS to guide you to your destination: a vehicle loan settled for pennies on the dollar. Here's the roadmap:

MILE ONE: GAS UP

Gather any and all documents from when you took out your loan. In addition, mail Letter F in Action Tools to request documents on your loan. In contrast to most other Debt Cleanse strategies, you want to build up your case early, even before you stop paying if possible. You want to be ready to jam up your lender if they try to repo. Most lenders will typically respond to your letter with at least some of the requested documents. If they ignore you, proceed anyway.

MILE TWO: FIND THE MOLE

Determine if there is a GPS disabler device installed on your vehicle. This should have been disclosed to you when you purchased your vehicle (if not, this is a deficiency which you can exploit later). When you stop making payments, the dealer or finance company can activate a remote kill switch to disable your vehicle, use the GPS to identify location, and pick it up.

If you are confident that one of these devices is not installed, skip to Mile Four.

MILE THREE: KILL THE MOLE

Remove the GPS disabler device. Some dealers and finance companies will insinuate that removing the GPS disabler device is illegal, akin to car theft. This is untrue. You own the car and they own a loan secured by the car. Therefore, you are legally entitled to remove the device, just like you could change the oil filter. Removing the GPS/kill switch device is likely a breach of your finance agreement, but so is not making your payments, so this has little impact.

If you are not mechanically inclined, you can review debtcleanse. com to find a local remover. If there is not one listed in your area, Google "GPS disabler removal" and the name of your city to find a local remover. If you cannot find anyone nearby, post an ad on craigslist or on social media: "I'm looking for someone who works on cars to remove a GPS disabler device from my car. If you can do this, please contact me."

The cost is typically around $100.

Alternately, you can remove the device yourself, or have a friend or family member with basic mechanical skills help you out. I learned most of the following from a post on instructables.com by "thematthatter."[53]

The first step is to locate the device, which typically needs access to the sky to engage the GPS, a clear shot to receive and broadcast

53 http://www.instructables.com/id/How-to-remove-a-GPS-disabler-from-a-vehicle/

a status signal through GSM, and is likely near the ignition due to the kill feature. These particulars narrow the potential locations. Access the underside of your dash and look for anything that appears added-on. Tip-offs include new wiring, new electrical tape, relatively thick wires and wires that connect to the roof. The disabler is about the size of half a baloney and mustard sandwich on Wonder Bread and typically is plastic and includes two wires, like strips of string cheese, which connect to the ignition.

The second step is to locate the components, which often have five wires:

1. GPS antenna wire or "eye," which you can likely follow to the top of the car by removing the plastic trim around the door.

2. GSM antenna wire, located next to the eye.

3. Ignition wire, which connects to the red wire on the ignition to provide power to the device.

4. Vehicle ground wire.

5. Relay wires, which are wired into the black wire to the ignition. When the device is "activated," the relay breaks contact with the black wire on your ignition key switch and kills your ignition.

The third step is to remove all five of the components. Before you do this, remove the negative cable off your car battery, which will broadcast to your dealer that the vehicle has no battery power. This will likely cause your creditor some concern and may prompt a call to you, which you can ignore. Remove the components by disconnecting the antennas at the receiver and pulling the eye or antenna apart.

The final step is to reassemble the ignition. Once the disabler is removed, reconnect the ignition wires so that the black wires are connected together, after which you can replace the plastic trim. Finally, reconnect the battery terminal and start your car, which your dealer or finance company can no longer disable or track.

Ignore any attempts by the dealer or finance company to contact you. As soon as the disabler is off, make sure to get your car off the street and into a locked garage, gated and locked driveway, or other secure area. If needed, take to a friend's or relative's home or business.

MILE FOUR: CUT THE CHEESE
Cut the money flow and stop paying. If your payment is conveniently debited from your bank account each month, now is the time to cancel the auto debit and make collecting inconvenient.

MILE FIVE: DUDE, WHERE'S MY CAR?
Always keep your car in a locked garage, behind a chained gate, or in some other secured area. I am repeating myself, but I don't want you to let your guard down and walk out to find your car jacked, whether by thieves or repo men. You need to protect your car from all kinds of predators.

Repo men generally may not breach the peace, so they cannot break into a locked area. When you park at work, or while you are out, be sure to park in secure areas whenever possible. Use gated pay lots if nearby. Consider swapping cars with a friend who is also participating in Debt Cleanse in order to keep the trail cold. Relax and enjoy your game of hide and seek.

Realize that repo men can be very persistent, so don't get lazy for a minute. If you have to run an errand, take someone with you who can sit in the driver seat while you step out. Over time, repo men get tired of chasing tough-to-find vehicles and look for easier prey. Nevertheless, act like you are always being followed. And remember, in some respects, you are.

Vehicles equipped with automated license plate scanners are cruising parking lots nationwide all day and night. These are "spotters" which feed scanned license plate images to private national databases. If a car wanted for repo is located, then the spotter is notified, almost instantly, and contacts a repo company in order to pick up the vehicle.

Even if a specific repo person cannot find your car, these spotters cruising the parking areas of high-density places such as shopping centers, apartment buildings, and sports events are a constant threat. To counter this new technology, always back into parking spaces if you live in a state in which a front license plate is not required. If you do have a front license plate in a state where one is not required, remove it.

If this sounds inconvenient, it is. However, the longer you go without paying and the longer your car is not repossessed, the less effort will be made to find your auto and the less likely that your vehicle will ever be repossessed. Target one year of not paying and parking strategically. The year will give you time to set aside enough payments in your settlement wallet to make a settlement offer and pay some legal fees, if needed. Take this day-by-day. Be patient and diligent.

MILE SIX: VETO THE REPO

A frustrated repo man, seeing that your car is behind a locked gate or speculating that the car is in your locked garage, may come to your door to ask that you hand over the keys and the car. Veto the repo. Unless they have a court order, just politely ask them to leave. You would have been notified if they have a court order.

You can lie to repo men, but not to police. Do not imply to repo men that your car was stolen (this would be lying about a crime), and definitely do not report your car lost or stolen to the police. You can tell the repo man that your friend borrowed the car and you haven't seen them in a while, that you parked it but can't remember where, or even that your kid's science fair project was to make a car drive on water. However, do comply with any legitimate court orders.

Keep your gas tank full in case repo men start following you. If you notice a tow truck on your tail, do not speed up, do not drive dangerously, and just proceed to your destination or other secure location. If you are driving by yourself to a location with a locked gate or non-automatic garage door, call someone and ask him or her to open it before you arrive, then close as soon as you get in. If you are being followed, do not get out of your car to open the garage or gate, as the repo person could hook your car and pull while you are out. They can move fast, sometimes without even getting out of their trucks. If no one is available at your destination, drive to a friend or family member who can assist.

Even if you have a garage door opener to open and shut the garage door without you having to get out of your vehicle, make sure to stay in your car until the garage door shuts behind you. An occupied car cannot be taken (this would be abduction) and you cannot be dragged out (battery & assault).

MILE SEVEN: GO SILENT

Go silent: ignore collection calls, letters, and any other outreach. Log the calls, any repo man interaction, and file away all correspondence. These steps will maximize the odds that you will keep your car and settle your unaffordable vehicle debt.

EIGHT MILE: I CAN'T LOSE MY JOB

Many employers have policies restricting personal phone calls in the workplace. Although exceptions are often permitted for family or urgent situations, this typically does not apply to calls from creditors.

Mail Letter B in Action Tools to shut down creditor calls to your workplace.

MILE NINE: DISPUTE & VALIDATE

For each party that contacts you in writing claiming to be attempting to collect your vehicle loan, respond with a Dispute & Validation Letter: Letter A in Action Tools.

File away whatever responses you receive. You may need to scour these later for deficiencies. You are building your defense —and even offense—component by component.

MILE TEN: STOP CONTACTING ME

If your loan is sold to a debt buyer or assigned to a collection agency, once you receive a response to your Dispute and Validation Request, send them Letter C to request that they stop contacting you.

MILE ELEVEN: GET AN ATTORNEY IN YOUR PIT

You might not need one, but get one ready to hop into the shotgun seat if you need help. See Chapter 3: Quick Start for guidance on selecting an attorney. However, hold off on paying the retainer—you might not need legal counsel.

MILE TWELVE: ARE YOU THREATENING ME?

Log and report threats. Repossession companies' employees are prone to stepping on the lines of what is legal, and even stepping over. The stress and high-pressure nature of their job may be their excuse, but that doesn't make their actions legal. Here are some real verbal threats from repo men, as captured on pennlawyer.com, a law firm that assists consumers with unaffordable debts:

"I gotta hear from you or I'm going to make this thing go legal."

Repo men cannot threaten you with an action they are cannot take. Repo companies are hired to pick up cars, not initiate legal action.

"I will be at your door every evening..."

Repo men cannot harass debtors with actions such as showing up at your door every day, or even threatening to do so.

"This is officer..."

Repo men cannot impersonate officers of the law.

"I will issue a warrant to the sheriff for your arrest."

Again, repo men cannot threaten you with what they cannot do. They cannot issue a warrant to the sheriff for your arrest.

If you receive any threats, log as much detail as you can with regard to the communication, along with the date and time. If in person, take video using your cell phone. If they leave a voice mail, save it. These records may be helpful if this is ever litigated.

MILE THIRTEEN: CONCEALMENT LAWS

In most states, you can actively hide your vehicle and not violate any laws. In Illinois, where I live, I could tell the repo man that the only reason they cannot find my car is because I am concealing it from them. There's no law against that. However, based on debt-slavery-like concealment laws in a handful of states, such as Texas and Georgia, repo men in many states (even those without concealment laws) readily hurl threats of imprisonment if delinquent debtors do not promptly hand over the keys to their cars. Concealment laws outlaw hiding collateral (such as a vehicle) that is subject to a security interest (such as a vehicle loan). These are typically misdemeanors.

Threats are frequently bluffs and are rarely carried out. Some repo men in Georgia have even been known to hand arrest warrant applications (filled-in, but never actually filed with the court) to debtors as a scare tactic. Realize that repo men want your car, and a misdemeanor charge against you does nothing to benefit them.

If any finance company, dealer, or repossession company ever threatens you with criminal action based on concealing collateral, not paying, or any other reason, or makes threats of any other kind, please input in your communication log and also register the threat at debtcleanse.com. The firm is likely violating the Fair Debt Collection Practices Act if they threaten you with criminal charges or other actions unless they intend and have the ability and authority to take such an action. If we can document these threats being utilized by companies that never follow through on them, then we have identified deficiencies that you and other debtors can exploit.

For instance, a hundred debtors may report on debtcleanse.com that ABC Repo (fictitious name) in Macon, Georgia threatened them with arrest warrants. However, if all hundred update the site each month and we find out after six months that ABC Repo never actually files a single arrest warrant application on any of them, then all one hundred debtors likely have a FDCPA violation as a deficiency. Additionally, other ABC Repo debtors being threatened would likely have peace of mind knowing that the jail threats are just a bluff.

To creditors' advantage, however, the threat of a misdemeanor charge will often convince debtors to hand over the keys. Tell me you're going to sue me, and my response will be, "Go ahead, and stand in line." Tell me I'm going to jail, my response becomes, "Wait, let me examine this situation a bit more carefully to make sure you're lying. But, if you are BSing me, I will throw the deficiency book at you."

Even if a creditor decides to try to get concealment charges filed, a hearing is typically required before a warrant can be issued. Your attorney can attend the hearing and defend the action. Someone needs to prove that you were hiding your vehicle from your creditor, as opposed to you being prudent and trying to avoid getting your car jacked. The creditor needs to prove they have a valid lien.

Here is a helpful summary from dallasconsumerattorney.com:

Texas Penal Code 32.33 contains the Hindering Secured Creditors crime. A person who has signed a security agreement creating a security interest in collateral, such as a car, may be convicted of hindering a secured creditor if, with the intent to hinder enforcement of the security interest, he destroys, removes, conceals, encumbers, or otherwise harms or reduces the value of the property.

First, though, the creditor must have made a demand for the collateral to be returned. Also, the statute says the property was taken outside Texas or across Texas lines without the consent of the secured party (finance company). Intent to hinder prosecution of the security interest must be proven as an element of the alleged crime.

For a person to be convicted of the crime of "Hindering Secured Creditors," the accusing party must prove the person INTENDED *to hinder enforcement by undertaking a specific act of "hindering." Merely refusing to turn over property will not support a conviction because that alone does not show active concealment, destruction, harming or removing the property from the reach of the secured creditor...Proving the charges is a high and difficult burden...I am not a criminal defense lawyer but I handled a case for abuse of process against a financial institution...the case resulted in a substantial settlement for my clients who had been arrested on such a charge.*

There are not supposed to be debtor's prisons in this country. These were abolished in the mid-1800s. However, concealment laws are tools of elite creditors and should be repealed. In the interim, we want to snuff out any use and abuse of these laws.

If a hearing on concealment charges is set, contact your attorney right away and jump to Mile Sixteen. Then, go to the Community

Chest at debtcleanse.com to start a crowdfunding campaign for your legal fees. We need to support you from start to finish on these actions, which means keeping you out of jail and suing the creditor for abuse of process. If debtors consistently present strong defenses, creditors will tire of employing this tool (which is rarely used anyway). Creditors talk money, so if a strategy loses money, creditors are going to stop utilizing that strategy.

At the hearing, your attorney can advise the court that the debt holder may not be entitled to the car or the amount claimed due to assorted deficiencies in the origination, servicing, and/or collection of your loan. With this, judges will likely recognize the dispute for what it is: a civil dispute that needs to be resolved in a civil court and not a criminal one. Ideally, the overzealous debt holders may settle for a big discount or even forgive what you owe, pay your legal fees, and—if the circumstances are just right—maybe even pay you a cash settlement.

MILE FOURTEEN: PREPARE FOR THE WORST

Do not keep personal items in your car. If the car gets taken, just let it go: you likely owe more than the car is worth, so you are losing nothing. However, by not leaving personal effects, you have no reason to follow up and pay to retrieve. Always carry your cell phone and money for transportation back to your home or work. Be prepared.

That said, if your car is repossessed, log every detail you can. In the event anything was improper about the process, this can create deficiencies that may help you settle the debt and get the car back. If you witness the repo, pull out your cell phone and videotape the proceedings. Object to the repo and demand that the repo man stop taking your car. Raise your voice so you are clearly heard:

"Mister, you can't take my car. That's my car. You can't take it. I'm objecting to you taking my car."

Be polite, but firm. Avoid cussing or being argumentative. Anticipate that the video may one day be viewed by a jury, or at least on YouTube. You want to be the mild-mannered reasonable one, and the repo man to be the aggressor.

Here are a couple potential repo deficiencies, as identified by Johnson Law Firm of West Des Moines, Iowa:

A. *The automobile was repossessed causing a breach of peace, such as taking your vehicle from your garage, taking your vehicle over your unmistakable objection, and/or shouting and yelling.* [54]

B. *A police officer facilitated the repossession. A police officer has every right to make sure the parties do not harm each other and to keep the peace, but a police officer is not allowed to take sides in a repo. You have as much right to your vehicle as the repo agent. Tell the officer politely that you will do whatever you are instructed to do, but you are not consenting voluntarily to the repossession of your vehicle.* [55]

If the repo man or police officer requires you to give up the vehicle over your objection, you likely have a deficiency that you may help get your car back, and settle the loan at a big discount.

MILE FIFTEEN: CHECK OUT THE ROAD AHEAD

Take a moment to assess your position. If all this sounds like you

---

54   http://www.johnsonlawfirmia.com/

55   Idib.

are going in to battle, you are. However, this is a fight you might win. Treat every day in which you do not pay and keep your car as a victory, as you keep adding money to your settlement wallet. If you can survive not paying for six months and you still have your car, there are six common outcomes (listed in order of most likely to least likely):

A. If all goes well, and particularly if your car or other collateral is of modest value, your debt holder may abandon repossession efforts. They may determine the amount that they could recover by repossessing and reselling your car and/or by suing you does not warrant further efforts. In this situation, there is a decent chance that your car never gets repossessed and you never get sued.

In 1996, I co-signed for an employee's car. After several months, the employee took another job and stopped paying on the car loan. It didn't feel right to pay. So I didn't. My phone would blow up with collection calls from time to time, and I had a blemish on my otherwise great credit. The car was never repossessed and after a year or so the lender wrote off the debt and sold to a collection agency. After seven years, the tar on my credit fell off and I could stop explaining what happened.

Keep driving the car until it dies. You can then sell to a wrecker for a token sum. If you decide to sell the car prior to that, you will need to reckon with the lender's lien. Think of the car lien like a mortgage on a house—this protects your creditor's loan until you pay or settle. If you want to sell, figure out how much you can sell the car for. Then contact the debt holder and offer to settle for 25% of what you will net from a sale. Being that the lien has been not been paid for an extended period of time, the debt will most likely have been sold to a debt buyer for pennies and they will likely welcome your heavily discounted offer.

Thus, you could drive the car for years without making a payment, fattening your settlement wallet. You then settle the debt when you sell the car, potentially netting money from the sale of the car that, when you stopped making the payments, was worth less than what you owed. Make sure that, as part of the settlement, you receive a waiver of deficiency so that the remaining debt is forgiven and you never have to pay another penny on this. Congratulations—you have now cleansed your unaffordable vehicle debt.

B. You "lose" and your car is repossessed. As you likely owed more than you could sell the car for, this is still a win: you got rid of a car with no equity and chances are that you saved some payments into your settlement wallet. Take that cash and buy a car outright. If you have $1,000, you can likely buy a running used car on craigslist.

When I moved from Cincinnati to Chicago in 2011, I sold my 2002 Isuzu Rodeo on craigslist for a thousand dollars. Even though the car had 170,000 miles on it, I had performed all the scheduled maintenance and the car ran great. The transaction yielded a happy seller and a happy buyer.

If you have saved more, you can buy a nicer car. Sure, it may be used, but you have no monthly payments. Besides, a new car depreciates the moment you drive it off the lot.

Unless you later get served with a lawsuit to recover the deficiency, this is your final step.

C. You receive a lawsuit or other court hearing notice from your debt holder trying to obtain a court order to turn over the car. Proceed to Mile Sixteen.

D. Everything outlined in outcome A about you keeping your car happens, except that the debt holder, or a debt buyer which buys your loan at a large discount, serves you with a lawsuit for the amount of the loan. Proceed to Mile Sixteen.

E. Everything in outcome B about your car being repossessed happens, except that the debt holder serves you with a lawsuit for the deficiency. Let's say you owed $10,000 and they repossess and sell the car for $5,000, the debt holder may sue you for the $5,000 difference. The now-unsecured debt is often written off by creditors and sold to debt buyers or assigned to debt collectors. These can often be settled for token amounts, or not paid at all. Proceed to Mile Sixteen.

F. You receive a notice of hearing on an application requesting an arrest warrant for concealment. Speed to Mile Sixteen.

MILE SIXTEEN: MERGE ONTO THE LEGAL HIGHWAY

Go ahead and pay the attorney you have chosen to work with using the funds in your settlement wallet. Share with your attorney the communication log, all notices and documents you have received, and any documents you have from when you financed the car.

MILE SEVENTEEN: DO A DIAGNOSTIC ON YOUR LOAN

Look under the hood on all the documents and interactions with your lender, dealer, repo men, collection agencies, and even the manufacturer. Identify deficiencies by looking for signs of trouble to exploit.

For instance, you may have qualified for an interest rate of 4%, but the dealer may have sold you on a 6% rate. Dealers are often paid bonuses if they can sell borrowers on rates higher than they qualify for, and dealers, in turn, frequently pay commissions to salespeople to take advantage of borrowers. This sounds like some under-the-table deal, but it's not: these kickbacks may be legal, but if this incentive arrangement contributed to your loan's unaffordability, then you can assert this deficiency. A Center for Responsible Lending report found that "consumers who indicated that they trusted their dealer gave them the best rate available paid between 1.9 and 2.1 percentage points more in APR, after controlling for credit risk, than those with a more skeptical outlook."[56] APR is Annual Percentage Rate, the yearly cost of the loan including interest and costs such as fees.

Dealers may be allowed unlimited markups, creating a wicked incentive for dealers to coerce borrowers to agree to the worst loans possible. This is a massive business—nationwide, consumers who purchased cars in 2009 paid $25.8 billion in additional interest due to dealers' markup of their rates.[57] Notably, borrowers whose loans are marked up are 33% more likely to fail and lose their vehicles to repossession.[58] Sadly, consumers are generally unaware of this abuse, as 79% of consumers surveyed in North Carolina were not aware dealers could mark up rates without their consent.[59]

56 Montezemo, S., "The State of Lending In America and Its Impact on U.S. Households, Center for Responsible Lending, http://www.responsiblelending.org/state-of-lending/reports/10-Payday-Loans.pdf (September 2013)

57 Kukla, C., "The Hidden Cost of Car Loans", US News & World Report, http://www.usnews.com/opinion/economic-intelligence/2014/02/27/how-auto-dealers-cheat-borrowers-with-interest-rate-markups (February 27, 2014).

58 Montezemo, S., "The State of Lending In America and Its Impact on U.S. Households, Center for Responsible Lending, http://www.responsiblelending.org/state-of-lending/reports/10-Payday-Loans.pdf (September 2013)

59 Id.

Instead, consumers are typically simply advised that they qualified for a certain payment, which may be at 8%. However, the consumer may have actually qualified for a 7% rate, so the lender will pay the dealer a fee based on upselling the borrower. These dealer incentives are not specifically disclosed to consumers. *Auto Dealer Monthly* justified this in a 2011 editorial:

> *Consumer advocates also believe that consumers should be told that the dealer keeps part of the finance charge and should be told the amount of the dealer's participation, notwithstanding the fact that nearly every* RISC *[Retail Installment Sales Contract] in use today discloses that the dealer keeps part of the finance charge and that the rate of finance charge is negotiable with the dealer. Additionally, the Federal Reserve Board has twice rejected the suggestion that the amount of dealer participation should be a required disclosure under Reg. Z, wisely concluding that the* APR, *which is a required federal disclosure, provides the best information to the consumer and that the disclosure of dealer participation would not benefit the consumer. The consumer advocates, however, claim to know better than the Feds.*[60]

Being that "the Feds" are the elite and often unduly influenced by lobbyists from all industries, including auto dealers, the conclusion that the government knows better than the people is naïve. Although this editorial asserts that a disclosure is typically made that "dealer keeps part of the finance charge", in practice these are typically buried in fine print and breezed over by sweet-talking salespeople.

---

60   Hudson, T., "Wrong Assumption on Dealer Participation Leads to Faulty "Study", Auto Dealer Monthly, http://www.autodealermonthly.com/channel/dps-office/article/story/2011/08/ wrong-assumption-on-dealer-participation-leads-to-faulty-study.aspx (August 2011).

Another deficiency could exist if you end up with a lemon of a vehicle because the dealer made promises, either in writing or orally, about the good condition of the vehicle. If so, the dealer may be required to live up to them. Statements about a product that you rely on as part of deciding whether to purchase the product constitute an express warranty that the dealer breaches if the promise turns out to be a lie. An "as is" contract does not disclaim an express warranty if one is made. To prove this, your attorney can prepare an affidavit about what the dealer told you, as well as one from any witness to the dealer's laudatory statements about the vehicle, plus copies of ads that state the car is in good shape, and anything else that will back up your story.

Many vehicle loans are unaffordable because much more than the car is being financed: Add-on products are often automatically included in the loan documents. Consumers are rarely advised that these are optional and that they can refuse these extra items which typically provide limited benefit to consumers, but dramatically increase the total amount financed and contribute to making loan payments unaffordable. The true "benefit" is increased earnings to salespeople and dealerships.

For example, Consumer Reports estimates that etching the vehicle identification number into car windows costs dealers about $90, but is often sold for up to $1,000.[61] The "service" is worthless, as the police will track a stolen car based on the Vehicle Identification Number (VIN), which the manufacturer marks your vehicle with. The Ohio Lemon Law Blog elaborates:

---

61 Max, J., "Beating the Car Salesman", NY Daily News, http://www.nydailynews.com/autos/beating-car-salesman-article-1.280327 (April 21, 2008).

Worse yet, in some cases we are now handling against one Dayton Ohio car dealer network, the internal dealer documents show a dealer cost of less than $10 for their $300 retail charge window etching and they are even installing it on cars that have real factory-installed alarm systems and theft deterrent devices. Folks, you don't need windows etched if you have a real alarm system already. So why do some folks end up with it? Some dealers apparently aren't telling the customer about the window etch theft guard that is being charged to them in their sales paperwork.[62]

For another example, GAP insurance is crammed into the finance contracts of more than a third of financed vehicles. This purports to cover the "gap" between the value of the car and the loan amount, as the loan amount often exceed the vehicle's value, which is a bad omen to begin with. The coverage protects the finance company. These policies typically costs dealers $60 to $100 and are resold for $300 to $500. Salespeople may wrongfully imply that financing will not be approved unless GAP coverage is purchased.

Perhaps the most common add-on is extended warranties. In the 3rd quarter of 2011, 46% of financed vehicles had vehicle service contracts packed into the monthly payment.[63] These contracts, which are often almost worthless, were frequently marked up 100% or more by the dealer and, on average, cost the consumer $1,790.[64] For the cost of this warranty, you could buy a decent used car outright on craigslist.

62   http://ohiolemonlaw.blogspot.com/2012/11/the-etch-sketch-window-etch-ripoff-scam.html

63   Montezemo, S., "The State of Lending In America and Its Impact on U.S. Households, Center for Responsible Lending, http://www.responsiblelending.org/state-of-lending/reports/10-Payday-Loans.pdf (September 2013)

64   Id.

Some of these potential deficiencies may be legal in some circumstances. However, lack of disclosure is not. Plus, there are plenty more: take a scenic drive through Deficiencies in Action Tools to peruse the many other potential deficiencies that you and your counsel can identify.

MILE EIGHTEEN: ZERO IN ON YOUR DESTINATION

Decide on a target settlement amount. Determine what your car would sell for by taking a gander at bluebook, craigslist, and online forums for private parties to sell used cars all-cash. Do not factor in any dealer sales, especially those with financing and warranties, which can distort the prices significantly upwards. Once you have determined what you could sell your car for, decide on a target settlement amount. I would propose that you target 50% of the likely resale amount. Thus, if you could sell your car for $5,000, then $2,500 will be your goal. Your loan amount may be over $10,000, but the focus is on what the debt holder could recover if they paid a company to repossess your car and then resold for cash. After costs, your $2,500 offer may be attractive. Furthermore, deficiencies that you and your attorney have identified may justify an even lower target settlement amount.

As with any debt, the longer you go without paying, the lower the amount you can likely settle for (and the more you can save into your settlement wallet). Have your attorney share your settlement offer with opposing counsel, and make sure that any resolution includes a waiver of deficiency.

MILE NINETEEN: CREATE SOME TRAFFIC FOR YOUR LENDER

Your attorney answers the lawsuit and files counterclaims and/or attends court hearing. The counterclaims are based on deficiencies by the debt holder, dealer, repossession company, and any other parties involved whose hands are dirty. Think of the litigation as their turn to wipe their hands of their misdeeds, and your opportunity to wipe away your debt.

Realize that any court action is costly for creditors. Therefore, court actions to repossess vehicles are not common, as the potential recovery often does not justify the cost. Most lenders just write off debts secured by low value cars. Nevertheless, court actions do happen, particularly on higher-end and newer cars on which the creditor believes they can recover a significant amount upon resale. Just because the creditor tells the court that you are not making payments does not mean that they are entitled to repossess.

Any court hearing is a great opportunity for your attorney to reiterate your settlement offer to the debt holder's attorney.

MILE TWENTY: TAKE APART THE ENGINE

Conduct discovery—the process by which your attorney requests that the opposition parties provide documents. In Mile Seventeen, you reviewed all the documents and records you possessed for deficiencies. Now, you get to see what your adversaries hold and review additional documents and records to find even more deficiencies. You are taking apart the whole transaction to find the problems.

Your attorney can even interview the opposition's drivers through interrogatories, requests for admissions, and depositions. The answering party is required to respond under oath to your attorney's questions. You may have the opportunity to question the dealer, lender, salesperson, repo men, collection agencies, and anyone else who may be culpable for deficiencies in creating and collecting on your unaffordable auto debt. Reference Action Tools for sample questions.

A deposition can be damning if, for instance, a salesperson admits that, unbeknownst to you, he or she inflated your income on the financing application. This may have helped him or her maximize commissions, but also saddled you with an unaffordable loan. Salespersons sometimes determine the amount that is needed to qualify a borrower for the desired loan amount, and then write the fabricated number in on the application. A 2014 New York Times investigation featured the story of Rodney Durham,[65] who stopped working in 1991 and was living on Social Security benefits. Nevertheless, his car loan application stated that he earned $35,000 annually working as a technician at Lourdes Hospital in Binghamton, New York. He says that he told the dealer that he had not worked there for over 30 years. "I am not sure how I got the loan," he said. After making five payments, he could not continue paying and Wells Fargo repossessed his car.

The report also uncovered dozens of other loans that included incorrect information about borrowers' income and employment, burdening consumers with unaffordable debt the minute they drove off the dealer's lot. Furthermore, the loans were typically for more than twice the amount of the used vehicles' actual values. Fraudulent practices such as these likely contributed to a 70% jump in the number of repossessions in the second quarter of 2014 compared to the second quarter of 2013, according to data provided by Experian.[66]

Did your dealer repeatedly sell the same car with unaffordable

65 Silver-Greenberg, J., and Corkery, M., "In a Subprime Bubble for Used Cars, Borrowers Pay Sky-High Rates" New York Times, http://dealbook.nytimes.com/2014/07/19/in-a-subprime-bubble-for-used-cars-unfit-borrowers-pay-sky-high-rates/?_r=0 (July 19, 2014).

66 Geier, B., "Can Subprime Auto Loans Crash the Financial System?", Fortune.com, http://fortune.com/tag/auto-loans/ (January 13, 2015).

terms, engaging in an illicit strategy of collecting down payments and then promptly repossessing in order to sell again? One in eight used car dealers sold at least one vehicle three or more times. In particular, Buy Here Pay Here used car lots which plague modest neighborhoods often repossess close to a third of the vehicles they sell, and then resell again, repeatedly fleecing consumers.[67] Research the vehicle history by obtaining a Carfax or AutoCheck report and then check the transfer history. Then, ask the dealer for their records to see if they match up and expose the fraud, or at least bad faith, perpetrated by the dealer in your transaction.

Discovery is your opportunity to get to the truth. If the opposition was not keen on settlement, uncovering misdeeds and flaws during discovery may change their stance.

If your case has gone this far, which is uncommon, then your attorney may let you know that the map has reversed: instead of trying to settle your debt at a discount, now you might be talking forgiveness of debt, payment of your attorney fees, and even some cash into your pocket for your troubles.

MILE TWENTY-ONE: TRY TO FIND THE MIDDLE ROAD

After serving discovery, your attorney should reach out again to opposing counsel with an offer to settle the matter. The sooner you can end this, the less legal fees you spend and the more you could presumably justify paying in a settlement. Never feel rushed or pressured to settle. Time is always the debtor's friend.

---

67 Quirk, M.B., "Investigation Finds Car Dealers Basically Setting Customers Up to Fail So They Can Repossess & Resell Vehicles", Consumerist, http://consumerist.com/2012/08/15/investigation-finds-car-dealers-setting-customers-up-to-fail-so-they-can-repossess-resell-vehicles/ (August 15, 2012).

MILE TWENTY-TWO: TAKE A LOOK AT THE NEW MAP

You and your attorney now get to review newly discovered documents and information for additional deficiencies.

MILE TWENTY-THREE: LET'S JUST BE FRIENDS

Request mediation. Getting all the parties in the same place may help you reach your destination and put an end to this drive. Typically, the mediator will split the parties up and go between the two of you to try to broker a compromise. For instance, if you owe $10,000 and are willing to pay $2,500, and the debt holder is willing to take $5,000, maybe the repossession company kicks in $1,000 and the dealer agrees to pay $1,500 plus another $1,500 towards your legal fees. Why would the dealer and repossession company contribute to the settlement? They want to settle the claims you are alleging against them. Your actions against them are a nuisance that is costing them legal fees, so better to end this with a modest contribution. Once the agreement is reached, a settlement agreement is typically drawn up in the subsequent week or two, then funds are paid and matter ended. The checkered flag is out. You are finished. Congrats!

MILE TWENTY-FOUR: SMASH 'EM UP

If mediation is not agreed to or is conducted but unsuccessful, then proceed with litigation and ultimately be willing to go to trial. Wow. By this time, most cases are taken care of. You sure must have some obstinate opponents. Settlement is usually appealing by now.

Taking a case to trial can be costly for all sides. Who knows who is going to win? Creditors usually can afford the souped-up engines and challengers are often trying to piece together second-hand parts. You represent millions of Americans who want you to win.

Go to the Community Chest at debtcleanse.com and start a campaign to crowdfund your legal fees. We want you to have all the resources you need. We will be in the stands cheering you on. In fact, post your trial date, time, and location on debtcleanse.com and some supporters might just show up to show solidarity in-person. Once the opposition realizes that you have the funds to take them on lap-by-lap and will not run out of gas, talks of settlement might materialize. They thought you couldn't afford to go all the way, didn't they?

If you win, you and your attorney agree to get the opposition to reimburse your legal fees so we can return funds to all your supporters, and the money can be recycled to assist our next driver on a collision course with the elite. If you lose, ask your attorney about appealing the decision or other alternatives. If you lose your vehicle, you still likely saved a big sum into your settlement wallet, which you can now utilize to purchase a replacement car for cash.

MILE TWENTY-FIVE: VICTORY LAP

We're all pulling for you to win. However, even if you lose, you're still a winner to us. Go to debtcleanse.com and let us know how it went down, mile by mile, so we can relive your race to the finish and learn from your mistakes and successes. Help improve the map for everybody.

Be prepared to enter a proverbial Indy 500 when you go through the miles of your vehicle loan Debt Cleanse. However, most of you will only need to drive a few miles before your creditor conks out, making your Indy 500 more like a few laps around the local Go-Kart track. Wherever your race takes you, know that the community on debtcleanse.com is there to wish you happy driving.

CHAPTER 7

STUDENT LOANS

Americans have over $1.2 trillion in outstanding student loans,[68] a level of debt exceeded only by mortgages. An eye-popping 11.5% of these loans are more than 90 days delinquent.[69] Even worse, 15% of recent graduates are delinquent,[70] demonstrating that the problem is getting worse, not better. Equally alarming, nearly 50% of recent private school graduates are delinquent.[71] This should come as no surprise: from 2005 to 2012, the average student loan debt rose by 35%[72], adjusting for inflation, while the median salary

68   Ellis, B. "40 Million Americans Now Have Student Loan Debt" CNN Money, http://money.cnn.com/2014/09/10/pf/college/student-loans/

69   http://www.newyorkfed.org/householdcredit/2013-Q4/HHDC_2013Q4.pdf

70   "Overdue Student Loans Reach "Unsustainable"15% Fair Isaac Says" http://www.bloomberg.com/news/articles/2013-01-29/overdue-student-loans-reach-unsustainable-15-fair-isaac-says

71   Dai, E., "Student Loan Delinquencies Surge" Federal Reserve Bank of St. Louis Publication, https://www.stlouisfed.org/publications/inside-the-vault/spring-2013/student-loan-delinquencies-surge (Spring 2013).

72   The Millennial Debt Sentence: Will They Ever Escape? Credit.com Blog, http://blog.credit.com/2014/10/the-millennial-debt-sentence-will-they-ever-escape-99964/

dropped by 2.2%.[73]

Student loans are a trap, selling students on their dreams and frequently not delivering. Instead, students are shackled with debt for decades and even lifetimes. Putting a financially naïve 18-year-old in front of a commissioned recruiter is like dropping a bloody steak in front of a tiger: the predator is going to annihilate. Furthermore, government-backed loans have been stripped of consumer protections and have no statute of limitations; are tough to discharge in bankruptcy; and possess super-collection powers, which allow creditors to bypass the judicial system and start garnishing wages, levying bank accounts, intercepting tax refunds, all without having to go to court to get judgments.

Here we'll provide you some super-powers of your own to settle your student loans for pennies on the dollar:

SUPER-POWER ONE: GET THE DOCUMENTS

Compile any and all documents from when you took out your loan. In addition, mail Letter F (as in the "F" grade you're going to give your student loan holder) in Action Tools to request documents on your loan. You can also call your lender to request these documents and/or, if you have a government-backed loan, forage through studentloans.gov to see what you can find. Either way, follow up with a written request as well. Most lenders will typically respond to your letter with at least some of the requested documents. If they ignore you, proceed anyway. At a minimum, you have proof that you submitted a reasonable request, which they refused to respond to. Round 1 will go to you.

---

73   Id.

SUPER-POWER TWO: STOP PAYING

Here's one lesson you probably did not learn in college: you cannot settle your student loan at a big discount until you stop paying.

Now, here's a math quiz:

Q: If you graduate with the average student loan amount of $28,400, how much should you try to settle it for if you stop paying?

A: Target $2,840, or 10% of whatever you owe. A distressed debt buyer can likely buy the debt for a nickel on the dollar, so a reasonable debt buyer open to a quick solution without any legal costs should be thrilled with doubling their money.

If you endure the multiple challenges the creditor and collection agencies may set out, you may never get anyone to agree to $2,840. Instead, you may pay $0.00 as your debt dies from nonpayment. In particular, government-backed loans often require a minimum lump-sum payment of 90% of your principal and interest in order to settle. That's not going to happen, so the goal is to pay zero. The loan lives on, but never gets paid.

What will happen to *your* debt? The truth is, you will never know until you take a deep breath and stop paying.

Now, let's continue with the quiz.

Q: There are 38 million Americans with student loans. 22 million (60%) are not paying, whether through deferments, forbearance, or just not paying. What if all 38 million just stopped paying? What would that mean to you?

A: You probably learned this in econ: if the supply of something increases, the prices fall. In this case, if everyone stops paying, then the supply of nonperforming student loan debt will increase. Thus, the prices at which all these bad debts sell for will drop.

If you encourage all your friends with student loans to stop paying, and they invite all their friends, then the law of multiplication kicks in. You might have learned that in marketing. Pretty soon, more and more people stop paying their student loans, flooding the market with nonperforming loans. That nickel price will drop to a couple of pennies. Maybe then you could reset your target settlement to a nickel on the dollar.

Stop paying and get an A+ on Super-Power Two.

SUPER-POWER THREE: DETERMINE IF YOUR LOAN IS PRIVATE OR GOVERNMENT BACKED

Private loans are generally easier to settle. Government loans have purported super-powers that will require a bit more work to defuse. You might have both, which is commonplace. Go ahead and identify which you have so you know what to expect.

Government-backed loans include FFELs (Federal Family Education Loans), GSLs (Guaranteed Student Loans), Stafford, Perkins, and PLUS (Piggish Loans Undermine Students). Just kidding on that last one: PLUS doesn't appear to stand for anything except another onerous type of student debt—it should be renamed MINUS. A guaranty agency will typically act as a middleman between the lender and the United States Department of Education. Each state has its own state guaranty agency and there are many private, non-profit, guaranty agencies like USA Funds (USAF) and the National Student Loan Program (NSLP).

SUPER-POWER FOUR: IGNORE CREDITORS

Ignore collection calls and file away all written communication. Don't talk to your lenders. Hope this goes away—it just might. However, it is more likely that you will get flurries of calls and letters. If you ignore them, then eventually the collection activity will die down as the collectors focus on those who are more responsive. If you don't pay for a long enough period of time, your debt is likely to be transferred to a collection agency or sold to a debt buyer, either of which is likely to subject you to another whirlwind of collection efforts. Expect these and know that the end will eventually come. Relax and think happy thoughts, like that day when you student loan is either settled or dead.

Do not waver from your resolve. If you give any indication that you might pay, you just encourage the collection efforts, which will intensify. No response is the best response.

SUPER-POWER FIVE: STOP CALLS TO WORKPLACE

65% of 2014 college graduates are employed.[74] However, 51% of the employed graduates are in jobs that do not require a college degree.[75] The 2014 graduating class was the most indebted ever, with the average graduate with student loan debt owing $33,000.[76] 32% of 2014 graduates identified the time it would take off to pay off

---

74 "Most 2014 College Grads' Jobs Don't Require Degree" Business Journal Daily, http://archive.businessjournaldaily.com/education/most-2014-college-grads-jobs-dont-require-degree-2014-10-21 (October 21, 2014).

75 Id.

76 Fortenbury, J., "How Much Student Loan Debt is Too Much?" USA Today College, http://college.usatoday.com/2014/08/26/how-much-student-loan-debt-is-too-much-2/ (August 26, 2014).

their student loans amongst their biggest fears after graduation.[77]

If you are lucky enough to be working, then getting collection calls at work can be troubling and likely against your employer's policies. Mail Letter B in Action Tools to stop calls to your workplace.

SUPER-POWER SIX: DISPUTE & VALIDATE

Each time the ownership or servicing of your loan transfers, you will likely receive an invitation to dispute the debt. Please RSVP using Letter A in Action Tools.

File away whatever responses you receive. Some creditors are not required to honor these requests. That's fine if they feel that way. Some students (including you) may feel disinclined to honor any requests they make of you. So, I guess you'd be even-steven.

SUPER-POWER SEVEN: CEASE CONTACT

If your loan has been sold to a debt buyer or assigned to a collection agency, and you receive a response to your Dispute and Validation Request, or 45 days pass without a response, mail in Letter C in Action Tools to request that collection outreach stops. They will typically be legally prohibited from calling or sending more letters, except for one to tell you what they are going to do and any documents necessary to proceed with litigation. Again, some creditors are not required to honor requests like this, feeling that they have special powers as an original creditor, or even the guaranty agency. That's cool—they're special, we get it. They can keep calling. You

---

77 "Most 2014 College Grads' Jobs Don't Require Degree" Business Journal Daily, http://
archive.businessjournaldaily.com/education/most-2014-college-grads-jobs-dont-require-
degree-2014-10-21 (October 21, 2014).

can keep ignoring. You're special too, even more so.

SUPER-POWER EIGHT: GET AN ATTORNEY ON-DECK
If you do not have an attorney, reference Hire an Attorney in Chapter 3: Quick Start. You might not need one, but it's best to get one on-deck. Find one you are comfortable with, and then get an engagement letter. Don't pay anything yet. No need to rush into an engagement, just know who you are going to turn to if this game heats up.

SUPER-POWER NINE: KICK IT
Wait. Be patient. Go about your life. Wait for your creditor to sue (private) or give you a Notice (government-backed). File away any other correspondence you receive and log the calls. Upon occasion, your lender will never take any action and you simply never pay. The more time that passes, the better for you. Kick it.

SUPER-POWER TEN: CREDITOR KICKS YOU
In most cases, your creditors will eventually make their move:

Private: you will be served with a lawsuit.

Government-backed: you will receive a Notice indicating that your wages will be garnished, bank account levied, tax return or Social Security benefits intercepted, and/or other adverse action. Before taking any of these actions, the U.S. Department of Education or a guaranty agency is required to send a Notice to your last known address. This Notice provides you rights to inspect and copy records related to the debt and to request a hearing concerning the existence, amount, or current enforceability of the debt.

In either case, share these immediately with your attorney. Now is the time to get engaged (congratulations, by the way!). Sign the engagement letter and pay the retainer to your chosen attorney, using funds from your settlement wallet.

SUPER-POWER ELEVEN: PREPARE FOR KICKFIGHT

Share with your attorney your communication log, correspondence, any documents you received in response to your document request, and any documents you still have from when you first obtained the loan.

SUPER-POWER TWELVE: IDENTIFY YOUR OPPONENT'S WEAKNESSES

Identify potential deficiencies. Every loan has some. Note that most deficiencies are not inherently fatal and just because you identify a deficiency does not mean that you will win your case. However, any deficiencies that you can identify will create leverage, which may encourage your opponents to settle your debt at a substantial discount. Quality of deficiencies is generally more important than quantity, as one major deficiency may be all that is needed to knock out a debt. On the other hand, a hundred, or even a dozen, minor deficiencies may demonstrate a lender's disregard for proper protocols and may kill your debt equally effectively.

For third parties to which you do not owe money, but which may be responsible for any act that resulted in your debt, the third-party may contribute to the overall settlement, or otherwise pay you to settle their portion of the matter.

To expose your opponent's vulnerabilities, take a look at the Deficiencies in Action Tools and identify those that apply to your debt. You and your attorney may add more based on the specifics of your case. There are typically plenty to be found.

For instance, according to a NBC News report, Sallie Mae paid $2 million in 2007 to settle allegations by the New York Attorney General[78] that "lenders pay kickbacks to schools based on a percentage of the loans directed to the lenders."[79] Additionally, "lenders have foot the bills for all-expense-paid trips for financial aid officers to posh resorts and exotic locations. They also provide schools with other benefits like computer systems and put representatives from schools on their advisory boards to curry favor."[80] If this illegal activity contributed to your unaffordable loan, then this is a deficiency that you can assert and exploit.

Additionally, "loan companies set up funds and credit lines for schools to use in exchange for putting the lenders on their preferred lender lists and offer large payments to schools to drop out of the direct federal loan program so that the lenders get more business." Lenders and universities paid millions to settle allegations such as these.

Kick back at kickbacks, and any other deficiencies you can identify.

SUPER-POWER THIRTEEN: WHAT WILL IT TAKE FOR YOU TO STOP KICKING?

Your lender may not know it, but you are about to throw down. Before you start getting merciless, let them know what you will pay them to walk away from this thumping.

---

78 "Large Student-Loan Firm Settles with N.Y. AG", NBC News, http://www.nbcnews.com/id/18055629/ns/business-personal_finance/t/large-student-loan-firm-settles-ny-ag/ (April 16, 2007)

79 "New York AG Alleges Student Loan Corruption", NBC News, http://www.nbcnews.com/id/17644168/ns/business-personal_finance/t/new-york-ag-alleges-student-loan-corruption/ (March 16, 2007).

80 Id.

Decide on a target settlement amount. This can be modest—I recommend 10% of the principal amount owed. Based on deficiencies identified thus far, your attorney may suggest an even lower starting point.

Whatever the amount you decide upon, make sure that you have this available in your settlement wallet. Only offer what you have available to pay. At this point, the debt holder may not be ready to approve the extent of the discount you seek. Deciding on a figure and sharing with the opposition early can be helpful. At some point, the debt holder may be inclined to settle and knowing what you want is useful.

Private: Skip to Super-Power Eighteen.

SUPER-POWER FOURTEEN: KICK BACK
Here, you get to kick back at your creditor and try to knock them down.

Government-backed only: You will have a choice of hearing types: in-person, telephone, or written. Request an in-person hearing. Choosing in-person will be more costly and burdensome for you, but also for the guaranty agency and Department of Education. Do not ask for an oral telephone hearing or a paper hearing. Getting in front of other human beings face-to-face is much more likely to result in progress, although keep your expectations low for a resolution at this juncture. Most importantly, in-person hearings maximize the likelihood for errors and missteps on the part of the creditor. Make sure that your attorney arranges for a court reporter to attend and chronicle the proceedings. You will need to pay for their time, but having this record later on may be helpful if you end up litigating.

As with anything government, there are extra layers of fat and inefficiencies. Instead of mailing one document to request a hearing, you need to send three, including Letter E from Action Tools and the two documents below. You can access fillable versions at debtcleanse.com.

First, use the government's official Request for Hearing form and fill in the blanks:

A. In "I," check box to select an in-person hearing.

B. In "II," check box 10 plus any others that apply. Then, enter total number of objections in the field at the end of the first paragraph of section II.

*   *   *

REQUEST FOR HEARING

If you object to garnishment of your wages for the debt described in the notice, you can use this form to request a hearing. Your request must be in writing and mailed or delivered to the address below.

Your Name: _____

SSN: _____

Address: _____

Telephone: _____

Employer: _____

Address: _____

Telephone: _____

Beginning Date Of Current Employment: _____

( ) CHECK HERE if you object on the grounds that garnishment in amounts equal to 15% of your disposable pay would cause financial hardship to you and your dependents. (To arrange voluntary repayment, contact customer service at the number below.) You must complete either the enclosed FINANCIAL DISCLOSURE FORM or a Financial Disclosure Form of your choosing to present your hardship claim. You must enclose copies of earnings and income records, and proof of expenses, as explained on the form. If your request for an oral hearing is granted, you will be notified of the date, time, and location of your hearing. If your request for an oral hearing is denied, the Department will make its determination of the amounts you should pay based on a review of your written materials.

NOTE: You should also state below any other objections you have to garnishment to collect this debt at this time.

NOTE: IT IS IN YOUR INTEREST TO REQUEST COPIES OF ALL DOCUMENTATION HELD BY THE DEPARTMENT BY CALLING THE CUSTOMER SERVICE NUMBER LISTED ON THE ENCLOSED NOTICE PRIOR TO COMPLETING A REQUEST FOR HEARING.

I. HEARING REQUEST (Check ONLY ONE of the following)

   ( ) I want a written records hearing of my objection(s) based on the Department's review of this written statement, the documents I have enclosed, and the records in my debt file at the Department.

   ( ) I want an in-person hearing at the Department hearing

office to present my objection(s). I understand that I must pay my own expenses to appear for this hearing.

I want this In-Person hearing held in: _____ Atlanta, GA. _____ Chicago, IL. _____ San Francisco, CA. (Check the location you wish for the hearing.)

( ) I want a hearing by telephone to present my objections. (You must provide a daytime telephone number at which you can be contacted between the hours of 8:00 am to 4:00 pm, Monday through Friday.) I can be reached at: ( ) _____-_____

II. IF YOU WANT AN IN-PERSON OR TELEPHONE HEARING, YOU MUST COMPLETE THE FOLLOWING: The debt records and documents I submitted to support my statement in Part III do not show all the material (important) facts about my objection to collection of this debt. I need a hearing to explain the following important facts about this debt: (EXPLAIN the additional facts that you believe make a hearing necessary on a separate sheet of paper. If you have already fully described these facts in your response in Part I, WRITE HERE the number of the objection in which you described these facts _____.)

Note: If you do not request an in-person or telephone hearing, we will review your objection based on information and documents you supply with this form and on records in your loan file. We will provide an oral hearing to a debtor who requests an oral hearing and shows in the request for the hearing, a good reason to believe that we cannot resolve the issues in dispute by reviewing the documentary evidence. An example is when the validity of the claim turns on the issue of credibility or veracity.

III. Check the objections that apply.

EXPLAIN any further facts concerning your objection on a separate sheet of paper.

ENCLOSE the documents described here (if you do not enclose documents, the Department will consider your objection(s) based on the information on this form and records held by the Department). For some objections you must submit a completed application. Obtain applications by contacting Customer Service at the number below, or go to the Department's Web site at: www.myeddebt.com, select Forms, then select the application described for that objection.

1. ( ) I do not owe the full amount shown because I repaid some or all of this debt. (ENCLOSE: copies of the front and back of all checks, money orders and any receipts showing payments made to the holder of the debt.)

2. ( ) I am making payments on this debt as required under the repayment agreement I reached with the holder of the debt. (ENCLOSE: copies of the repayment agreement and copies of the front and back of checks where you paid on the agreement.)

3. ( ) I filed for bankruptcy and my case is still open. (ENCLOSE: copies of any documents from the court that show the date that you filed, the name of the court, and your case number.)

4. ( ) This debt was discharged in bankruptcy. (ENCLOSE: copies of debt discharge order and the schedule of debts filed with the court.)

5. ( ) The borrower has died. (ENCLOSE: Original, certified copy, or clear, accurate, and complete photocopy of the original or certified Death Certificate.) For loans only.

6. ( ) I am totally and permanently disabled—unable to engage in substantial gainful activity because of a medically determinable physical or mental impairment. (Obtain and submit a completed Loan Discharge Application: Total and Permanent Disability form. This form must be completed by a physician, except if you are a veteran, in which case you can submit required documentation from the U.S. Department of Veterans Affairs. Refer to the application for all requirements.) For loans only.

7. ( ) I used this loan to enroll in _____
_____(school) on or about ___/___/___, and I withdrew from school on or about ___/___/___. I paid the school $_____ and I believe that I am owed, but have not been paid, a refund from the school in the amount of $_____. (Obtain and submit a completed Loan Discharge Application: Unpaid Refund form. ENCLOSE: any records you have showing your withdrawal date). For loans only.

8. ( ) I (or, for parent PLUS borrowers, the student) used this loan to enroll in _____
(school) on or about ___/___/___ and was unable to complete the education because the school closed. (Obtain and submit a completed Loan Discharge Application: School Closure form. ENCLOSE: any records you have showing your (or, for parent PLUS borrowers, the student's) withdrawal date.) For loans only.

9. ( ) This is not my Social Security Number, and I do not owe this debt. (ENCLOSE: a copy of your driver's license or other identification issued by a Federal, state or local government agency, and a copy of your Social Security Card.)

10. ( ) I believe that this debt is not an enforceable debt in the amount stated for the reason explained in the attached letter. (Attach a letter explaining any reason other than those listed above for your objection to collection of this debt amount by garnishment of your salary. ENCLOSE: any supporting records.)

11. ( ) I (or, for parent PLUS borrowers, the student) did not have a high school diploma or GED when I (or, for parent PLUS borrowers, the student) enrolled at the school attended with this guaranteed student loan. The school did not properly test my (or, for parent PLUS borrowers, the student's) ability to benefit from the training offered. (Obtain and submit a completed Loan Discharge Application: False Certification (Ability to Benefit) form. ENCLOSE: any records you have showing your withdrawal date.) For loans only.

12. ( ) When I borrowed this guaranteed student loan to attend _____ (school), I (or, for parent PLUS borrowers, the student) had a condition (physical, mental, age, criminal record) that prevented me (or, for parent PLUS borrowers, the student) from meeting State requirements for performing the occupation for which the school training was provided. (Obtain and submit completed Loan Discharge Application: False Certification (Disqualifying Status) form. For loans only.

13. ( ) I was involuntarily terminated from my last employment and I have been employed in my current job for less than twelve months. (Attach statement from employer showing date of hire in current job and statement from prior employer showing involuntary termination.)

14. ( ) I believe that _____ _____ (name of individual or other party) without my permission signed my name or used my personal identification data to execute documents to obtain this loan, and I did not receive the loan funds. (Obtain and submit a completed False Certification (Unauthorized Signature/Unauthorized Payment) discharge application or Identity Theft Certification). Enclose any records showing your withdrawal date). For loans only.

IV. I state under penalty of law that the statements made on this request are true and accurate to the best of my knowledge.

DATE: _____

SIGNATURE:_____

SEND THIS REQUEST FOR HEARING FORM TO:

US DEPARTMENT OF EDUCATION ATTN: AWG HEAR-
INGS BRANCH
PO BOX 5227
GREENVILLE, TX 75403-5227

*   *   *

Next, list the deficiencies you discovered on the Reasons for

Objection to Garnishment, Letter E in Action Tools. If needed, add additional pages.

Finally, add the letter below, based on a sample from Goingo & Orth, P.A., a Florida law firm, which specializes in student loan defense:

* * *

DEMAND FOR DISCOVERY & IN–PERSON ADMINISTRA-TIVE HEARING

Your Name
Your Address
Your City, State & Zip

VIA CERTIFIED MAIL/RETURN RECEIPT REQUESTED/ COPY RETAINED

Date

US DEPARTMENT OF EDUCATION
ATTN: AWG HEARINGS BRANCH
PO BOX 5227
GREENVILLE, TX 75403-5227

Re: Demand for Discovery and In-Person Administrative Hearing.

Account Number:_____

My name is _____ and I am the alleged debtor in this matter. Please accept this letter as a formal demand for discovery and an in-person hearing before a U.S. Department of Education approved hearing officer. I intend to challenge the existence of the alleged debt and the amount of the alleged debt, including the reasonableness of collection costs. You are advised that the hearing will be recorded by a certified court reporter.

Prior to assigning this case to a hearing officer and scheduling a hearing date, I request that the following documents be provided to me within 30 (thirty) days of the date of this letter:

1. A copy of the front and back of the promissory note as it exists today, including all assignments, endorsements and allonges thereto;

2. Payment history for the life of loan, including a detailed breakdown of payments posted to the account and application of those payments to principal, interest, and any other type of charges;

3. A detailed breakdown of any collection costs and the basis therefore;

4. As a request for admission, please admit that the promissory note is being enforced as a negotiable instrument pursuant to the Uniform Commercial Code, along with any supporting documentation.

I would also like to formally request an opportunity to inspect the original promissory note. Along with your responses to the Discovery Requests, please provide me with reasonable locations for inspection and at least five proposed dates and times, or in the alternative, provide me with the name and direct contact information for the individual responsible for scheduling the inspection of a promissory note.

Once the above documents and information have been properly provided to me, I am requesting written notice of the time and place for the in-person hearing be forwarded to me immediately, with at least fifteen (15) days' notice prior to the hearing. Please be aware that scheduling such a hearing before fully responding to the discovery requests above would be a violation of the law and contrary to my rights.

I am also asserting my right to an Administrative Procedure Act-type judicial review in federal court once the administrative hearing has been completed.

Thank you in advance for your anticipated cooperation.

Sincerely,

Your Signature
Your Name

cc:

Lender or Servicer
Guaranty Agency
Board or Department of Education in your state
U.S. Congressperson in student's district

* * *

Mail in all three together and attach a copy of the government's

Notice to you. Send by certified mail, return receipt requested. The cc's can be sent by regular mail. Keep copies of everything you send.

You need to request records within twenty days of the date of the Notice, and request a hearing within thirty days. The only exception is for Federal Family Education Loans (FFEL), for which requests need to be made within fifteen days.

Provided that your request is made before the deadline, garnishments, levies, and other adverse actions are on hold until they prove that you owe the money, that the amount they claim is due, that they own the loan, and that they have the books and records to prove all this.

Note that even if the government has already started garnishing your wages or taken similar adverse action, you can still request documents and a hearing. However, the garnishment or other action will typically continue until the matter is resolved.

SUPER-POWER FIFTEEN: GET CALLED INTO THE PRINCIPAL'S OFFICE

Government-backed: You will receive a notice of your hearing date, time and place. Kind of like getting called into the principal's office, except here you can send someone else to stand in for you. When I was a kid, they used to have a paddle on the wall in there. I never got hit, but soon enough you will get to use a proverbial paddle to swat your lenders into submission.

Hearings are usually held in Atlanta, Chicago, and San Francisco. Typically, only an attorney needs to attend on your behalf. If your attorney is not near one of these cities then, instead of incurring travel costs for your attorney to attend, suggest that your attorney engages another attorney near the hearing location attend along with a court reporter who can provide a record of the hearing. This is commonplace and your attorney will understand the request, and would likely propose this if you don't. In each of the cities in which hearings are held, the directory on debtcleanse.com will identify attorneys familiar with the process and available to attend. Your attorney will provide details to local counsel, including deficiencies and agreeable settlement terms.

The following Department of Education regulations outline the government's perspective on defaulted student debts:[81]

(a)(1) We have the burden of proving the existence and amount of a debt.
(2) We meet this burden by including in the record and making available to the debtor on request records that show that—
(i) The debt exists in the amount stated in the garnishment notice; and
(ii) The debt is currently delinquent.
(b) If you dispute the existence or amount of the debt, you must prove by a preponderance of the credible evidence that—
(1) No debt exists;
(2) The amount we claim to be owed on the debt is incorrect, or
(3) You are not delinquent with respect to the debt.

At first glance, this may look tough to win. However, in many cases, the original note "proving the existence and amount of a debt" has been lost. Alternately, any of the assignments of the debt may be missing, so the government may be unable to prove who owns your debt. The purported note holder may not be able to break

81   34 CFR 34.14

down how they arrived at "the amount stated in the garnishment notice". Can they provide a life-of-loan payment history proving that "the debt is currently delinquent"? I mean, are you sure this wasn't a grant instead of a loan? Find enough errors and this will be a grant, or close to it.

SUPER-POWER SIXTEEN: YOU'RE NOT A LOSER, BUT YOU MIGHT LOSE THIS ROUND

Your attorney, or their local representative, and a court reporter will attend hearing in front of an administrative law judge.

Expect to lose, but your attorney or their local representative should take the opportunity to share the amount you are willing to settle for with the debt holder's representative. This is likely the first time anyone on the debt holder's side with some authority is focusing on resolving your debt.

SUPER-POWER SEVENTEEN: THE DECISION—YOU LOSE! (BUT THIS TIFF AIN'T OVER)

Within 60 days after the hearing, the administrative law judge will issue a ruling. You likely lost. No biggie. Look at this like practice sparring with the enemy. You just need to get through these steps to get to the main event.

SUPER-POWER EIGHTEEN: ENTER THE RING FOR THE MAIN EVENT

Private: file answer and counterclaims against debt holder, servicer, school, and any other responsible parties.

Government-backed: file lawsuit against guaranty agency, U.S. Department of Education, debt holder, servicer, school, and any other responsible parties.

When you answer or file a lawsuit, always remember to request a jury trial. There are a lot of out-of-work graduates out there who will be thrilled with the up to $50 per day which is paid for jury service. Let's hope some of them are on your jury.

SUPER-POWER NINETEEN: FEEL OUT YOUR OPPONENT

Look for more of your opponent's shortcomings. Conduct discovery—the process by which your attorney requests documents and prods and probes your opponent(s) via interrogatories, requests for admissions, and/or depositions. Even if you have copies of these documents from origination or from the government-backed loans document request, ask for these again as part of the court case. You want to see what the opposition holds. See Action Tools for sample requests.

For instance, schools often set up students to fail by providing loans with payments that would be unaffordable based on the average income of recent graduates in the same field of study. This would be easy to measure and a prudent practice, but no one does it. Instead, student lenders and their associates are reckless and predatory by making loans they know, or should have known, are frequently impossible to repay.

For instance, let's say you went to ITT for an Associate's Degree in drafting and design. The recruiter told you about the high placement rates for well-paying drafter positions. The finance person then hooked you up with a zero-interest "Temporary Credit" loan. You were on the right path to your dreams. You studied diligently, graduated with great grades, and then discovered that there are few opportunities for entry-level drafters, and most do not pay very well.

To compound the misery, as the Consumer Financial Protection Bureau recently announced in a lawsuit against ITT, you and many other students were not told that, after a year, the "Temporary Credit" loan converted to a high-cost private loan at 16.25% interest. "ITT marketed itself as improving consumers' lives but it was really just improving its bottom line," said CFPB Director Richard Cordray. "We believe ITT used high-pressure tactics to push many consumers into expensive loans destined to default."[82]

Now, imagine ITT's representative deciding whether to board a plane to answer questions regarding their fraudulent tactics that created your financial hardship, if not ruin. If I were the ITT rep, I am going to strive for a settlement now and avoid the deposition. If you are the aspiring draftsman, ITT should pay off your loan, pay your legal fees, and maybe even pay you some cash—maybe $5,000 or $10,000—for your troubles.

ITT's vulture-like tactics are commonplace at many private colleges. However, even if you went to a well-known public school such as UCLA or OSU, the tactics are often similar, just subtler. Did anyone actually explain the amount you were borrowing, the interest rate, and share any kind of guidance as to whether your degree is likely to result in a job that provides you a reasonable ability to repay? Those are the types of questions you get to ask opponents as part of discovery.

SUPER-POWER TWENTY: CAN'T WE ALL JUST GET ALONG?

After serving discovery, your attorney should reach out to opposing counsel with an offer to settle the matter. Share your target amount.

---

82 CFPB, "CFPB Sues For-Profit College Chain ITT For Predatory Lending" Consumer Financial Protection Bureau, http://www.consumerfinance.gov/newsroom/cfpb-sues-for-profit-college-chain-itt-for-predatory-lending/ (February 26, 2014).

This may or may not be appealing to the opposition at this point, but start to set expectations of what you want. The sooner you can end this, the less legal fees you spend and the more you could presumably justify paying in a settlement. Never feel rushed or pressured to settle, as time is always the debtor's friend.

SUPER-POWER TWENTY-ONE: KICK UP MORE DIRT

You and your attorney can now review newly discovered documents and information for additional deficiencies. They're ready for plucking. Think of the deficiencies as shin guards, which not only defend you in the kick-fight, but also power you. Kick your creditor in the back of the knees!

First, though, let's try one more time to settle the score in a more civilized manner.

SUPER-POWER TWENTY-TWO: GIVE PEACE A CHANCE

Getting all the parties in the same place in mediation may help get you the result you want: a discounted settlement. Typically, this is done away from the courthouse and the mediator will split the parties up and go back and forth to try to broker a compromise. For instance, if you owe $100,000 and you are willing to pay $10,000 and the debt holder is willing to take $15,000, maybe the school agrees to kick in the other $5,000 to satisfy your claims of fraud and non-disclosure against them. Once the agreement is reached, a settlement agreement is typically drawn up in the subsequent week or two, then funds are paid and the matter ended.

SUPER-POWER TWENTY-THREE: BECOME THE MAIN EVENT

If mediation is not agreed to or is unsuccessful, then proceed with litigation and ultimately be willing to go to trial. At some point, a settlement should become appealing to the opposition. Although debtor/creditor cases often do not go to trial, be prepared to go all the way if needed.

If you do go to trial, you become the main event for millions of student loan debtors, and every American fed up with the pillaging of the American people. We all want to help you win. The legal fees for trial can be substantial and this often gives an edge to lenders and schools.

We are going to kick away their advantage: access the Community Chest at debtcleanse.com to start a crowdfunding campaign and get what you need to pay your legal fees for trial preparation and representation. We all need to support those that go to trial. Together, debtors can become more powerful than creditors. Some well-funded courtroom victories, or even the threat thereof, will entice creditors to settle other lawsuits, like maybe yours, early on.

There have already been victories. Former delinquent student loan debtor Stefanie Gray shared in a 2014 post in *The Guardian* that Sallie Mae brought four lawsuits against her for unpaid student loans. With the assistance of New York Legal Assistance Group, she:

> ...discovered, and brought to the attention of the court, that in three of the four suits, I was being sued by an entity—'SLM Education Credit Finance Corp'—that wasn't even registered to do business in New York State, and the plaintiffs couldn't produce any evidence that the entity in the fourth suit—'SLM Private Credit Student Loan Trust VL Funding LLC'—even exists. Sallie Mae's own lawyer was dumbfounded. The judge threatened them with a $10,000 sanction for their 'nonsense', then dismissed their case against me because they lacked standing. Their attempt to

overturn the judge's decision was denied, and they were told that, if they want to sue me again, they'd have to register to do business in New York (and pay millions, if not billions, of dollars in taxes) first. I had won.[83]

SUPER-POWER TWENTY-FOUR: SHARE THE OUTCOME

Post ongoing progress, final disposition, and settlement results, as well as review of your attorney, to debtcleanse.com. Ask your attorney to post copies of pleadings and any insight gained. These will be helpful to others facing similar predicaments. We are all in this together.

Rather than helping build America, student loans are shredding the future of America: our youth. Now is the time for all students to become super-heroes, shred their loans and re-build America.

---

83 Gray, S., "I Beat Sallie Mae at the Student Loan Game—But Nobody Should Face Financial Ruin For an Education" The Guardian, http://www.theguardian.com/commentisfree/2014/nov/24/sallie-mae-student-loan-financial-education (November 24, 2014).

CHAPTER 8

BUSINESS LOANS

I lost everything in the aftermath of an ice storm that ravaged Woodland Meadows, an apartment complex I owned in Ohio. Before the storm, I never imagined that I would not win. I had succeeded repeatedly in building a portfolio of over 4,000 apartment units across the country. I was so confident that whenever any business creditor asked me to sign a personal guarantee, I never hesitated to grab a pen and scribble my signature. After all, if I refused to sign the guarantees, then I would not have been able to obtain as much financing. However, each stroke of my pen made me personally responsible if the business was unable to pay. When my real estate empire collapsed, the personal guarantees represented the largest creditor claims against me, over 80% of my total debt. If I hadn't made any personal guarantees, the debts would have died with the LLCs that owned the properties. My crash would have been hard, but not nearly as catastrophic.

I could not afford to pay any of them: Key Bank, Vestin Mortgage, and All California Funding were claiming over $5 million each;

Franklin Capital, Aztec Financial, Peninsula Finance and Danco Inc. were close to $2 million each. Plus, there were dozens of smaller claims from vendors and contractors that had my guarantee.

Most business creditors are realistic about whether collection efforts warrant spending money on legal fees. Based on experience, many realize that a business failure will sometimes render the personal guarantor unable to make good. Any money they spend on collection efforts is typically regarded as throwing good money after bad. As a result, I was sued on two of the three personal guarantees over $5 million and none of the guarantees around $2 million. Most of them had their attorneys send saber-rattling letters threatening legal action, but then they didn't actually do anything.

Several of the smaller creditors sued me and many won uncontested judgments. At the time, I thought like most debtors: I owed the money and there was nothing I could do to beat the creditors. I had yet to learn the Debt Cleanse strategies that I'm sharing with you here. These could have prevented the judgments. Nevertheless, as I learned my lessons, I successfully defended paying the judgments, many of which eventually went dormant and died.

If you obtained a loan guaranteed by the Small Business Administration, you almost certainly signed a personal guarantee and are likely to be pursued. Although this may require some patience and diligence, I'll share strategies to free you from the SBA.

If the only obligor on your debt is your entity, such as an LLC or Corporation, and there is no personal guarantee, the unpaid debts will generally go down with your business. In these cases, do nothing and let the creditors have at it. Unless you signed a guarantee, there is nothing they can do against you personally.

Here are 19 steps to Debt Cleanse your Business Loans:

STEP ONE: ARM YOURSELF

Deficiencies are your ammunition to shoot down your unaffordable business debts, and you can mine these from documents and records on your loan. Assemble every document from when you took out your loan. Also send in Letter F in Action Tools to your loan holder or servicer to request documents on your loan. You will generally receive a response with at least some of the requested documents. If there is no reply, no worries. Move on.

STEP TWO: CLOSE SHOP

As soon as you realize that your business is going to fail, conserve all your cash and stop paying everyone. Stop the bleeding and shut it down. Sell whatever inventory, equipment and other stuff you have, and keep the cash. If you are on a lease, stop paying and walk away. Even if you have a personal guarantee, stop paying. Many guarantors are not pursued on these obligations.

STEP THREE: CLOSE YOURSELF

Close yourself to your creditors. Don't talk to them. Just ignore them.

Some business debt collectors feel that they can do anything they want. We had a collector calling me at AHP continuously, 20 or more times in succession, to collect a Woodland Meadows-era debt from me. I told reception to hang up on him and eventually we blocked his number. Others have threatened me with hollow threats of criminal charges and government audits. Although the FDCPA specifically prohibits these actions, the FDCPA does not apply to business debts. Nevertheless, these actions may amount to harassment and many states have laws to prevent this type of behavior, even for business debts.

Log all the calls, keep all the correspondence, and use these if you end up in litigation.

Other than that, hang up on callers and block the numbers they are calling from.

STEP FOUR: SAFEGUARD COLLATERAL

If there is any collateral securing your debts, keep this inaccessible in a non-public area. See details on hampering repossession in Step Five of Chapter 9: Secured Personal Loans.

STEP FIVE: CHILD'S POSE

In yoga, child's pose is a restful pose. Breathe deep and relax.

Once you awaken, focus on rebuilding, look forward, and glean whatever lessons you can from your defeat. You always learn more from your failures than your successes. Many wildly successful people have also wildly failed. I aspire to be one of them.

My greatest business asset is my mind, educated in part by the lessons that have been seared into my brain as a result of my failures. Recognize that although you lost your business, you may have gained something more valuable, something no one can take away from you.

Ordinarily, I vigilantly hold my focus forward. Glancing backwards can often stunt progress, as thoughts of regret infest my mind. "If only I did this differently, if only this or that had happened." The "what if" rabbit hole is one that is best avoided.

Nevertheless, looking backward can be useful if you're doing it with a specific purpose: to identify why your business failed. List the top ten factors that contributed to the failure of your business. Be realistic and shoulder some of the blame, if appropriate. By reflecting now and identifying shortcomings, you lessen the likelihood of repeating the same missteps in your future endeavors. Equally importantly, this will help identify any parties that may share some responsibility for your unaffordable business debt.

Here's my list:

1. The ice storm, December 24, 2004. This storm just devastated Woodland Meadows. This was the largest federally declared disaster in Ohio history, and Woodland Meadows may have been the largest single loss in the state. Our older radiant heating system, which pumped hot water from boilers through every apartment's pipes (which froze and burst post-storm, flooding buildings), partially subterranean first floor units (into which several feet of water accumulated), and massive size (1,100 units in 122 buildings over 52 acres) contributed to the extraordinary impact.

2. Me. I made plenty of mistakes in my response. I could have closed the property right away. I could have explored the City's suggestion of vacating the complex and moving the HUD contract to another location. I could have made any number of different choices, which may have yielded a better outcome. Instead, I had tunnel vision that I was going to rebuild Woodland Meadows, no matter what.

3. The City of Columbus, which seized on the opportunity to get rid of Woodland Meadows and gain control of one of the

largest single properties in the city. The property's location was prime: across the street from the newly built Veterans Administration Hospital, just blocks from the airport, and backing into the prosperous Bexley neighborhood. The city was underhanded and deceitful, made unfounded allegations, wrongfully interfered with my business, and helped wage a smear campaign against me.

4. Me (Again). I was slow to comprehend that Woodland Meadows might not survive. I was not nimble and spry. I did not take time to assess the overall landscape. I needed to recognize that the playing field had changed and I could not play the game as I did before.

5. Taking debt secured by other properties. When the insurer balked at paying, I borrowed on my other properties to fund Woodland Meadows' restoration. Woodland Meadows should have stood on its own. If the insurer did not pay, I shouldn't have restored the property until they did. This would have forced me and everyone else to reckon with the problem earlier. Instead, I handicapped all my other holdings. I had hoped that the eventual settlement would pay off the debts encumbering the other properties. Instead, I lost my other holdings as well. This is one of the challenges with debt.

6. Belfor, an international disaster remediation contractor that wined, dined, and otherwise pleasured insurance adjusters in order to get their inflated bills approved. However, the billings became so mammoth and the scope of work so enormous that the insurer refused to pay, no matter how hot the naked stripper sitting on their adjuster's lap was.

7. *Columbus Dispatch*, which unleashed a barrage of yellow journalism, turning public opinion against Woodland Meadows and me. A "blame the victim" strategy was executed with great aplomb.

8. RSUI and Lloyds of London, the insurers who refused to pay our full claim and instead forced us to litigate, eventually wearing me down until I capitulated and accepted a big discount on the insurance settlement.

9. HUD, which gave in to City pressure to give us 30 days to rebuild what a court had just given us six months to accomplish. This came in December, just two months after HUD performed a REAC inspection that gave Woodland Meadows high marks and commended our progress in rebuilding from disaster.

10. Me (Again and Again). I am not entirely sure of what else I did wrong, but the end result speaks for itself. There must have been something more or different I could have done to achieve a better result.

Look at your list. If you named yourself, congratulations. This means you have learned something from your failure, and you have gained from your challenges. This will help you in future ventures.

Now, focus on other people or entities that share some of the blame. On my list, I have the City of Columbus, Belfor, *Columbus Dispatch*, RSUI, Lloyds of London, and HUD. They all bore some responsibility for the outcome and I should have sued them all, or added them as cross complainants when I answered a big creditors' lawsuit.

If any other person or company shares culpability, bring them into the litigation to spread the burden. Culprits could be franchisors, business partners, contractors, suppliers, lenders, SBA, insurers, and any number of others. You can't sue yourself, though, no matter how much at blame you might be. Sorry.

Finally, to inspire your comeback, look to Henry Ford. He started two automobile companies, both of which failed and left him broke. Learning from his failures, on his third try he founded the Ford Motor Company, which went on to become extraordinarily successful. Improving worker conditions and salaries while concurrently producing affordable automobiles proved to be a winning combination. Remarkably, at the time, Wall Street criticized Ford's labor practices when he began paying workers enough to buy the products they made.

Over time, competing manufacturers ate into Ford's dominant market share by offering financing on their vehicle sales. Ford initially resisted, insisting that such debts would hurt the consumer and the general economy. I concur with Ford's initial assessment.

STEP SIX: SEEK COUNSEL

You might need an attorney to help. Take a look at Hire an Attorney in Chapter 3: Quick Start. Review a few to find one you are comfortable with. Ask them to provide you an engagement letter and then hold onto to it until you are certain you need it. If your creditor drops the matter, there is no need to pay the retainer.

STEP SEVEN: WHAT'S YOUR TYPE?

Are you more SBA or private? You either have a loan guaranteed by the Small Business Administration, or you have a private loan without an SBA guarantee. Now is the time to figure out which.

If yours is SBA, you'll have some extra work to do. Unless your business was well established with lots of assets and ample collateral, you likely signed a personal guarantee. The SBA, Treasury Department and their cronies have powers that would be illegal for any private business or person in the U.S.:

1. Garnish wages, levy bank accounts, and intercept tax refunds and a portion of Social Security payments—all without a court order.

2. Hold hearings at which debtors can contest SBA collection actions. However, the officials presiding over the hearings are SBA employees.

3. Refer to private collectors who can add collection fees of up to 30% of what debtors owe.

These are mob-like tactics. Where is our government to intervene in this? Oh, wait—SBA and Treasury are the government. Don't fret. I'll share some strategies for you in the upcoming steps.

Many of you will be like me and just have private business debts. If your business tanked, even those with SBA loans probably have plenty of private debts as well. Private business debts are generally easy-peasy. Just follow the steps and feel like a firefighter as you extinguish one bad debt after another.

STEP EIGHT: BE REACTIVE

In most cases, once you get past a flurry of collection calls and correspondence, eventually your creditors will ideally write your debt off. Although being proactive is often helpful in life, now you are best off being reactive: just wait and respond to whatever actions your creditors take. There might be nothing more for you to do except to move on with your life with your business debt no longer burdening you. On the other hand, you will need to react if your matter is escalated with a notice:

Private: You will be served with a lawsuit.

SBA: You will receive a 60-day Notice indicating that the SBA is transferring your debt to the Treasury for collection. This notice also includes an invitation to (1) inspect and copy SBA records related to your debt and (2) request a review of SBA's claim that you owe the debt.

Once you receive either, pay the retainer to your attorney and get engaged.

STEP NINE: FIND FAULT
Business loans are as laden with deficiencies as consumer loans. Share all your loan documents, the lawsuit, your communication log and any correspondence with your attorney. Go through them all and compare to the Deficiencies in Action Tools.

For example, you may have received a 1099-C from your debt holder, which submitted the form to the IRS to notify them that your debt has been cancelled. The downside is that the 1099-C may create a potential tax liability. See "Resolve To Pay No Tax on Forgiven Debt" in Chapter 2: Pre-Cleanse to learn how you can likely avoid this tax.

However, even if you are not required to pay the tax, you can argue that you cannot be saddled with a potential tax liability and be forced to pay the debt. The creditor, and any subsequent holders of your debt, can have one or the other. This creates a challenge for creditors, as many times they are legally required to issue the 1099-C even if they believe that the debt is still collectible. Yet, some recent court decisions have ruled that the issuance of a 1099-C cancels the debt and the creditor can no longer collect. This is not a universal opinion amongst courts, but presents the prospect of costly losses for creditors.

Alternately, your rights may have been violated if any of the following were not included in the SBA's 60-day Notice and similar communication notifying you that your debt was being transferred to the Treasury Department:

A. Nature and amount of the debt, including the basis for the debt.

B. Explanation of how interest, penalties, and administrative costs are added to the debt.

C. Date by which payment should be made to avoid late charges and enforced collection (generally 30 days from the date the demand letter is mailed).

D. Name, address, and phone number of a contact person or office within the creditor agency.

E. Explanation of the agency's intent to enforce collection if debtor fails to pay.

You are sure to find more, as creditors large and small all seem to run a side business churning out deficiencies for you to exploit.

Private: Skip to Step Thirteen.

SBA: List deficiencies in Letter E from Action Tools and submit with "Request to Inspect & Copy SBA Records" in the next step.

STEP TEN: ARM YOURSELF, THE SEQUEL

More documents, more problems. This is good news. Submit the request below, and check any boxes that apply, but be sure to always check line #8.

∗   ∗   ∗

REQUEST TO INSPECT & COPY SBA RECORDS

Your Name
Your Address
Your City, State & Zip

VIA CERTIFIED MAIL/RETURN RECEIPT REQUESTED/ COPY RETAINED

Date

To: OFFICE REPRESENTATIVE
U.S. SMALL BUSINESS ADMINISTRATION
Address
City, State, Zip

Re: Request to Inspect & Copy Records

Account Number:_____

My name is _____ and I am the alleged debtor in this matter. Please accept this letter as a formal request for the opportunity to inspect and copy any and all records pertaining to the SBA's claim of my alleged debt. Please furnish me with:

1. A copy of the front and back of the promissory note as it exists today, including all assignments, endorsements and allonges thereto;

2. A copy of the front and back of the security agreement, including any assignments;

3. Payment history for the life of loan, including a detailed breakdown of payments posted to the account and application of those payments to principal, interest, and any other type of charges;

4. A detailed breakdown of any collection costs and the basis therefore.

I would also like to formally request an opportunity to inspect the original promissory note. Along with your responses to the Discovery Requests, please provide me with reasonable locations for inspection and at least five proposed dates and times, or in the alternative, provide me with the name and direct contact information for the individual responsible for scheduling the inspection of a promissory note.

In addition, I am requesting a formal review of the SBA's claim that I owe this debt for the following reasons:

1. _____ The amount the SBA claims that I owe is inaccurate and does not take in to account the payments I made towards the balance of the alleged debt. Evidence of payment is enclosed

with this letter. (ENCLOSE: copies of the front and back of all checks, money orders and any receipts showing payments made to the holder of the debt.)

2. _____ I am making payments on this debt as required under the repayment agreement as agreed between the creditor and myself pursuant to the [insert date of signed agreement] repayment agreement, which is also enclosed with this letter. (ENCLOSE: copies of the repayment agreement and copies of the front and back of checks where you paid on the agreement.)

3. _____ I currently have pending bankruptcy filed on or about [insert date]. (ENCLOSE: copies of any documents from the court that show the date that you filed, the name of the court, and your case number.)

4. _____ This debt was discharged in bankruptcy. (ENCLOSE: copies of debt discharge order and the schedule of debts filed with the court.)

5. _____ The borrower has died. (ENCLOSE: Original, certified copy, or clear, accurate, and complete photocopy of the original or certified Death Certificate.)

6. _____ I am totally and permanently disabled and am unable to engage in substantial gainful activity because of a medically determinable physical or mental impairment. Therefore, I have submitted a Loan Discharge Application dated [insert date] which is enclosed with this letter. (Obtain and submit a completed Loan Discharge Application: Total and Permanent Disability form. The form must be completed by a physician if you are a veteran, in which case you can submit required

documentation from the U.S. Department of Veterans Affairs. Refer to the application for all requirements.) For loans only.

7. _____ This is not my Social Security Number, and I do not owe this debt. (ENCLOSE: a copy of your driver's license or other identification issued by a Federal, state or local government agency, and a copy of your Social Security Card.)

8. _____ I believe that this debt is not an enforceable debt in the amount stated for the reason explained in the enclosed letter. (Attach a letter explaining any reason other than those listed above for your objection to collection of this debt amount by garnishment of your salary. ENCLOSE: any supporting records.)

9. _____ I was involuntarily terminated from my last employment and I have been employed in my current job for less than twelve months. A statement from my employer verifying this information is enclosed. (Attach statement from employer showing date of hire in current job and statement from prior employer showing involuntary termination.)

10. _____ I believe that _____ (name of individual or other party) without my permission signed my name or used my personal identification data to execute documents to obtain this loan, and I did not receive the loan funds. A False Certification Discharge Application and/or Identity Theft Certification were completed and submitted on [insert date] and are enclosed with this letter. [Obtain and submit a completed False Certification (Unauthorized Signature/Unauthorized Payment) discharge application or

Identity Theft Certification)]. Enclose any records showing
your withdrawal date).

Sincerely,

Your Signature
Your Name

cc:

Lender or Servicer
U.S. Congressperson in your District

*   *   *

Mail in with Letter E from Action Tools and itemize all the deficiencies that you have identified. When you send in the request,
attach a copy of the government's notice to you and send by certified mail, return receipt requested. Mail to the SBA's address
indicated on the letter you receive. If there is no address under
the "Request a Review of your Debt," then mail to the address
under "Agree to a Repayment Plan." The cc's can be sent by regular
mail. You need to submit within sixty days of the date of the Notice
indicating that the SBA is transferring your debt to the Treasury
for collection.

The SBA will likely provide at least some documents to you. If there
are a substantial number, they may request a fee for copying. Pay
the fee, which is likely to be modest. In order to inspect original
documents, such as the note, the SBA will likely make the original
available for inspection at one of their offices. The SBA review of
your obligation is likely to affirm that you owe the money. However,

there are additional opportunities to crush your debt.

STEP ELEVEN: REQUEST ADMINISTRATIVE HEARING

If the SBA or Treasury opts to garnish your wages (typically up to 25% of disposable income), intercept a tax refund or a portion of your Social Security check, or take collection action against a specific asset or income source, they are required to mail a notice to your last known address at least 30 days prior to proceeding. This gives you time to object, which is what you are going to do. You will have 15 days from the date of the notice to submit your reply. Use the form below, fill in the blanks which apply and always check the boxes to dispute the "Existence of the debt" and the "Amount of the debt." You require evidence of the debt, such as the promissory note that you signed, evidence that the Treasury or SBA is the lawful holder of the debt, and that the amount claimed is correct. In the "Debt Amount" field, input the amount claimed and write the words "is the amount claimed by creditor" just to reiterate that you don't know the actual amount due, at least until you receive and review a payment history and other records:

* * *

Hearing Request

Administrative Wage Garnishment

MAIL OR FAX FORM TO: FAX: (855) 292-9623
EMAIL: AWGhearingrequest@fms.treas.gov
Debt Management Services
Attn: AWG Analyst
Post Office Box 830794
Birmingham Al 35283-0794

Debtor Name _____

FedDebt Case ID Number _____

Federal Agency _____

Federal Agency Account Number _____

Debt Amount _____

If you object to garnishment of your wages for the debt mentioned above, you can use this form to request a hearing. Please check the appropriate box(es) below. Your request for a hearing must be in writing, signed, and delivered to the address above. EXPLAIN any additional facts concerning your objection on a separate sheet of paper and, together with all supporting documentation, enclose it with this request. Your objection(s) will be considered based on the information and documents you provide with this form, and any records held by the agency.

_____ Existence of the debt—I do not owe the debt.

_____ Amount of the debt—I do not owe the full amount of the debt.

_____ Garnishment Amount—Proposed garnishment would cause financial hardship.

NOTE: You must provide a signed financial statement along with copies of earnings and income records and proof of expenses. To obtain a copy of the financial statement form, go to http://fms.treas. gov/debt/consumer_finstmt.pdf or call the number listed above.

_____ I was involuntarily terminated from my last employment, and I have been employed in my current job for less than 12 months.

NOTE: You must provide a signed financial statement along with copies of earnings and income records and proof of expenses. To obtain a copy of the financial statement form, go to http://fms.treas.gov/debt/consumer_finstmt.pdf or call the number listed above.

Debtor Address _____

Debtor Phone Number _____

Employer Name and Address _____

Employer Phone Number _____

I have read and understand the Important Notice about Administrative Wage Garnishment.

I understand that if I make or provide any knowingly false or frivolous claims or statements, representations, or evidence to a Federal Agency, I may be subject to penalties under the False Claims Act, 31 U.S. C. 3729-3731 or criminal penalties under 18 U.S.C. 286, 287. 1—1, and 1002.

Signature _____

Date _____

* * *

Mail in with the same Letter E you submitted in Step Ten. Provided that you mail the request before the deadline, garnishments, levies, and other adverse actions will be on hold until they prove that you owe the money, that the amount they claim is due, that they own the loan, and that they have the books and records to prove all this.

Note that even if the government has already started garnishing your wages or similar steps, you can still request documents and a hearing. However, the garnishment or other action will usually continue until the matter is resolved.

STEP TWELVE: CAN YOU HEAR-ING ME NOW?

Hearing is quite a generous term in these circumstances: an SBA official will review your request and will then subjectively decide if this warrants an oral in-person, telephone, or "paper" hearing. The former is ideal, but you don't get to choose. The latter typically involves both sides submitting written evidence, with the hearing office then rendering a decision. No matter the hearing type, emphasize any deficiencies.

If the SBA grants you an oral hearing, your attorney should attend along with a court reporter that can provide a record of the hearing. Your attorney can hire the reporter and your side gets to pay. If the hearing is not local, your attorney can engage a local attorney to attend the hearing on your behalf.

These hearings are partial to the SBA. The administrative courts are run by the government agencies themselves, "much as if the police department could make up its own prosecutors, judges and courts of appeals," observed Charles Murray in *The Wall Street*

Journal in May 2015.[84] They might hear you, but they won't hear you. You know what I mean? Just expect to lose. It's cool. This is just one step on your journey.

STEP THIRTEEN: WHAT'S IT WORTH TO KISS AND MAKE UP?

Decide on a target settlement amount. This could be zero or $1, or hundreds of thousands. This should be a lump sum that you can afford, and which takes into account your creditor's perception of your collectability as well as the potency of any deficiencies you have uncovered.

If you found some strong deficiencies, then you and your attorney might start discussing what the opposition should pay you. Likewise, if you have no assets and are self-employed (paid by your own LLC), the appropriate amount may be nothing. If there are a few modest deficiencies, and you have steady work, a house with equity, and stocks and bonds or other significant assets, you might want to up your offer a bit, maybe 10% of what is owed.

With SBA loans, your attorney can make an Offer in Compromise. With private loans, your attorney can simply contact the attorney representing the lender to tender your offer.

STEP FOURTEEN: FILE LAWSUIT OR ANSWER WITH COUNTERCLAIMS

Private: File an answer and counterclaim against debt holder, servicer, franchisor, business partner, contractors, vendors, lenders, and/or anyone else responsible for your unaffordable business debt.

---

84 Murry, C., "Regulation Run Amok—And How to Fight Back" The Wall Street Journal, http://www.wsj.com/articles/regulation-run-amokand-how-to-fight-back-1431099256 (May 11, 2015).

Government-backed: File lawsuit against debt holder, servicer, SBA, Treasury, franchisor, business partner, contractors, vendors, lender(s), and/or anyone who had a hand in the downfall of your business and the resultant debts.

STEP FIFTEEN: SCRATCH UNTIL YOU FIND THE FLAWS

Ask opposition parties for documents and answers through the discovery process, utilizing Action Tools. As there are many factors, and often many parties, which contribute to a business failure, you and your attorney are likely to come up with several requests.

For instance, Quiznos settled several franchisee lawsuits in 2010, agreeing to pay $206 million to settle allegations of violations of U.S. racketeering and corruption statutes.[85] One of the issues was that Quiznos required all franchisees to purchase food and other supplies through an affiliated supplier at above-market prices. Oftentimes, the costs were so high that franchisees could not financially survive.[86] Quiznos and their affiliated supplier were "a highly profitable cash engine even while franchisees lost money and closed their doors by the hundreds."[87]

Discovery is your opportunity to uncover, for example, a memorandum drafted by a Quiznos lawyer in 2003 that stated, "40

---

85 Janet Sparks, "Quiznos Disclosure Shines Light On Settlements, Litigation" *Blue MauMau.* December 13, 2012, http://www.bluemaumau.org/12139/ quiznos_disclosure_shine_light_settlements_litigation

86 Ibid.

87 Jonathan Maze, "Quiznos Faces Some New Lawsuits" *Restaurant Finance Monitor,* July 13, 2013, http://www.restfinance.com/Restaurant-Finance-Across-America/February-2013/ Quiznos-Faces-Some-New-Lawsuits/

percent of Quiznos units are not breaking even".[88] This would be very helpful if you bought your franchise any time after the memo date, as failure rates that high should have been disclosed to prospective franchisees. Similarly, if the SBA produced statistics revealing that 23.4 percent of Quiznos franchises with SBA loans failed,[89] they would need to answer why they nevertheless proceeded to approve a loan for you to open a Quiznos franchise. Particularly when, in contrast, SBA loans for Subway franchises had a 4.8 percent failure rate.[90]

Once discovery is served, your attorney should reach out to opposing counsel with an offer to settle the matter. Let them know your target amount, which eventually may become appealing to the creditor.

STEP SIXTEEN: FIND EVEN MORE FLAWS
You and your attorney can review newly discovered documents and discovery responses for additional deficiencies.

STEP SEVENTEEN: SETTLEMENT BETTERMENT
Get all parties in a room and try to make a deal. Mediation can be court-ordered or both sides can agree to mediation directly. Typically, an independent third-party mediator will go back and forth between the sides and try to broker a deal. Litigation is annoying and incalculable for all sides. Agreeing to a compromise is worthwhile if you end up settling your debt at a big discount.

88 "Franchise Perils: A Look at the Impending Quiznos Bankruptcy" *Mailbox And Business Center Developers,* accessed August 7, 2015. http://mailboxdevelopers.com/news/franchise-perils-quiznos/

89 Tad DeHaven. "Investigative Reporters Tackle the Small Business Administration", *CATO Institute.* April 8, 2013. http://www.cato.org/blog/investigative-reporters-tackle-small-business-administration

90 Ibid.

STEP EIGHTEEN: TRIAL IN STYLE

If all else fails, go to trial. We want you to put your best foot forward, so go to trial in style: Level the litigation playing field by accessing the Community Chest at debtcleanse.com and crowdfunding your trial preparation and litigation budget. However, if you win, make sure that the legal fees are part of the award and you return these contributions to your supporters.

Best wishes in court. Your attorney will be your guide once you set foot in the courtroom. We will all be rooting for you.

STEP NINETEEN: LET US IN ON IT

Remember to let us know what happens every step of the way, as other debtors will benefit from your experience.

We live in challenging economic times. More small business are closing than are starting.[91] "I don't want to sound like a doomsayer, but when small and medium-sized businesses are dying faster than they're being born, so is free enterprise," said Gallup CEO and Chairman Jim Clifton in January 2015. "And when free enterprise dies, America dies with it." [92]

If your business died, now is the time to cleanse your unaffordable business debt and start a new business—this time without debt (see "Starting a Business" in Chapter 14: Aftermath: Living Debt-Free).

---

91 Clifton, J., "American Entrepreneurship: Dead or Alive" http://www.gallup.com/businessjournal/180431/american-entrepreneurship-dead-alive.aspx

92 Id.

CHAPTER 9

SECURED PERSONAL LOANS

"Let's play Monopoly!"

When I was a young boy, I spent many lazy summer afternoons with my brothers and some neighborhood kids playing the board game Monopoly. We learned real-life lessons in negotiation, decision-making, cash management, diversification, and dealing with luck and adversity. One day, my brother Charles and I were doing well and built up some monopolies. We put up a bunch of hotels and houses, giving my brother Alastair few places to land without paying rent. We refused to trade with him, so he was forced to pay rent which rapidly depleted his Monopoly money. His string of adversity left him bankrupt and unable to pay his debts. He got so upset that he overturned the board, scattering game pieces all over, and ran to his room, slamming the door behind him. We had to start the game over without him.

I never thought about where our Monopoly game came from. My guess is that my parents purchased the game new for a few dollars, or one of my two older sisters received it as a birthday or Christmas present. When we were all older, the well-worn game was sold in a yard sale for a dollar.

Today, I could commit to pay $6.99 monthly at 24.99% percent interest to buy the Monopoly Junior board game for $23.99 (not including interest) at Fingerhut.com. Alternately, I could buy the game at Wal-Mart all-cash for $11.99 and have no payments. I could even buy a used game on eBay for around $6.50 (or at a yard sale for a buck or two). Instead, though, some consumers choose to pay the inflated price at Fingerhut.com for the privilege of buying on credit.

You're never going to buy Park Place or Boardwalk if all you focus on is the monthly payments, rather than the true cost of what you are purchasing. Selling consumers on monthly payments is not exclusive to marketing Monopoly board games:

Fingerhut offers a Samsung 32" 720p LED TV for $499.99 at $34.99 monthly, whereas the same TV is available at Best Buy for $189.99.

LutherSales.com offers the Whirlpool 18.2 Cu. Ft. Monochromatic Top-Freezer Refrigerator for $1,550 at $81.18 monthly, but you can buy the same item at Home Depot for $689.

ElectroFinance.com offers the MacBook Air 2015 11.6" for $1,349 at $46 per week, whereas BHPhotoVideo.com sells for $799.99.

Financing transactions like these occur many times every second in America to sell goods, services, and even medical procedures such as breast implants and dental work. The consumer—maybe you—needs something, but doesn't have the cash. The seller offers financing by hooking you on the monthly payment. You sign and initial all the documents, but often have no idea how much you are borrowing, what the interest rate is, or even how many years the payments go on for. These numbers are buried in the documents and rarely pointed out by the sweet-talking salespeople.

All you are told is the monthly payment. The salesperson may cram add-ons, such as almost-worthless warranties and insurance, into the financing. If the loan is long enough, the payment may appear affordable. On the other hand, paying in cash would have kept whatever you wanted out of reach. However, by financing, you have surrendered another share of your monthly income for years or even decades, further enslaving you to the elite.

We need to put an end to "Buy Now, Pay Later." If you owe unaffordable debt for stuff, the following are 17 steps to do like my brother: overturn the board, slam the door and start over (but keep your wheelbarrow, battleship, Scottie dog, boot, iron, thimble, top hat or whatever collateral secures your loan).

STEP ONE: SEE WHAT THEY HAVE

Gather any and all documents from when you took out your loan. In addition, mail Letter F in Action Tools to request copies of your loan documents. You need to arm yourself early on, even before you stop paying if possible.

STEP TWO: DON'T GIVE 'EM A PENNY MORE

Not paying a loan for stuff is a cinch when you are in a pinch: just stop paying. Make sure to cancel any automatic payments. Take a deep breath and relax. Everything will be fine. No slamming of doors is necessary at this point.

STEP THREE: IGNORE THEM ALL

Creditors will call and write letters. I yawned as I wrote this—excuse me. Feel free to yawn, too. Expect a whole bunch of noise from your creditors, but not much action. Utilize a simple response: ignore them all. Block your creditors' numbers and hang up if you inadvertently pick up, log any calls you errantly answer, and file away any correspondence you receive.

STEP FOUR: STOP CALLS TO YOUR WORKPLACE

If you stop paying, your creditor can call you at home (for the dwindling few of you who still have a home phone), work, or on your cell phone. They probably have your number(s) from your initial application. Even if you change numbers, most creditors have access to databases such as LexisNexis, which will often readily provide creditors with your recent phone numbers and other data, such as current employer.

You need to be sweating over the work generated by your regular job, not in response to your creditors trying to make you sob. Thus, mail Letter B in Action Tools, then smile. Just the act of smiling will make you feel good. Really. Plus, those around you will wonder what you are up to. Well, you are happy because, once you mail Letter B, your creditors are legally restricted from calling you at work.

When you first stop paying, calls may come from the original creditor, which may be subject to an action by the Federal Trade Commission if they call you at work if they know, or should have known, that your employer disallows personal calls. This letter lets them know this. If they still call you, log the time and date of the call(s) to use as a deficiency in any future litigation.

If the call comes from a debt collector which is working on behalf of the creditor or which bought your nonperforming loan, the FDCPA bans them from calling you at work once the above letter is received. If you do receive a call, log the time and date. This is a deficiency that you can exploit later if the debt is litigated.

STEP FIVE: PROTECT YOUR STUFF

Always keep your property secured by a loan in a non-publicly accessible area. Furniture, equipment, a Jet Ski and/or boat should all be stored in secured areas, such as a locked garage or behind a locked gate. If you don't have one, ask a friend or family member to use theirs. Repo men generally may not breach the peace, so they cannot break into locked areas.

If a repo man shows up, do not let him or her in. Slam the door if you feel like it. You are not required to provide them access into your home or any other private area, unless the creditor first obtains a court order. If your property is worth less than a couple of thousand, then it's typically not worthwhile for a creditor to go to court. For insight into what your stuff is likely worth, go to craigslist, eBay or some other forum for private parties to sell items like yours used for all-cash. Disregard or adjust dealer sales, which are typically labeled as such, as prices are often distorted upwards due to financing.

Let's say you are having trouble making the $6.99 monthly payments to Fingerhut for that Monopoly Junior game. As a result, you might consider encouraging your kids to play Monopoly at a card table in the backyard, not the ungated front yard. Otherwise, you might reason, if they all go inside for some Kool Aid and cookies, they might return to the front yard to find the game repossessed.

Yet, think about it: used Monopoly Junior games sell for $6.50 on eBay. Is Fingerhut really going to send a repo person out to try to pick up a game and recoup $6.50? Never going to happen. Laptops, refrigerators, TVs? Until you creep over a couple of thousand dollars in resale value, if you don't voluntarily hand over the goods, most creditors will write off these debts. As a result, these unpaid loans are frequently sold at big discounts to debt buyers, which will typically let borrowers keep their stuff and attempt to collect as they would unsecured loans. You can usually kill these debts in Steps Six and Seven.

However, if your equipment is of high value, such as a boat, Jet Ski, or even an airplane, then your lender may sue you, and even schedule a court hearing to request an order that you turn over your stuff. In rare situations, a creditor could request criminal charges of concealment against you.

The FDCPA and state laws prohibit debt collectors and collection agencies from threatening you with criminal prosecution for not paying a debt. Nevertheless, a creditor could allege that you are concealing, or "hiding," the collateral. They may believe that you should make repossession easy by moving your recliner to the porch or your ATV to your open driveway. However, they cannot dictate what you do with *your* property. No "Get Out Of Jail Free" card is needed. Instead, review Mile Thirteen: Concealment Laws in Chapter 6: Vehicle Loans for insight into what to expect and how to respond.

STEP SIX: DISPUTE AND VALIDATE

Eventually, with continued nonpayment, your loan will likely be sold to a debt buyer or transferred to a collection agency. These entities may perceive themselves as vultures attempting to strip what they can from you financially. However, first they need to mail you an invitation to dispute and validate the debt you purportedly owe. Respond by mailing back Letter A in Action Tools to dispute and request validation of your debt. Whoever purports to own your debt needs to have the documentation and records to prove that your debt is alive, that they own it, and how big it is. In many cases, the creditor will be unable to do so and the vulture will leave you alone and turn their focus to the majority of debtors who are not disputing their debts.

Without the documentation to validate, this one simple letter may be the death sentence for your debt. Go about your life and enjoy your sofa, pet cockatoo, rims, trombone, or whatever.

STEP SEVEN: STOP CONTACTING ME

Now is the time to tell your creditor to "shut up!" When you receive a response to Letter A (or if you have not received a response 45-days after mailing), mail in Letter C from Action Tools. Once you do this, debt buyers and collection agencies are prohibited from contacting you. All they can do is send you one more communication letting you know what they are going to do as well as serve any documents required to proceed with a lawsuit. You have called their bluff. Now you get to see if the creditor wants to make good on those threats to sue your pants off, garnish your wages, levy your bank account, or put a lien on your home. Dare them to "walk the walk… talk ain't necessary", as Nigerian strategist George Akomas Jr. said. Chances are your creditor will do nothing and your debt will shrivel up and die. I am happy for your loss. Splendid. You get to keep your stuff.

However, note that original creditors can typically still contact you after receiving this letter. If you continue to withstand their annoying efforts, eventually they are highly likely to sell your debt to a debt buyer or transfer to a collection agency. When you receive notice that this has occurred, repeat the process of mailing Letter A followed by Letter C to each new holder of your debt. Your goal is that they eventually loosen their grip and allow your debt to hurl to a timely death.

STEP EIGHT: HIRE AN ATTORNEY

If you get served with a lawsuit, take three steps:

1. Breathe in, open your mouth wide, and yawn.

2. Log the date you were served, and write the date on the lawsuit document (Summons & Complaint).

3. Hire an attorney by following the steps in Chapter 3: Quick Start.

You might think hiring an attorney is overkill for such a small debt. However, if the debt holder is insisting on keeping this alive, knocking on *your* door is more like trick or treat: you and your attorney have a whole bag of tricks. If everything goes just right, your debt holder might make enough mistakes that you and your attorney may realign your sights. Instead of simply settling your debt at a big discount so you can keep your stuff, now you also want a big bag of candy: the debt holder pays your attorney fees plus maybe even a cash settlement *to* you.

STEP NINE: DEFICIENCES ARE WORTH WAY MORE THAN MONOPOLY MONEY

The outfit selling you financed products typically arranges the loans on your stuff. For instance, that loan on an engagement ring was probably signed at a jewelry store and the easy financing on breast implants was likely set up at a cosmetic surgeon's office. Your contact was likely with a clerical employee who ran through the agreement and disclosures with you: "sign here," "initial there," "accept this," "yes here…" These employees would be prudent to go through each document slowly and disclose each feature of the loan. However, their commission is usually earned once the documents are signed and transmitted to the finance company.

As a result, disclosure is not a priority and most borrowers have no idea what they are signing. Frequently, the employees selling the financing really do not understand much either. They were typically hired because of their knowledge of the product they are selling, such as appliances, electronics, musical instruments, or whatever, not because of their financing background. Thus, with so much fine print and legalese, no one really knows what is being signed. Commissions to salespeople based on financing and add-on products often contribute to saddling consumers with unconscionable debt burdens

Let's say you purchased a guitar and the salesperson, without mentioning to you, stuck an extended warranty in as part of the purchase. This is akin to going to the grocery store to buy a box of Cheerios. When you get to the cashier, she is super friendly, all smiles, talks about the weather, and throws in a warranty that the Cheerios are edible. The box of Cheerios costs $5 and the warranty costs $2. Amidst chatter about the sunny skies, you do not realize that you paid an extra $2 when you swiped your credit card. Chances are you'll never even know that you purchased a warranty and you'll eat the Cheerios, they were edible, and the cashier earned a fat commission on that warranty sale. Besides, I expect that General Mills, the manufacturer of Cheerios, would gladly replace any box of Cheerios that proved inedible, so the $2 warranty provided duplicate coverage and was worthless.

Many salespeople earn little or no commission for selling the actual product, be it a refrigerator or a box of Cheerios. Instead, their incentives are pegged to the add-ons, often grossly overpriced and of little value, such as extended warranties and insurance products. These optional add-ons are typically marked-up excessively, generating high profit margins. According to checkbook.org, "in 2005, about a third of Best Buy's profits came from warranty sales, which carried profit margins of roughly 50 percent, as opposed to margins of just a few percent for many of the products covered by the warranties. That was the last year Best Buy reported details on the profitability of extended warranties. No wonder: Some analysts estimate that all of Best Buy's profit now comes from the sale of extended warranties." The whole situation is ripe for breeding deficiencies for you to exploit. And you must exploit.

Thus, gather up all the documents and records you have from when you first took out the loan, any you received in response to your document request, your communication log, as well as correspondence received. Share these with your attorney and perform a debt autopsy: pore through every piece of data and identify Deficiencies by referencing Action Tools.

STEP TEN: FILE ANSWER AND COUNTERCLAIMS
Your lender wants the equipment, money, or both. Well, you did borrow the money and got the equipment or service. Thus, the judge is going to immediately rule in the creditor's favor, right? Nope, not if you file an answer and counterclaims against the lender, the servicer, the dealer who provided the product and arranged or referred the lender, any warranty or insurance provider, and/or

any other party responsible for your unaffordable debt. By doing so, your case becomes a contested matter and your creditor will need to prove to the court that you owe what they allege. As always, request a jury trial. There are certainly some jurors who owe money on stuff they own and might better relate to you than the elite creditor (plus you are probably a more likeable person). Many creditors simply dismiss cases when an answer is filed.

If your lender has requested a hearing in an attempt to pursue concealment charges against you, your attorney will counter that the financing is disputed and the creditor's right to repossess is therefore jeopardized. How can you conceal collateral from a lien-holder whose rights to the lien are in question? Most judges will likely dismiss the matter and suggest that the dispute is resolved in civil court.

If you are arrested for concealment, go to the Community Chest at debtcleanse.com and start a crowdfunding campaign to raise funds to defend yourself in the criminal action and then file a separate civil action against the creditor for abuse of process. America does not have debtors' prisons, and using criminal courts to attempt to coerce collection of debts is repugnant. We will all support you to keep you out of the slammer, plus sue your creditor, ideally extracting a settlement to compensate you for your trouble and reimburse your supporters.

STEP ELEVEN: LET'S MAKE A DEAL

You have collateral of reasonably high value like a bird, a plane, even a Superman painting. You want to keep the collateral, but your lender wants the item or money. "Let's make a deal," as Monty Hall said for years, to euthanize your debt.

In Step Five, you determined the likely sales price for your stuff in used, as-is condition. Now, offer 25% of that as your cash settlement amount to end the litigation and avoid a judgment. So, if you have a boat worth $10,000, offer $2,500. In doing so, what you're really offering your creditor is an outcome that is certain. No more Chance. Some debt buyers will take the deal, or counter at something reasonable. Don't be afraid to ask for what you want.

To help justify your offer, now is the time to share any flaws in the collateral's condition with your creditor, emphasizing any repairs needed. "I just want to let you know that my boat is scratched in several places, the engine keeps overheating, has trouble shifting, and the steering feels like its frozen in place. There's some mold in the cabin which I am having trouble getting rid of, plus I am scared to take it out because the oil looks kind of like chocolate milk." Maybe provide a repair estimate. If you present the facts appropriately, with some supporting photos and documentation, then your $2,500 offer may appear quite generous.

Finally, if you have identified any particularly egregious deficiencies, then offer even less, or nothing. Let your attorney guide you on this, plus check debtcleanse.com for outcomes in similar matters, especially against the same creditor. Request that any final settlement includes a waiver of deficiency. Have your attorney make the settlement offer to the opposition. They may not be ready to make a deal yet. However, the creditor is risking a sure $2,500. They could get stuck with the goat behind Door #2.

If the creditor rebuffs your offer, fine. Just keep trudging forward. The longer you go without paying, the lower the amount you are likely to ultimately settle for and the more you can save into your settlement wallet.

STEP TWELVE: TELL ME EVERYTHING

Learn something new by asking your creditor for everything they have on your debt. You and your attorney can conduct discovery by asking your creditor and their associates for documents and answers to questions about your debt. Reference the sample requests in Action Tools. Your attorney will likely come up with more based on the specifics of your case. Your creditors and any other parties you are suing are legally compelled to furnish any and all documents that are responsive to your requests.

As an example, many promissory notes and loan agreements dictate that notices are sent to debtors to advise them of their default. Further, many states require that creditors send out specific notices in order to take collection actions. This patchwork of laws is often difficult to keep up with, and required notices are sometimes overlooked. Have your attorney identify every notice required in your loan documents, as well as any required by law, then request that the debt holder provides. Any missed notices are likely deficiencies which you can exploit.

As needed, your attorney can request depositions, interrogatories, and requests for admissions from opposition parties. With any of these devices, your attorney gets to dig deep into the birth, life, and background of your debt and the people and entities that have handled (or mishandled) the purported obligation. These proceedings are likely to expose additional issues.

STEP THIRTEEN: KILL MY DEBT ALREADY, WILL YA?

The likelihood of personal property collection actions getting this far in litigation is slim. By now, your creditor should have either agreed to a settlement or dropped the matter entirely. If not, after serving discovery your attorney should reach out to opposing counsel to offer—again—to settle the matter. Repeat your same target settlement amount. At some point, your number should become interesting.

STEP FOURTEEN: MORE DOCUMENTS, MORE PROBLEMS

Review newly discovered documents and responses for additional deficiencies.

STEP FIFTEEN: IF WAR IS THE ANSWER, WE ARE ASKING THE WRONG QUESTION

Request mediation. Getting everybody together may help get you the result you want: peace, and a discounted settlement. After the mediator sets out the session's plans, the parties are usually split up and the mediator goes back and forth between each side to try to broker a compromise. Call it war with a go-between who tries to accelerate a resolution. Your attorney will typically take the lead with the mediator, and you can be open and upfront in any communication. The mediator cannot share anything you say with the debt holder, unless you authorize.

To start, offer the settlement amount you offered in Step Eleven. As part of the back-and-forth, maybe increase your offer by a modest amount, to $2,600. Let's say that the other side is stuck at $5,000. If you named the dealer who sold you the boat as a party in the suit for failure to properly disclose the terms of the financing, for instance, the dealer may kick in the remaining $2,400 and pay your legal fees. If everyone is legitimately working towards a settlement, a deal agreeable to all can sometimes be struck. If so, a settlement agreement is typically written up in the following week or two, then funds are paid and the matter ended.

If mediation does not prove fruitful, expect to escalate.

STEP SIXTEEN: WAR CHEST VS. COMMUNITY CHEST

If the opposition refuses to settle, get ready for trial. Be willing to go to war.

Your creditor's war chest is likely well-stocked with cash for legal fees and is indubitably bigger than yours. However, you are one of us, the majority of Americans who have unaffordable debts, and your battle is our battle. Collectively, we can crowdfund a Community Chest large enough to take your creditor on at trial. Post your request at debtcleanse.com.

Due to the unpredictability of trials, creditors will often cave at the end and attempt to settle. Don't get starry-eyed and try to hold out for some big win, which may or may not occur. If you can get your debt settled at a big discount and maybe your legal fees paid, take the deal. Trial outcomes are uncertain for both sides and, even if you win, the creditor may appeal in order to drag this out. Settlement is betterment.

STEP SEVENTEEN: SHARE YOUR STORY AND YOUR PROGRESS

Keep us abreast of your progress on debtcleanse.com. Your win is our win, and, if you suffer a setback, we all want to know so we can help you get back in the game.

"Own It All" is Monopoly's slogan. This appears to have been adopted by America's elite, the creditors who eat away at families' incomes by aiding and abetting the sale of overpriced goods and services, often with high-margin add-ons of little value. Monthly payment plans are often marketed to seduce and betray consumers. We need to take back our incomes and, if stuck with one of these loans, we need to "Own It All" by settling our secured personal debts for pennies on the dollar (or even nothing) and keeping our stuff. Just like that lazy summer day decades ago, let's do like my brother and upend the monopolies which the elite hold on our country. Board overturned. Door slammed. Free Parking. Let's start a new game.

CHAPTER 10

CREDIT CARDS & UNSECURED PERSONAL LOANS

The average U.S. household with debt owes $15,611 on their credit cards as of December 2014, according to Federal Reserve statistics.[93] Luckily, credit cards are among the simplest of all debts to cleanse. There's no collateral, loan amounts are relatively small, and there are often missing data and documents. All of this weighs to the advantage of you, the debtor. Cutting up all your cards and settling your credit cards for pennies on the dollar is typically simple.

A 2008 Federal Trade Commission report concluded that, based on an analysis of prices paid by debt buyers in more than 3,400 portfolios, debt buyers paid an average of 4.0 cents per dollar of debt face value.[94] If you owe $5,000 on your credit card and stop paying,

---

93   https://www.nerdwallet.com/blog/finance/money-taboo-and-credit-card-debt-survey/

94   https://www.ftc.gov/sites/default/files/documents/reports/structure-and-practices-debt-buying-industry/debtbuyingreport.pdf

eventually your credit card debt will likely be sold for around $200. The minimum payment on a $5,000 balance is typically $100, so your debt is sold for the equivalent of two payments.

The debt buyers who buy massive pools of this defaulted debt often try to collect 100% of what is due; yet they end up collecting nothing from guys like me. I had multiple Visas and MasterCards, along with American Express and some store cards from Sears and Macy's. When I went through my financial chaos, these all went unpaid. I got a bunch of calls and letters, but eventually they all ran out of steam and died off. There were a couple with fat balances, over $10,000, and they perished alongside the $200 I owed to Sears.

Unsecured personal loans are the same. In recent history, banks have tended to market credit cards much more aggressively than unsecured personal loans. However, over the last few years, unsecured personal loans have become increasingly popular on peer-to-peer lending platforms such as Lending Club and Prosper. If you need a personal loan of $35,000 or less, you can go to these sites and apply. At Prosper, the APR ranges from 6.68% to 35.97%. If approved, funds are often transferred directly to your bank account within a week.

When these sites first started around eight years ago, "peers" funded most of the loans. Regular people would chip in $25 or more and earn most of the interest generated. However, the elite eventually elbowed their way in and now Wall Street-type firms fund the majority of the loans. The sites are models of efficiency as a go-between for creditors and debtors. As we have built debt-cleanse.com, we have often looked to lendingclub.com and prosper.com for inspiration. Whereas these lending sites put borrowers into debt, debtcleanse.com will get borrowers out of debt.

When a borrower stops paying a peer-to-peer loan, the challenges for the creditor in collecting are the same as credit cards. This is Prosper's strategy in the event of a default, per a 2012 post at lendacademy.com:

> *98% of borrowers are on an automatic ACH withdrawal, so Prosper is alerted immediately if there are not enough funds to make the loan payment. Here is the procedure they follow when that happens:*
>
> 1. *With an ACH failure an email is immediately sent to the borrower.*
>
> 2. *Make two more attempts at ACH payment, notifying the borrower each time there is a failure.*
>
> 3. *Make regular phone calls to the borrower until they are able to get an answer. Try and work out some kind of payment on the loan.*
>
> 4. *If after 30 days no payment has been made, hand off borrower to the collection agency, Amsher.*
>
> 5. *Amsher will send letters and continue to make phone calls. Amsher emphasizes the peer-to-peer aspect of this debt to try and persuade the borrower to pay back the loan.*
>
> 6. *If Amsher is unsuccessful after 120 days past due the loan is charged off.*
>
> 7. *The loan is then often handed to a different collection agency, IC System, where they continue to try and collect on the charged off loan.*

Prosper does not file judgments against borrowers at this time primarily because of the court costs involved. Before the financial crisis they used to get judgments against homeowners and attach liens. But with so many homes underwater this strategy is no longer effective. The real estate market would have to improve for Prosper to consider this again.

In a bankruptcy filing they will immediately pull the loan back from collections. If it is a Chapter 7 filing then all debts are discharged so Prosper will usually get nothing. With a Chapter 13 filing, the borrower has to file a plan to make payments and Prosper will file a proof of claim in those situations.

Prosper's approach is similar to most credit card issuers and personal loan providers. As you have likely detected, there really is not much that can be done to force you to pay. You'll be threatened with court action but, most of the time, the costs do not make this worthwhile. Even if your creditor files a lawsuit, you can often kill the creditor's progress by simply filing an answer.

If you look at the title of this book, it ends with "And Not Pay Some At All." Well, credit cards and unsecured personal loans generally fall into this category. Here's the blow-by-blow of blowing off your unaffordable credit cards and unsecured personal loans:

BLOW ONE: STOP PAYING

Stop paying. Cancel any automatic payments. If you have checking or savings accounts with any banks that have issued you credit cards, close the accounts and open elsewhere. Otherwise, the bank could offset your checking or savings account for your unpaid payments. Remember to notify any sources of direct deposits, such as employers, of the new account change.

BLOW TWO: GO INCOMMUNICADO

As soon as you stop paying, your phone and mailbox will overflow with communication from your creditors. Please disregard. There is no benefit in responding.

BLOW THREE: MY EMPLOYER IS A MEANIE (BUT MY CREDITOR IS WORSE)

Your employer may be tough on policies, such as receiving calls at work. Turn your employer's iron fist onto your creditor by mailing Letter B in Action Tools. This will help your employer enforce the rules and keep your creditor from calling you at work. What a great employee you are.

BLOW FOUR: GIVE YOUR CREDITORS A BLOWOUT

Mail Letter C in Action Tools.

Most non-original creditors, such as debt buyers and collection agencies, are legally barred from communicating with you upon receipt of this letter. If they do contact you, make sure to log the communication. This represents a deficiency that may be helpful later. Although original creditors may not be legally required to stop contacting you, many will honor your request.

Although they cannot call or mail you collection letters, they still have one option left: file a lawsuit. They are entitled to serve you any documents pertaining to a legal filing. You have given them an option: sue me, or don't contact me.

Luckily, as most will not sue you, this is the end. Your credit score will be shot but, outside of that, nothing more happens. It kinds of feels like this all ended before it got started.

BLOW FIVE: CHILLAX

Chill. Relax. If any of the original creditors attempt to communicate, ignore them. Just go about your life and wait. Most of the time, creditors will not send you a notice that your debt is dead. You just need to assume this when you go a long period without hearing about it.

BLOW SIX: BE OBJECTIONABLE

As you fall six or more months behind, most creditors will either sell your debt to a debt buyer or assign to a collection agency, sometimes on a contingency basis. You will typically be notified that a new company will now attempt collection. The notice will include an invitation to dispute the debt. Go ahead and take the creditor up on the invitation by sending Letter A in Action Tools.

Expect your debts to be sold multiple times. Each time, you will receive a new letter and invitation to dispute. Keep re-sending the same letters, and include Letter C to make sure that they know not to try to contact you again unless they sue.

Original creditors are excluded from the FDCPA and therefore can ignore these requests. Nevertheless, many will comply in an abundance of prudence.

The vast majority of credit card and unsecured personal loan debts are on death row by now. Sometimes, however, credit card companies and debt buyers will not go away so easily.

BLOW SEVEN: YOU'VE BEEN SERVED!

If you are served with a summons and complaint, which begin a lawsuit, log the date you were served and write the date on the actual court document. The countdown to answer starts on this day. The specific number of days you have to answer, often 20-30, will be indicated on the summons.

The amounts in dispute in a credit card matter are often relatively modest. There is also no collateral, such as a house or a car. Your goal is to simply encourage the credit card company to go away and leave you alone. Even though you may be able to beat this on your own, get some help.

BLOW EIGHT: DON'T HIRE A BLOWHARD

Hire an attorney if you have not done so yet. See Chapter 3: Quick Start for some tips to make sure you don't retain a blowhard by mistake. If you hired an attorney for another debt, the same counsel can probably assist on your credit cards and other debts as well.

BLOW NINE: BLOW HOLES IN YOUR DEBT

At the beginning of the book, I shared a quote from Judge Noach Dear, who observed that creditors in 9 out of 10 credit card lawsuits cannot prove they own the debt. Defects are rampant with these small, unsecured loans. Odds are great that the lawsuit and debt include a whirlwind of deficiencies.

Share all the documents you have compiled, including any received in response to your request for verification, with your attorney. In addition, provide your communication log. Then power up Action Tools to review common deficiencies—especially those related to missing documentation and standing to sue—which can be particularly common in credit card debts.

Additionally, credit card issuers sometimes increase interest rates without justification, which is a deficiency you can now exploit. You may simply receive a notification that the interest rate has been increased. You may have already charged up thousands of dollars thinking you were paying a lower rate, and now you need to repay at a higher rate. This predatory, illegal lending practice may replace an affordable interest rate with an unaffordable one. The creditor knew, or should have known, that you did not have the ability to pay the higher rate. Nevertheless, you were given no choice but to pay the increased rate.

With credit cards, there is often no contract to evidence the debt. If the creditor has anything at all, it's often just a brochure or boilerplate card member agreement, without anything specifically identifying the borrower. The creditor may allege that this is sufficient, but you can argue that it's not. Further, these agreements may not name the correct original creditor. This may have been easy to remedy at the outset, but it's not so simple years later when you are challenging the current debt holder. Also, peruse the deficiencies pertaining to negligent and abusive collection practices, which are often employed in the collection of credit card debt. Since there is no collateral to seize, bullying credit card debtors is often collectors' most effective strategy. For instance, the FDCPA identifies that the hours between 8:00AM to 9:00PM are typically assumed to be convenient for debtors to receive calls. [95] Did you receive calls outside of these hours? If so, now is the time in which your communication log can be reviewed and any identified deficiencies exploited.

Next, let's put these deficiencies to work.

BLOW TEN: BLOW BACK
Answer and file counterclaims against whoever is suing you, and

---

95   15 U.S.C. 1601, et. seq.

maybe add the original creditor, whoever signed the affidavit, the notary, and any other culpable parties.

More than 93% of credit card lawsuits are unchallenged by debtors.[96] Just by answering the lawsuit, in many cases the creditor will elect to dismiss the matter. Most collection agencies will file hundreds of these suits at a time, expecting to win on some and lose on others. They are going to lose on yours—the only question now is how much. If you and your attorney have uncovered some encouraging deficiencies, your attorney should demand fees and a cash settlement before agreeing to any dismissal.

BLOW ELEVEN: MIND BLOW

Request everything from the creditor: the application and disclosures from when you obtained the credit card, the signed credit card agreement, billing statements, any assignments, a copy of the debt holder's collection license for your state, all correspondence, and anything else pertinent and helpful. Additionally, ask for a life of loan payment history, as well as a breakdown of the amount due into interest, late fees, and other charges. You want the creditor to show how they arrived at the total balance they claim is due. All these requests—and hundreds more—are in Action Tools. Even if you already have these documents, ask the creditor to produce again. Any inconsistencies may expose additional deficiencies.

In all likelihood, the party suing you is missing some, if not all, essential documents. The FTC report revealed that, for most portfolios, debt buyers did not receive any documents at the time of

---

96 http://www.huffingtonpost.com/2014/06/02/debt-collectors-wages-savings_n_5364062.html

purchase. [97] Instead, "buyers were given a defined amount of time, typically between six months and three years, to request up to a specified maximum number of documents, e.g., equal to 10% to 25% of the number of debts in the portfolio, at no charge. After that, buyers were given an additional, defined amount of time to request documents for a fee, usually between $5 and $10 per document, with a maximum number of documents again specified. Debt sellers usually had substantial time, typically between 30 and 60 days, to respond to requests for documents. Availability of documents was not guaranteed. Most purchase and sale agreements stated that documents may not be available for all accounts."[98]

As a result, debt buyers rarely, if ever, have any documents containing your signature or any evidence that the amount claimed is correct, or even that the debt exists. All the debt buyers typically receive is a bit of electronic data showing the name, address, social security number, account number and a dollar amount supposedly due. This is a systematic weakness that you can exploit to your great benefit.

Frequently, creditors try to cover-up shortcomings in records and documentation by providing affidavits to the court. An employee for the creditor signs a template document stating the date the account was allegedly opened and how much is purportedly owed. This is supposedly based on a review of the creditor's records. The document is then often notarized, providing an official look. However, the affidavit frequently was not prepared based on a review of the creditor's books and records, as the person signing the affidavit did not have access to these. Even if the books or records are

97   https://www.ftc.gov/sites/default/files/documents/reports/structure-and-practices-debt-buying-industry/debtbuyingreport.pdf

98   Id.

available, these affidavits are often lacking pertinent data and the purported review was not completed.

Your attorney can depose the person signing the affidavit, the notary, and a representative of whoever is suing you. Odds are that the debt holder is not local, so they'll have to fly someone in. This is a supreme annoyance and can also expose shoddy practices, and is likely to prompt a resolution.

You are applying pressure to entice the opposition to settle and well they may. Depose to impose. Discover to uncover. Hit 'em on the chin to win.

BLOW TWELVE: THE BIG BLOW

The creditor is likely to settle before the trial. However, if needed, go to trial. You are likely to win, or achieve a favorable settlement. Most of the times, you will be in small claims court, so the trial is fast and furious (and relatively cheap).

Going to trial in a higher court on a credit card or unsecured personal loan is rare, unless the balance due is very high. If this is your situation, crowdfund the trial and legal fees by accessing the Community Chest at debtcleanse.com. If necessary, we want you to go all the way.

BLOW THIRTEEN: BLOW UP

Let's blow Debt Cleanse up. Go to debtcleanse.com and blow other debtor's minds with every little detail about your debt battles, even if you only had to go as far as the Cease Contact letter. We want to know who, where, what, why, and how. Assuredly, another debtor is about is about to blow off the same creditor(s) and can learn from your experience.

CHAPTER 11

MEDICAL BILLS

42% of Americans surveyed do not trust doctors, according to a 2014 Harvard School of Public Health study.[99] "What's driving [trust levels] down is that physicians in the U.S., as groups and leaders, are not seen as broad public advocates for health and health care issues," said Robert Blendon, a Harvard professor of health policy and political analysis, to *Live Science*.[100] "In the U.S., they're seen more as a group concerned with their own professional problems and economic issues."[101] He observed that U.S. physician groups have been largely absent from discussions regarding means to bring down health care costs, contributing to public distrust.

Why are health care costs so high in the U.S.? Factors include excessive administrative costs, drug costs that are 50% higher than

---

99   http://www.livescience.com/48407-americans-trust-doctors-falling.html

100 Id.

101 Id.

in other developed countries, and high physician compensation (partially necessary for many doctors to pay the massive student loans often needed to complete medical school). Also, a sue-happy culture, as I guess I am perpetuating in this book, has resulted in many physicians practicing defensive medicine. Being overly-prudent, doctors often order unnecessary tests in order to justify whatever care they administer.

As a result, medical bills often include excessive charges and are chockfull of services that patients did not need. Patients typically have no say in what hospitals and doctors charge. Frequently, patients do not approve the costs of treatment beforehand, especially in emergency situations.

Most frustrating, points out bronxlawguide.com, "is that the amount that the hospital will bill you is many times higher than when they would charge an insurance company, Medicaid or Medicare.[102] You would think that if a person could not afford any or better insurance, then the hospital would bill less not more, but the exact opposite is true. For example, a CT scan might normally cost $900 and an insurance company may pay less than half of that. But if...you're uninsured, the hospital may charge you $4,000 to $5,000..."

Jarringly, the uninsured are not the only ones struggling with health care costs. 43 million Americans, many of whom have insurance, are struggling with unpaid medical debts. According to a 2014 Kaiser Family Foundation report, "an estimated 1 in 3 Americans report having difficulty paying their medical bills—that is, they have had problems affording medical bills within the past

102 http://www.bronxlawguide.com/credit7.html

year, or they are gradually paying past bills over time, or they have bills they can't afford to pay at all."[103] This includes those with and without insurance.

Health care is the number one cause of bankruptcy in America today. However, you don't need to file bankruptcy to get rid of your unaffordable medical debts. Instead, just follow this pill-by-pill prescription:

BILL PILL ONE: TAKE A DEEP BREATH, RELAX, & BLOW YOUR UNAFFORDABLE DEBTS AWAY

Open wide and say "ahhhhhh". You look okay, a bit stressed maybe, but that's common amongst those afflicted with unaffordable debt. You need to relax. Take a deep breath in, as much air as you can, and hold it a few seconds.

Now exhale and empty every inch of your lungs. Do this twice a day, morning and evening, for a minute at a time. By emptying all the stale air out of your lungs, you replace it with fresh (at least relatively fresh, if you live in a polluted metropolis) air. Your stress will dissipate and you will feel rejuvenated.

After one week of this twice-daily routine, you will be ready to advance. Assemble all your unaffordable medical bills and, after making sure they are scanned and uploaded to debtcleanse.com, crumple each bill into a ball. Next, place a trashcan under the edge of the table or desk you are sitting at. Then place one of the crumpled bill balls about six inches from the edge of the surface overhanging the trashcan.

---

103 http://kff.org/private-insurance/report/medical-debt-among-people-with-health-insurance/

Now, stand up, take a deep breath and blow your bill off the surface and into the trashcan. That felt good, huh? Sense the power of taking control of your unaffordable bills. Now, repeat for each and every bill ball until they are all gone.

If you have unaffordable medical bills, this is how to start on the path to a cure: do not pay. Instead, crumple the bills into balls and blow them away.

BILL PILL TWO: KILL PILLS

When you receive a medical bill, take a look: did you request all the services? Were all those tests and procedures really necessary? Were you advised as to the full costs prior to treatment? Was a more cost-effective and/or medically beneficial remedy available?

What follows are kill pills, which you can complete, sign, and forward to the source of your discomfort: the hospital or doctor that is sending you these unaffordable bills. The letters are based on samples from bronxlawguide.com. There's a separate kill pill for services administered at a hospital and another for those provided at a doctor's office. Be careful not to mix up the kill pills!

In each kill pill, check all the lines that apply. For instance, if you suspect that the provider bills insurance companies less that they billed you for the same service, go ahead and check that line and let the provider prove it's not true:

* * *

DISPUTE OF CHARGES & SERVICES (use for hospitals)

Your name

Your Address
Your City, State Zip

**VIA CERTIFIED MAIL/RETURN RECEIPT REQUESTED/
COPY RETAINED**

Date

Medical Provider Name
Address
City, State Zip

RE: Invoice/Account/Medical Record Number: _____

Please be advised that I am disputing your bill (copy attached) for
the following reasons:

_____ Some or all of the charges are incorrect.

_____ I believe that I should have been provided free or discounted
services as I am uninsured and have little income.

_____ I believe that some or all of the charges are for services that
were not requested and/or agreed to by me and were not medically necessary.

_____ Your representatives led me to believe that I would not be
charged for some or all of the charges in your bill.

_____ The charges are excessive and greatly exceed the amounts you
accept for the majority of your patients.

_____ The charges violate the agreement between your institution and my insurance company which I believe provides that you are required to accept my insurance solely.

_____ Your institution has not timely or properly submitted the bill to my health insurance company/Medicare/Medicaid/No-Fault Insurance and/or Workers' Compensation as required.

I hereby demand that within thirty (30) days of this letter you:

*Provide me with a full copy of my Uniform Bill including all DRG/ICP/CPT codes for diagnosis and treatment claimed to have been rendered by your institution.

*Provide me with a breakdown of reimbursement rates for Medicare/Medicaid/and all third-party payors for the DRG/ICP/CPT codes for my treatment evidencing the customary rates you are paid for similar services so that the reasonable rates for your services may be determined.

*Provide me with a copy with any and all Financial Responsibility Agreement signed by me.

*Verify in writing the medical necessity for each medical procedure, test, and medication, etc. contained in your bill.

Please be further advised that pursuant to the Fair Debt Collection Practices Act, I do not want to be contacted by phone, at home, at work, or on my cell phone by anyone from your institution or any collection agency authorized by you regarding this claimed bill. Any contact must be in writing only.

In addition, if this bill is reported to any credit-reporting agency, it must be listed as "disputed."

Sincerely,

Your Signature
Your Name

*   *   *

DISPUTE OF CHARGES & SERVICES (use for doctor's offices)

Your name
Your Address
Your City, State Zip

**VIA CERTIFIED MAIL/RETURN RECEIPT REQUESTED/
COPY RETAINED**

Date

Medical Provider Name
Address
City, State Zip

RE: Invoice/Account/Medical Record Number: _____

Dear Dr. _____(insert name of doctor who treated you)

Please be advised that I am disputing your bill (copy attached) for the following reasons:

_____ Some or all of the charges are incorrect.

_____ I believe that some or all of the charges are for services that were not requested and/or agreed to by me and were not medically necessary.

_____ You or your staff led me to believe that I would not be charged for some or all of the charges in your bill.

_____ The charges are excessive and greatly exceed the amounts you accept for the majority of your patients.

_____ The charges violate the agreement between your institution and my insurance company which I believe provides that you are required to accept my insurance solely.

_____ Your office has not timely or properly submitted the bill to my health insurance company/Medicare/Medicaid/No-Fault Insurance and/or Workers' Compensation as required.

I hereby demand that within thirty (30) days of this letter you:

*Provide me with a full copy of my Uniform Bill including all DRG/ICP/CPT codes for diagnosis and treatment claimed to have been rendered by your institution.

*Provide me with a breakdown of reimbursement rates for Medicare/Medicaid/and all third-party payors for the DRG/ICP/CPT codes for my treatment evidencing the customary rates you are paid for similar services so that the reasonable rates for your services may be determined.

*Provide me with a copy with any and all Financial Responsibility Agreement signed by me.

*Verify in writing the medical necessity for each medical procedure, test, and medication, etc. contained in your bill.

Please be further advised that pursuant to the Fair Debt Collection Practices Act, I do not want to be contacted by phone, at home, at work, or on my cell phone by anyone from your institution or any collection agency authorized by you regarding this claimed bill. Any contact must be in writing only.

In addition, if this bill is reported to any credit-reporting agency, it must be listed as "disputed."

Sincerely,

Your Signature
Your Name

*　*　*

DRG/ICP/CPT? I didn't know what these meant either, so I had to Google the terms: DRG = Diagnosis Related Group, ICP = Integrated Care Program, CPT = Current Procedural Terminology.

Even with the full words, I do not pretend to understand their full meaning. Nevertheless, go ahead and send in the letters to get these disputes started.

BILL PILL THREE: WORKPLACE TRANQUILIZERS
A workplace should be off-limits to your creditors, a no-call zone

where you can toil away in peace. Use Letter B in Action Tools as a workplace tranquilizer to sedate your creditors.

One workplace tranquilizer per creditor is all that's necessary to quash phone calls at work. If a debt buyer or collection agency receives a tranquilizer and continues to call you at work, draw a happy face in your log: they just created a deficiency and an FDCPA violation, which could result in a monetary award of up to $1,000 to you. The penalties assessed are typically calculated per occurrence, so let them call—then make them bleed.

In the event that your debt is sold, you will need to administer a new tranquilizer to each new debt holder.

BILL PILL FOUR: CORPSE POSE

Remember those breathing exercises you learned at the top of the chapter? Get ready to use them again. As the hospital or doctor realizes that you are not responding to friendly reminders, they may step up their attack. You may be bombarded with calls and letters. Here is what you do to cope: corpse pose.

Corpse pose is a resting pose in yoga in which you lie flat on your back with your eyes closed, breathe, and detach from the outside world. Breathing is one of the essential components of yoga.

When you pick up the phone and determine that the caller is a creditor, breathe in deep, exhale, and hang up. Then add the phone number to a call blocker app. If you receive any correspondence from a creditor, scan and upload to debtcleanse.com, then crumple and use the strength of your breath to blow your medical bills away, just like you practiced in Bill Pill One.

There is one exception: when you receive a notice that your debt has been sold, which is highly likely, then you need to catch the dispute-eez.

BILL PILL FIVE: THE COOTIE SHOT

Dispute-eez: a condition that empowers debtors to take control and dispute their unaffordable debts.

Cooties: a condition that debilitates debtors due to uncertainty of what will happen if they stop paying their unaffordable debts.

Like a disease which gets passed from host to host, your debt will likely get handed off from creditor to creditor, often multiple times. In an effort to bleed cash from nerve-wracked debtors, creditors typically try to spread the cooties to get afflicted families to exhaust any resources they have left. As a disease-control measure, creditors are required to notify you each time your debt is sold.

Once you receive this notification, give yourself The Cootie Shot. Hold out your arm, and use your other arm's index finger to trace circles and dots on your forearm. Repeat the following: "Circle, circle, dot, dot—Now I've got the cootie shot!"

Next, let your creditor know of your immunization by mailing Letter A in Action Tools.

BILL PILL SIX: I DON'T WANT TO TALK TO YOU ANYMORE

Once you receive a response to your Dispute-eez (or 45 days has passed since you mailed Letter A), send the choker: Letter C in Action Tools, which advises your creditor that you never want to talk to them again unless they want to go to court.

BILL PILL SEVEN: RUN FREE!

The Bill Pills you have utilized thus far are often sufficiently potent to kill your unaffordable medical debts. You are now free to enjoy your presumably medically improved body. Run free!

Perchance, the disease may return. Although unlikely, be prepared for the return of the unaffordable medical bills.

BILL PILL EIGHT: RASH FOR CASH

Doctors and hospitals are unlikely to sue if you don't pay. However, like a rash whose cure is cash, debt buyers or collection agencies may sue you for not paying doctors and hospitals. If the rash appears, your creditor should be asking Dr. Phil for some advice, because they are wasting their time and money. You are about to go Jerry Springer on them. Chaos will reign. Soon, your debt will be the one in need of treatment.

See a specialist immediately. Review Chapter 3: Quick Start on how to hire an attorney and, with the urgency of a speeding ambulance, get your new care-provider all the documents you have accumulated on this disease. Together, we are going to find a cure and make this all better.

BILL PILL NINE: TURN THE DISEASE ON ITSELF

Medical debt is generated when you have a need, sometimes a desperate need, for medical help. A medical staff member will ask you to sign some forms, often with little explanation as to what you are signing. Frequently, there is little disclosure as to just what services you are getting, why they are needed (or even if they are needed), and what they cost. You have to sign the forms to get the treatment, so you sign.

This environment is ripe for breeding deficiencies. Now is your time to turn the disease against itself. Share all your documents, your communication log, and all correspondence, with your counsel. These are the ingredients of your remedy. You and your attorney can prescribe yourself a cure by reviewing Deficiencies in Action Tools to identify shortcomings that you can exploit.

BILL PILL TEN: SEIZE THE DISEASE

Take control and seize the disease. Utilizing the deficiencies identified, answer the lawsuit and cross complain against whoever is suing you, the medical provider, doctor, and anyone else who may bear responsibility for your unaffordable debt. In attempting to alleviate your pain and suffering with the help of a medical professional, you have incurred fresh pain and suffering at the hands of the same medical professional and their cohorts as they try to collect excessive amounts for often unnecessary and/or over-priced services.

Request a jury trial, as most regular Americans will better understand your plight. Judges earn an average of over $100,000 annually and tend to be from the elite, or at least buddies with them, and may feel more strongly for their friends. [104]

BILL PILL ELEVEN: PROBE & PROD

Your answer should have killed the opposition's lawsuit, just like medical professionals kill patients. A 2013 Patient Safety America study estimated that between 210,000 and 440,000 patients die annually after going to a hospital and suffering some type of

---

104 "The Highest-Paying Jobs With the Most Time Off" AOL Jobs, http://jobs.aol.com/ articles/2011/09/09/the-highest-paying-jobs-with-the-most-time-off/ (September 9, 2011).

preventable harm at the hands of medical professionals.[105] Medical errors are the third-leading cause of death in America.

Doctors may be too busy killing patients to reason that killing your debt is their best option. Thus, prod and probe: you and your attorney can conduct discovery powered by the 750+ sample requests in Action Tools. Your attorney can request depositions of the debt holder, the doctor and staff who treated you, and anyone else responsible for your unaffordable medical debt. The more, the deadlier. However, while depositions are costly and inconvenient for your opposition, these can also be costly and inconvenient for you. Thus, your attorney should also serve the more cost-effective interrogatories and requests for admissions where appropriate.

BILL PILL TWELVE: SETTLEMENT HARMONY

Your debt should be ripe for settlement at this point, so have your counsel offer up to 5% of what you owe as payment in full. Ideally, you have saved this amount in your settlement wallet. If not, only offer what you have. You want a lump-sum settlement, not a payment plan. This is a prescription that makes sense and which the opposition should accept or counter within some reasonable range.

If your creditor refuses to negotiate, I proffer that you may be dealing with none other than Dr. Seuss, who once said, "I like nonsense; it wakes up the brain cells."

Alternately, discovery may have unearthed evidence of something malignant, more like the work of Dr. Hannibal Lecter. In these cases, your attorney may demand that the debt is forgiven, that

---

105 James, J. "A New, Evidence Based Estimate of Patient Harms Associated with Hospital Care", Journal of Patient Safety, Volume 9(3) (September 2013).

your attorney fees are paid, and that you are paid a settlement for your troubles. That would be harmony.

BILL PILL THIRTEEN: MEDICATION, MEDITATION, MEDIATION

If your case has not settled by now, go ahead and have your attorney request mediation. This may be the best medication. Reiterate your offer of maybe 5% of the amount due. If you are feeling frazzled, try some meditation. Breathe.

BILL PILL FOURTEEN: CLINICAL TRIALS

If the opposition pushes you to trial, conduct a crowdfunding campaign using the Community Chest at debtcleanse.com to fund trial preparation and representation. If you win, make sure settlement includes reimbursement of your legal fees so you can return money to your crowdfund supporters. The outcome is uncertain, as with any clinical trial, so you might lose. However, these trials are often most valuable in testing theories in real-life circumstances.

If you win or lose, let us know what happened at debtcleanse.com. Others will benefit from your experience. If you lose, you and your attorney should discuss an appeal. Even without an appeal, remember that all the opposition wins is a judgment. They still have to collect. There are antidotes in Chapter 4: Judgments that can make collection on your judgment difficult, if not impossible.

Medical needs are often unanticipated and can result in life-altering financial consequences. Whether you are uninsured or underinsured, an unexpected medical event may put you in the uncomfortable position of deciding whether to choose your creditor by paying huge, oppressive medical bills or choosing yourself and your family by not paying, and working towards a settlement or possibly never paying. Every time you encounter such a fork in the road, always choose yourself and your family. Doing so is likely to save you worry and stress, and this really will improve your health. Relax. Breathe.

CHAPTER 12

PAYDAY LOANS

I have been burdened with almost every kind of debt—mortgages, credit cards, personal loans, business loans, vehicle loans—I even financed some toilets I bought for Woodland Meadows. One debt I have never experienced is payday loans.

In my weakest moments of 2006 and 2007, there were periods when I had no cash at all. There was always some money anticipated soon, a commission or other payment, and that kept me going. However, if I needed basics and someone offered me $350 and required that I repay $400 in two weeks, there were times I would have happily agreed. "*The fee is only $50*," I might have reasoned. However, if I pay $50 to borrow $350 and subsequently do not have the funds to repay, I would likely need to pay another $50 to extend for an additional two weeks. If these extensions go on for a year, I would pay $1,200 in fees on the original $350, a cost of over 300%. This may seem preposterous, but scenarios like this play out daily for millions of financially struggling Americans.

Payday loans are high-cost small loans averaging $350, which typically must be paid in a single payment after two weeks and are designed to create a long-term debt trap, according to a report from The Center for Responsible Lending. Although the name "payday loans" implies that borrowers need to have jobs, that is not the case. Many lenders will arrange payday loans to be repaid by unemployment, disability, Social Security, and other recurring payments that are directly deposited into borrowers' bank accounts. Even without direct deposit, if you can evidence that you receive a recurring payment, chances are good someone will agree to advance money against it.[106]

Nowadays, payday loans can often be obtained online—frequently through Indian tribes, which claim to be above licensing laws and corresponding restrictions on fees and interest rates. The convenience and efficiency of the Internet are being utilized by Native Americans to enslave non-Native Americans. Seems like Karmic payback for how our founding fathers treated the Indians. However, scratch a little and you will discover that—surprise, surprise—the elite are typically "renting-a-tribe"—simply paying a fee to the tribes to gain sovereign immunity. "Evidence we have collected reveals that a number of these Internet payday lenders have little or no true connection to the tribes and simply use the nominal relationship as a cover for their illicit practices," wrote Michael Blume, director of the Justice Department's consumer protection division, in a September 2013 memo.[107]

Whether borrowers receive the loans online, in storefronts, or

---

106 Montezemo, S., "The State of Lending In America and Its Impact on U.S. Households, Center for Responsible Lending, http://www.responsiblelending.org/state-of-lending/reports/10-Payday-Loans.pdf (September 2013)

107 Id.

through banks, the vast majority of borrowers cannot both repay the loan and cover basic living expenses until their next payday. They can do one or the other. As a result, borrowers typically take out multiple loans within a short timeframe, often from multiple payday lenders and repeatedly paying high fees to do so. A recent CFPB report found that for about 50 percent of payday loan borrowers, taking a single loan ends up resulting in a series of ten loans.[108] On average, borrowers take out eight 18-day loans during the year and are indebted 144 days, paying an average of $520 in fees alone for an initial loan of $375.[109] Payday loans frequently create a debt treadmill that makes struggling families worse off than they were before they received the loan. John Oliver, host of "Last Week Tonight," observed that, "basically, payday loan companies are the Lay's potato chips of finance," he said. "You can't have just one and they're terrible for you." [110]

Let me walk you through the steps of how to get rid of your payday loan(s) for next to nothing, or even zilch. You might even pick up a few dollars for your trouble.

STEP ONE: COMMIT A CRIME
Stop paying. It's not a crime, but your payday lender may imply that it is.

"The most common threat we get from panicked clients is they were

---

108 http://www.consumerfinance.gov/f/201403_cfpb_report_payday-lending.pdf

109 Montezemo, S., "The State of Lending In America and Its Impact on U.S. Households, Center for Responsible Lending, http://www.responsiblelending.org/state-of-lending/reports/10-Payday-Loans.pdf (September 2013)

110 Woodruff, M. "The Reign of Payday Lenders May Soon Be Over" Yahoo Finance, http://finance.yahoo.com/news/the-reign-of-payday-lenders-may-soon-be-over-201715917.html (August 13, 2014)

told they were going to jail, or the police were going to arrest them for some sort of crime related to their borrowing money. This is patently false," states the Daffy Law website in a post pertaining to Payday Loans in Pennsylvania.[111]

Go ahead and close the bank account from which you gave the payday lender a post-dated check or authorized an electronic debit. If you have other accounts at the same bank, close them all and open at a different bank. When the payday lender's check or debit hits your account, this will generate a Non-Sufficient Funds ("NSF") fee or two (they will likely redeposit a second time) and you don't want this to impact any of your other accounts.

When you open the new account, transfer any recurring direct deposits such as paychecks or government checks to the new account. As a bonus, several banks frequently offer promotions in which you can earn $100 or $200 for opening a new account and transferring a recurring direct deposit. This could be the seed money for your settlement wallet, so you get paid for the extra effort of switching banks.

If you cannot close your account before the payday lender's debit hits, just withdraw all your money and the bank will eventually close the account for you.

However, if you use this passive route, your account will likely be assessed NSF fees. The bank may send you letters and try to collect these, but you can easily get rid of these by following the steps in Chapter 10: Credit Cards & Unsecured Personal Loans. Ultimately, though, it's easier to just proactively close the accounts.

---

111 http://bankruptcyblog.mduffylaw.com/2012/06/four-facts-about-so-called-payday-loans.html

If you must keep the account open because you cannot change a direct deposit in time or for some other reason, then place a stop payment on your ACH debit or check. This will cost you some fees. If you authorized an automatic debit, mail the letter below to your payday lender. Then take a copy of the letter to your bank and request a stop payment on the electronic authorization. If your loan documents included a wage assignment, provide a copy of the letter to your employer. These notifications generally need to be completed at least three days prior to the scheduled payment.

✳   ✳   ✳

REVOCATION OF AUTHORIZATION TO DEBIT BANK ACCOUNT

Your name
Your Address
Your City, State Zip

VIA CERTIFIED MAIL/RETURN RECEIPT REQUESTED/ COPY RETAINED

Date

Payday Lender Name
Address
City, State Zip

RE: Loan #_____

I am revoking authorization for ACH withdrawals and also any wage assignments I may have signed. I have given a copy of these revocations to both my bank and my employer. Any future attempts to collect funds in this manner will be blocked.

Please also consider this correspondence as a formal request to cease and desist all contact with me. Please also cease and desist any contact with my references, family, friends, neighbors, employer, or anyone else regarding this matter. Should you fail to heed this request, I will take action against you under the Fair Debt Collection Practices Act.

Should you fail to comply with any of these requests, I will not hesitate to take action against you with the appropriate authorities for your predatory lending practices.

Have a wonderful day,

Your Signature
Your Name

*   *   *

STEP TWO: MAINTAIN A PEACEFUL WORK ENVIRONMENT
If you are working, wait a couple of days after Step One actions, then mail Letter B from Action Tools. This should block any calls to your workplace.

The FDCPA outlaws debt collectors from calling you at work once this letter is received. If a debt collector nevertheless calls you at work, this creates a deficiency to exploit in the event of litigation.

Most payday lenders are likely treated as creditors, though, and are not covered by the FDCPA. Helpfully, the Federal Trade

Commission prohibits unfair and deceptive trade practices including calling you at work when a creditor knows, or should have known, that your employer forbids personal calls. If, despite receiving the letter, your payday lender calls you at work, this creates a deficiency.

STEP THREE: BECOME A PAYDAY LENDER AVENGER

Once you stop paying, your payday lender will start calling you incessantly, and maybe write you some nasty letters. Just ignore them. Block their calls. If you pick up and then realize it's them, hang up. Or say, "Knock, knock". "Who's there?" is how they will likely respond. "Lender." "Lender who?" "Lender Avenger, stop calling me." Then disconnect. There is no benefit in going back and forth with them. Using debtcleanse.com or a pad of paper, log all communication, even their futile attempts, and file away all written correspondence.

Because you stopped a check or cancelled an ACH authorization, some payday lenders will suggest that your action was criminal and tantamount to writing a bad check or fraud. This is not true. You are an avenger, not an offender. The lender knew, or should have known, when they took your check or authorization that you likely did not have the money in the account. At that time, you intended to repay them. If you later decided not to pay, or that you could not pay, that's your choice. There is no fraud or other criminal action in that. However, if a creditor says or implies anything about having you arrested or sent to jail, jump for joy. This is an FDCPA violation:

> *807 15 USC 1692e (4): The representation or implication that non-payment of any debt will result in the arrest or imprisonment of any person or the seizure, garnishment, attachment, or sale of*

any property or wages of any person unless such action is lawful and the debt collector or creditor intends to take such action.

Such action is not lawful. Log the communication and exploit this deficiency if you end up in litigation.

STEP FOUR: LEAVE ME ALONE

Mail Letter C in Action Tools to shut down contact from Debt Buyers and Collection Agencies. Always keep a copy and mail certified, return receipt requested.

Payday lenders that are considered creditors under FDCPA may not be legally required to honor this letter. Nevertheless, they may respect your request. However, if they do keep attempting to contact you, continue to ignore.

STEP FIVE: BEST SAVINGS PLAN EVER: DON'T PAY YOUR UNAFFORDABLE BILLS

Save the money that you would otherwise use to pay your payday loan. Deposit that sum into your Settlement Wallet and watch it grow. Relax and unwind. Let's turn your "payday loan" into a "payday."

STEP SIX: PROVE IT

If you receive a notice that your payday loan has been sold or the account has been transferred for collection to another firm, do a little jig and rejoice! Your payday lender has essentially conceded defeat. At the bottom of the letter, there should be an invitation to dispute and validate the debt within 30 days. Go ahead and mail Letter A in Action Tools to the debt holder to dispute and request validation. If another party, such as a debt buyer or collection agency, attempts to collect the same debt at a later date, re-send

Letters A and C to the new party.

This is likely the beginning of the end for your debt. The small amount of most payday loans does not justify additional resources to collect. Welcome the demise of your debt.

STEP SEVEN: JOIN THE ACTION

Check debtcleanse.com for any class action lawsuits you can join against your payday debt holder, or Google the name of your payday lender followed by "class action lawsuit" to determine if there are any active suits pending against your lender. If you find one, please share on debtcleanse.com. If you cannot find one, propose one on debtcleanse.com and we'll see if other potential class-action members want to join and an attorney wants to take up the case.

Class action suits are particularly effective weapons for small, meddlesome debts such as payday loans. When possible, join the action. Don't expect to get rich off any settlement, but there have been several successful class actions in which loans have been forgiven and small cash settlement checks paid to payday borrowers. This may preclude you from suing your payday lender but, since payday loans are typically so small, potentially getting your loan forgiven and a few dollars in your pocket is a great result, especially when you do not need to front any legal fees.

In March 2014, Loan Point USA agreed to forgive the payday loans of 406 borrowers plus pay a $233,000 settlement, which included $60,000 for legal fees and the cost of locating borrowers and mailing checks.[112] The checks went to borrowers who had already repaid their loans. Again, these were small checks, but the loans were small in the first place.

Some payday lenders have buried fine print in loan agreements that bars borrowers from participating in class-action lawsuits. Instead, disputes must be decided by arbitration. These provisions are typically not pointed out by payday lender employees and, in some cases, courts have ruled that borrowers had no idea that they have forfeited their rights and, as a result, have allowed class action suits to go forward.

STEP EIGHT: SEE YOU IN COURT

Despite the relatively puny size of most payday loans, some of these guys do not know when to give up. If your lender wants to push this further, you might be served with a lawsuit. Write the date you were served on the document and log.

The payday lender is likely expecting that you, like most borrowers, will not answer the lawsuit. As a result, they expect to obtain a default judgment against you for the amount of the loan, interest, and costs. Most borrowers assume they owe the money. They figure the judge will side with the creditor, so they don't respond. As a result, they lose, and the creditor receives a judgment easily and cheaply. The creditor will even add their court costs and fees to the judgment.

You can win—or at least stall—the litigation by simply answering the lawsuit. Some creditors will dismiss the cases against the

112 Keiler, A. "Montana Consumers Win Fight Against Online Payday Lender, Loan Debt Will be Forgiven", Consumerist, http://consumerist.com/2014/03/20/montana-consumers-win-fight-against-online-payday-lender-loan-debt-will-be-forgiven/ (March 20, 2014).

borrowers who answer and focus their efforts on the majority of debtors who do not answer.

STEP NINE: LET ME TALK TO MY ATTORNEY

Retaining an attorney on a measly debt such as a payday loan may seem like an extraordinary reaction. However, the payday lender is the one escalating the matter. It's kind of like when you were a kid and you shrieked when a sibling poked you: "She started it!" This time, you get to be the one to finish it.

Your goal is not simply to defend your lawsuit. Instead, you want to win, have your debt forgiven, get your legal fees paid, and maybe even get a cash settlement. Many attorneys will take these cases on contingency, in which they receive a percentage of any settlement. This is an ideal alignment of interests.

If you have not retained an attorney, see Chapter 3: Quick Start. Note that you can use the same attorney for all your debts in most cases, and this will typically save you some money. Just keep the attorney on deck; ready to step in when you have a challenge for which you need legal help.

Best of all, it sounds kind of cool to say, "Let me talk to my attorney."

STEP TEN: MAYDAY FOR PAYDAY

Payday lending is a high-volume business of multiple small-transactions routinely completed by clerical employees. This maximizes the likelihood of incomplete and sloppy documents and disclosures. Likewise, if a payday lender files suit, the legal pleadings may be prepared in a high-volume fashion by overworked paralegals. Combine all this and you and your attorney are likely to tap a gusher of deficiencies, which can then be exploited.

In order to originate a loan, most states require that lenders are licensed. This is particularly challenging for online payday lenders, several of which have been accused of operating in states where they do not have the proper licenses.

Some states have online databases, which you can search to determine if your payday lender is licensed. Some lenders' ads, websites, and documents may display their license numbers as well. If you cannot find the license number, allege that your lender is unlicensed. The lender must then prove otherwise.

Additionally, brokers, finders, and lead generation firms often market to produce borrower "leads" and are then compensated by the lender. Unless these firms are licensed as lenders, the compensation and even the advertising may be illegal.

Further, many states have enacted legislation to cap the rates and fees of payday lenders. A small, inadvertent calculation error may make your loan illegal, and even criminal. Illegal loans do not need to be repaid.

Finally, if you have been extending payday loans, or getting new loans to payoff old loans, and this continues for over a month, then the payday lender is no longer providing a short-term solution. Instead, the lender has created a burdensome long-term debt with the oppressive high costs of short-term debt: a debt trap. Having all the licenses and forms in order should not excuse that.

Take a look at Action Tools and you will find dozens of other potential deficiencies.

STEP ELEVEN: YOU ONLY NEED ONE ANSWER

You just need to file one answer to respond to your payday lender's lawsuit. In addition, file counterclaims against the payday lender, their bank and, if applicable, the lead generation company and any other culprits. For instance, the payday lender's bank may have tried to process an ACH debit from your account to repay what may have been an illegal loan. Many banks have stopped providing services to payday lenders in order to avoid potential liabilities such as these.

STEP TWELVE: TELL ME SOMETHING I DON'T KNOW

Your attorney will request documents and written responses to assorted questions from the payday lender and their cohorts. You want to be privy to whatever documentation and information the opposition holds. These may uncover additional deficiencies that can then be used against them. See the sample discovery requests in Action Tools.

For instance, if you did not receive copies of the documents when you signed them, your lender likely messed up and this is a potential deficiency. As always in litigation, be truthful—in some cases, your lender may have videotape of your transaction. These can be advantageous to you and, through the discovery process, you can likely obtain copies of these tapes.

If needed, conduct depositions of opposition parties. These are basically in-person interrogations in which the other party is required to respond under oath to your attorney's inquiries (such as those listed in Deposition Questions in Action Tools). You might feel the impulse to waterboard your opponents, but that's likely unnecessary. Even creditors tend to tell the truth when under oath. You can also submit interrogatories and requests for admissions to get written responses to your inquiries.

If the proceeding gets this far, the attorneys for the creditor will likely contact your attorney to propose settlement. You started out wanting to settle your debt for little or nothing. If all goes well, you will pay nothing and your legal fees will be paid. Ideally—although not all that likely—you and your attorney will also share in a modest cash settlement.

STEP THIRTEEN: YOU'RE SAYIN' THERE'S EVEN MORE PROBLEMS?
You and your attorney can scroll through any discovery responses and deposition transcripts in order to identify additional deficiencies.

STEP FOURTEEN: TRIAL OF ERRORS
The odds of a payday loan collection case going to trial are about as likely as Payday candy bars going out of style. Most cases will be settled well before trial. However, be prepared to go all the way if needed. The costs can be steep, though. To combat this, go to debtcleanse.com's Community Chest to start a crowdfunding campaign to help offset legal fees for trial preparation and representation. By supporting those who do go to trial, all debtors benefit. With a few debtor victories, creditors will become more inclined to seek out early, favorable settlements.

At trial, you and your attorney will exploit your opponent's errors. We'll be cheering for you.

STEP FIFTEEN: STAY IN TOUCH
Whether your lender writes your loan off early or you go all the way to trial, let us know. Share your progress, outcomes, tips, victories and losses on debtcleanse.com. Also, review your attorney if you

used one. This information will be helpful to others following in your path.

Payday loans are addictive, high-cost products peddled to vulnerable populations. By design, these loans set up borrowers to fail. However, if you focus on escaping the trap, you can succeed in settling payday loans for pennies, or not repaying at all.

CHAPTER 13

COLLECTION ACCOUNTS

Debt in collections is death row for debts. Any debt you do not pay is likely to eventually end up there. 77 million Americans have debt in collections.[113] That is almost a third of the 242 million adults in America, and 35% of Americans with credit files. Look at it like this: there are 74 million Americans between the ages of 18 and 34, so imagine everyone in this country in that age group having a collection account. You could even throw in the 2 million Americans over age 90, and you'd still have more Americans with collection accounts. The point is that collection accounts are really popular. However, there is nowhere to apply for one. Not to brag, but I have a whole bunch of them. If you don't have one, though, don't fret: you'll probably get one, or even many, once you start your Debt Cleanse. The best news is that collection accounts are the easiest debts to cleanse. Oftentimes, you can pay nothing and in time the debt is dead.

---

113 http://money.cnn.com/2014/07/29/pf/debt-collections/

Since the account is in collections, you presumably stopped paying. This could result from almost any kind of bill—utility, credit card, medical, payday loan, an old cell phone bill, maybe even that Bally's Fitness membership contract you signed up for but then only went a couple of times. After enduring some collection efforts (congratulations, by the way), your debt was eventually either assigned to a collection agency or sold to a debt buyer. Voila! You incurred your very own collection account. Now, here are the steps to get rid of it.

STEP ONE: KNOCKOUT PUNCH

You will typically receive an introduction letter from the collection agency. This is no different than the later stages in most of the debt-specific chapters. To summarize the contents: "Hi. You owe us money because we just bought (or were assigned) the debt you owed someone else. However, if you dispute anything about this debt, please RSVP within 30 days."

Well, since they did say please, go ahead and oblige by mailing Letter A in Action Tools.

The odds that the collection agency will be able to validate your debt are close to 50/50, similar to the odds that an average American will spend more than they earn today. If the debt cannot be verified, this may be the end. The FDCPA prohibits debt collectors and debt buyers from pursuing unverified disputed debts, although they can sell the debts. Even if the collection agency verifies your debt, the simple act of sending the dispute letter lets the opposition know that you are not a pushover: they are in for a fight. As a result, less than 5% of verified disputed debts are resold, and less than 1% of unverified debts are resold.[114] Even if you didn't keep going to Bally's, you summoned Debt Cleanse power to deliver a knockout punch to level your collection account in just one step.

If somehow the collection agency gets up and wants to keep fighting, now is time to give them the gag order.

STEP TWO: GAG ORDER

See Action Tools and mail Letter C, which acts as a gag order and will stop all communication from the collection agency, except for a lawsuit. That's right: if they want to communicate with you further, all they can do is serve you documents required to litigate this debt.

Now, if the collection account is less than a couple of thousand, chances are that the expense of litigation is not worthwhile. Thus, the collection agency will just write it off and leave you alone. Cool. Being alone is great.

If the debt is larger, the collection agency needs to decide whether they want to press forward and risk spending legal fees that they may never recoup. Most of the time, they'll determine that it's easier for them to focus on the debtors who are more receptive to their unseemly advances.

STEP THREE: R&R

Time is always the debtor's friend. Patience and anxiety-management are greatly rewarded qualities in Debt Cleanse. Hopefully by reading this book you will know what to expect and this will

114 https://www.ftc.gov/sites/default/files/documents/reports/structure-and-practices-debt-buying-industry/debtbuyingreport.pdf

make being patient easier. The older an unpaid debt gets, the less valuable it becomes. Unless the amount owed is substantial and the debt is less than a year or two old, chances are good that you will not hear more about your collection account.

Historically, recently defaulted debt is statistically more likely to be repaid. Many families have lost a job, incurred an unforeseen medical expense, or otherwise suffered some temporary financial setback. Once they recover, they catch up on their bills. However, if a debt goes unpaid for years, the likelihood of repayment plummets. As a result, fewer resources are devoted to older debts and, over time, the frequency and intensity of collection efforts will diminish.

If there is no collection activity, relish the tranquility. Not hearing anything about the debt is positive. Get some R&R (Rest & Relaxation). Chances are good that you will not hear more about your collection account.

STEP FOUR: GOONIES
If sued, take the lawsuit to your attorney. These collection company goons didn't get the message did they? Instead of turning it down, they are escalating the situation. This gives you no option but to do the same. You can go goon, too. See Chapter 3: Quick Start to find an attorney and take the collection agency to the mat.

STEP FIVE: WHY ARE YOU ALWAYS LOOKING FOR PROBLEMS?
Take all documentation you have from when you first incurred the debt; what was provided to you in response to your validation request (if anything); correspondence; billing statements; communication logs; and anything else from the original creditor, any prior collectors on this debt, and the company suing you. Then sift

through Deficiencies in Action Tools to find potential deficiencies.

As an example, does the company suing really own your debt? Maybe they do, but proving it can be another matter. A common deficiency is that whoever is suing you does not have standing, meaning that they cannot prove that they own your debt. Frequently, assignments of the debt may be missing. For instance St. Mary's Hospital may have sold your debt to ABC Collections, which then sold your debt to XYZ Collections, which sold your debt to Last Chance Collections. Maybe the ABC to XYZ assignment is missing, meaning that, according to the documents, ABC still owns your loan and that Last Chance does not have standing to sue or take other collection action. Allege lack of standing and let the debt holder try to prove you are wrong.

Any misstep should be exploited.

STEP SIX: GO AHEAD, ANSWER BACK—IT'S OK

Answer the lawsuit and file counterclaims against the company suing you, the original creditor, any other collection agencies that tried to collect this debt, and any other parties that may bear some responsibility for this unaffordable debt.

All successful collection agencies are tenacious or they would not stay in business. However, they also need to make money to stay in business. Pushing forward in a money-losing effort after you have demonstrated no interest in paying is not a wise business decision for them. As a result, simply filing your answer will takedown many collection agency lawsuits. The end should be now.

STEP SEVEN: RESEARCH & DEVELOPMENT

They want to keep jabbing? Truly, going mano-a-mano in a

contested collection lawsuit is borderline inconceivable, unless your debt is substantial. You are not going to pay—can't they see that? But, if they want to rumble, let's ask them for all the documents they have plus some answers under oath. You can find everything you need in Action Tools.

For instance, the debt holder may be claiming the wrong amount, or even the right amount but is unable to prove it. One of your discovery requests should be a life-of-loan payment history. If your loan has been sold, especially multiple times, these are often difficult for the debt holder to obtain from prior holders. These may take months to obtain, and may be impossible—prior holders or servicers may be out of business or bought out. The debt holder needs to prove every penny of the claim.

If the pay history identifies any fees or charges assessed to the account, such as legal or inspection fees, request back up. Even if the charges are justified, you need back up documentation and, if your debt has been sold multiple times, then the current holder may be unable to provide. If the debt holder demanded $50,152.31, but can only prove that you owe $45,312.76, then they may need to re-start or amend whatever action they are taking to correct the amount claimed. Satisfying your requests can take months, losing time and money for the debt holder but gaining time and money for you as debtor.

Time is always on your side. At some point, your debt may become too old to collect: the statute of limitations sets a time limit within which a creditor may sue for payment of a debt. The amount of time varies from state to state, frequently ranging from 3 to 6 years, and even varies between different types of debt. The date of default (typically, thirty days after the last billing statement issued before you stop paying) determines when the statute of limitations begins to run.

You want to find out what they missed, and then hammer them with your proverbial fist. Do your research, then develop your findings into a defense, and even an offense.

STEP EIGHT: TAKE TIME OUT TO WORK IT OUT

File for mediation. If the collection agency is still fighting, you owe them a lot, or for some reason they really believe they can win. Offer a token sum, maybe 5% of what is due, at mediation and try to work something out.

STEP NINE: V FOR VICTORY

If mediation fails, get ready to go all the way. We will support you. You are on our team and this is our country. Go to the Community Chest at debtcleanse.com to start a crowdfunding campaign to pay for trial preparation and representation. All it takes is what you got. Victory is the goal. Determination gets you there. Your attorney will be there in person to help, and all of us will be sending good thoughts. You can win this.

STEP TEN: VICTORY PARADE

Let us know what goes down at debtcleanse.com. If you win, make sure to get the opposition to pay your legal fees so that all your debtcleanse.com supporters can get their money back and help others in similar clashes. If you lose, talk to your attorney about appealing. Even if this battle is lost, the war ain't over. Now these nitwits need to collect. See the tactics in Chapter 4: Judgments to make sure that judgment they fought so hard for is worthless. No matter what, you're a winner to all of us.

CHAPTER 14

AFTERMATH: LIVING DEBT-FREE

Debt Cleanse is your once-in-a-lifetime opportunity to rid yourself of unaffordable debts and pledge to never again take on debt. But how can you live debt-free in modern-day America?

For a moment, reflect on your life and what you want from your existence, why you are here, and what you can contribute. So often, people get so caught up in day-to-day routines that stepping back can feel foreign. The best debtors possess admirable qualities, like the best slaves: predictable, obedient, fearful, and consistent. They stick to the same routine day after day, month after month, and year after year. They go to college and take on a student loan, buy a car and take on an auto loan, buy things and take on credit card debt, buy a home and take on a mortgage, maybe start a business and take on a SBA loan, age and take on some medical debt. Debt is there every step of the way; boxing in our lives so sticking to the routine is the only means to survive.

Remove the box of debt and what do you do?

WHAT MAKES US HAPPY

"I can't wait until you finish writing this book so we can spend time together again," my wife Verria said to me as I was typing away on my laptop at our dining room table in the one-bedroom apartment we share. "I want my regular Jorge back, not the tired, I-was-up-all-night-writing Jorge."

"I can't, either," I responded. I have spent many evenings and weekends since June 2014 writing this book. Many weekends she wanted to go out or see a movie and I felt compelled to keep writing instead. "I had no idea how long this would take."

"We need to go on more hikes," she said. Before I started writing this book, we frequently took weekend trips to destinations within a couple of hours of where we live in downtown Chicago. Most of our trips are highlighted with time on trails, just walking, talking, laughing, and fending off bugs.

"We'll go soon," I said. My favorite trails are just half an hour from Chicago at Morton Arboretum, a 1,700-acre nature park full of stately trees, which bring back memories of Woodland Meadows. "I am almost done."

"You've been saying that for months," she responded. Since I started writing this book, our adventures have been less frequent. However, my wife appears patient, recognizing my tunnel-vision determination when I set my mind to something.

"I know. This time, I really am close," I replied. I do feel guilty, though. Like my wife, I would like nothing more than to be on a trail with her right now. "How would you most like to be spending your time?"

"I want to spend more time with you," she replied. I have heard this before. The number one request from my wife is not jewelry, trips or gifts, but my time. Since I work a lot, one solution was to have her work with me. Verria is AHP's Chief Operating Officer.

"What else would you really enjoy spending your time on?" I asked. "What do you daydream about? Give me the top five."

"Besides spending time with you, time with friends and family, working out, cooking," she said, "I would also like to teach people with health challenges like I had. I want to show them how to get well." Verria's mother was forty-three when she lost a battle with cancer. Verria was twenty-five at the time and had been very close to her mother. The loss devastated her. She suddenly developed a debilitating illness, which multiple doctors could not diagnose. It took years for her to get through it and, in the end, no doctor could help. She cured herself through a stringent diet and lifestyle changes. Even so, some of her health issues still linger. When we first met in 2005, I was in the midst of my Woodland Meadows turmoil. I think that we both recognized vulnerability in each other and this shared sense of loss drove us together.

"What about you?" she asked.

"Time with you, time with family and friends, my work at AHP," I replied. "Writing, and running, especially by myself on trails." These are important to me.

Now, take out a sheet of paper and list what you would like to be doing with your time right now. I do realize that reading this book might be fun and informative, but I am okay if you leave reading *Debt Cleanse* off the list. Recognize that time is your most precious possession and significant gift. "If you want your children to turn out well, spend twice as much time with them, and half as much money," wisely advised Abigail Van Buren of *Dear Abby* fame. Avoid responses such as "have a Ferrari" or "own a mansion." We anticipate that these will bring us happiness, but often they do not. Instead, think about what you really enjoy spending your time doing and who you savor spending time with. Include activities in your life now, which you wish you could spend more time on, as well as pursuits you can reasonably expect to add to your life soon. Set yourself up for success.

"Do you realize that, out of all the things we listed, none of these cost much money?" I asked. "Do you think this is the same for most people?"

"I think so, some might want to take more trips and travel," my wife responded. "Also, when I worked in corporate America, I didn't really like my job, so some people might say they don't want to work."

"Yes, but that's probably more a reflection of not enjoying the work they have," I said.

My dad kept working until he was 91, when he designed a rotisserie chicken restaurant near the intersection of Slauson and Overhill in Los Angeles. He was in the midst of a years-long battle with cancer, yet he relished solving architectural problems and work gave him this outlet. He was in and out of the hospital during this period, and he could sometimes be seen in his hospital bed sketching out solutions. I thought of author and civil rights activist James Weldon Johnson's astute words, "Labor is the fabled magician's wand, the philosopher's stone, and the cap of good fortune."

Towards the end, when he could no longer drive, my dad walked with a cane and took three buses to get to the space that would become Wings N Greens. He fell once getting on the bus. He was not badly hurt and continued on his journey. My brother Alastair asked him why he didn't just stay at home. "I love my work," he said.

What do you love? Recognizing the value of your time, write down the five pursuits you spend the most time on. Chances are sleep and work or school may make the top five. For me, work, sleep, writing, running, and time with my wife is the recent mix, in that order. Although these are generally healthy choices, I recognize that I need to spend less time working and more time on the other four. Check in with this list periodically as time passes and your priorities change.

Working two jobs because you enjoy it, and not because you feel forced to in order to pay debts, might be fine if you are single and enjoy the work. However, if you are married and/or have children, and the reason for all the work is to pay your otherwise unaffordable debts, your life is likely imbalanced.

Bonnie Ware, an Australian nurse who spent several years working with patients in the last twelve weeks of their lives, wrote a book called *The Top Five Regrets of the Dying*,[115] which she identified as the following:

1. *I wish I'd had the courage to live a life true to myself, not the life others expected of me.*

---

115 Ware, B. "The Top Five Regrets of Dying" Hayes House (Reprint March 20, 2012)

2. *I wish I hadn't worked so hard. (This was a particularly common response from men).*

3. *I wish I'd had the courage to express my feelings.*

4. *I wish I had stayed in touch with my friends.*

5. *I wish that I had let myself be happier.*

If you had twelve weeks to live, how would you spend your time? Freed of your unaffordable debts, how would you spend your time? Adjusting priorities and rebalancing your time typically result in incremental changes that can lead to a more rewarding and enjoyable life.

MAKING MONEY

Walking to work with Verria is ten minutes of together time for us. We chat, check emails on our phones, and complain about the weather, be it too hot, too cold, too wet, or too windy. Chicago is a beautiful city, but the weather wears a bit on my wife and I as we both grew up in season-neutral and eternally pleasant Southern California.

"What's that guy carrying under his arm?" I asked as we walked down Roosevelt Road towards State Street. There were two elderly men in front of us with their arms locked, walking together slowly. One was white. One was African American and had something protruding under his right arm.

"I can't tell," said Verria. "But it looks like he has his arm in a sling."

"You're right," I said. We were catching up due to their leaden progress. "Looks like a ski pole?"

"No, that's a cane," she said. We were now closing in and getting ready to pass. "The kind that blind people use to kick the ground in front of them."

As I realized what was going on, my eyes welled. The African American man was blind and must have fallen and injured his now-slung arm. We passed in silence.

"That teaming up of humans," I said. "That's how the world is supposed to work."

"How so?" she asked.

"The blind man was not relying on his cane, but was instead relying on another man to guide him," I said. "The second man had a skill or capability that the blind man needed."

"The ability to see?" asked Verria.

"Exactly," I said, as we walked north on Wabash Avenue past Trader Joe's. "Just like the blind man likely has a skill or capability that someone else needs. We all have and can learn skills and capabilities which others need."

"All of us?" she asked, pondering my statement.

"Yes, sure," I said. "Everyone. If you can see, you can hear, you can speak English, or you can walk. Someone always needs the skills someone else has. Think about it."

"I guess you're right," she said.

"And, look back at those two," I said. "I'm certain that the blind man does not care if his guide was white, African American, Asian, or Hispanic. "

"With or without vision, race should be of no consequence," Verria, an African-American, said as she glanced back. "But we both know that's often not the case.

"I remember at Woodland Meadows," I said. "Sometimes the most important person to me was a plumber." Often, toys, tampons, and other intruders would somehow find a way into the pipes and everything would get backed up. Then a tenant would call to report that the bathroom was flooding.

"We didn't even need a master plumber," said Verria, who assisted me during Woodland Meadows' final days. "We just needed someone who knew how to snake the pipe and clear it out."

"Exactly," I said. "Me and almost any other property owner or tenant in that position does not care about the drain unclogger's gender, race, or sexual preference. Even if the unclogger dropped out of high school, is terrible at math, doesn't speak English or has a felony record. All we want is the pipes clear."

"They get paid well," she said. "If they're dependable, on-time, and price fairly, people will pay good money. Plumbers are always in demand."

"That exchange of services," I said. "That is how the world should work, and sometimes does."

Human nature is to focus on what one does not have, versus on what one has. Whether your challenge is blindness, bad credit, a criminal record, poor math skills, a lack of formal education, or whatever, you nevertheless have skills that someone wants. I have bad credit, dropped out of high school, millions of dollars in unpaid judgments against me, and Google searches turn up stories of me arrested, accused of felonies, and labeled "schemer" by government officials who publicly "declared war" against me. If I only focused on these, I could not accomplish anything.

STARTING A BUSINESS

"Even if people get rid of their unaffordable debt, they still need to make money to survive," my wife said as she looked out the window. We were on a Southwest Airlines flight to Los Angeles to visit our families. I was pecking away at my laptop and munching on some free peanuts. "A lot of Americans make less today than they did a decade ago. Cleansing the debt people cannot afford is a step, but what if they cannot find jobs, or can only get jobs that barely pay enough to survive?"

"The cost of living has gone up, while wages have fallen for the majority of Americans," I said. "That's a problem. However, instead of getting frustrated, people need to start their own businesses."

"But don't people need to get loans to start a business?" she asked. "If they cannot afford the debts they have, who is going to give them a loan to start a business?"

"The key is to not take on debt when you start a business," I said. "Your chances of success are much higher. Twenty-five years ago, a partner and I each kicked in $50 to start a mortgage company. After that, we just reinvested our earnings and never put in another dollar of our personal money."

"I don't think there are many businesses someone can start for $50," she said.

"Sure there are," I said, reaching up to adjust the airflow as the plane seemed to be getting a bit warm. "Let's say someone is mechanically inclined. You know those GPS disabler devices that dealers put on financed cars?"

"Yes," she said.

"If someone learns how to remove those devices, they could start a business for less than $50. Their only startup cost would be the tools."

"What about advertising?" she asked. "How would they get clients?"

"Put an ad on Craigslist, list on debtcleanse.com, post to social media, tweet about your new service," I said, "Advertise to remove those devices for $100. I bet they'll get all kinds of people willing to pay $100. If they do good quality work, are reliable and charge fairly, they've just started what should be a successful business."

"No business loan needed," said Verria.

"Exactly," I said. "Whatever skill they have, they should share online. Fix cars, or teach others to fix cars. Be a handyman, a painter, computer technician, or babysitter. Help others with writing blog posts, marketing, or graphic design. Whatever skill or interest you have, someone is willing to pay you for it, and they could care less about your credit score or that you have judgments. Best of all, if you *do* have judgments, self-employment earnings are much more difficult for creditors to intercept."

Over the past several years, more small businesses have been closed in America than started up. We need to reverse this. By definition, small businesses can start very small—just you. Grow as you earn. If you start by yourself as a handyman, you can later hire other handymen and eventually a dispatcher. You could also drive people around using Uber or Lyft, rent out rooms through Airbnb, walk or house dogs using Dogvacay, and use any of the other online service marketplaces.

"What about a business plan and stuff like that?" asked Verria.

"The plan is provide a good service, charge a fair price, and get good word of mouth," I said. "The next day, you do the same. Learn as you earn. You don't need a business plan or financials for that. Those are often just needed for a loan."

PATIENCE

"So, how long will this take, for everyone to stiff all their creditors?" my wife asked. We were hiking in Topanga Canyon, California, and just crested a long uphill stretch. We were taking a break from the family visits. "Sorry, I mean to get rid of all of their unaffordable debts?"

"Months, years," I said. "The timeframe will depend on who the creditors are, the size of the debts, and whether any are mortgages or larger loans."

"Humor me with a guess," she prodded.

"Most consumer debt will take one to three years. Stuff like large business debts and mortgages could take longer. I stopped paying everyone in 2005 and 2006 and I still have a couple of battles going on a decade later. You learn to live with the effort. It's like a part-time job."

"What if Debt Cleanse doesn't work?" she asked.

"We'll deal with whatever obstacles come up as they appear," I said. I thought of the words of Eckhart Tolle, author of *The Power of Now*, who keenly wrote, "Ask yourself what problem you have right now. Not next year, tomorrow or five minutes from now. You can always cope with the now, but you can never cope with the future. Nor do you have to. The answer, strength and the right action will be there when you need it. Not before or after."

"So everyone should take these steps forward on this path," she said. "But no one knows where it will lead?"

"Yes, but we will take comfort in being with friends, family and the Debt Cleanse community. We will trust in a power greater than each of us individually," I said, reflecting on the guidance of Alcoholics Anonymous. "Besides, I know Debt Cleanse will work. I've done it, and I have witnessed debtors and attorneys use bits and pieces of the same strategies against AHP and other debt holders. Debt Cleanse just puts all these fragmented strategies together into one efficient process."

"How do you know how the big banks are going to react?" my wife asked as we walked through a small meadow. "Can't they go to their friends in the government and try to find a way to force everyone to pay, or should I say, *encourage* them to pay?"

"The United States is a great country in many respects because of our justice system," I said. "But it's far from perfect. There is too much improper government influence. Still, I believe right will win out."

"Well, everyone not paying their unaffordable debts is not exactly most people's definition of right," she said.

"Agreed. But families sacrificing their lives to pay their creditors is also not right," I said. "Truth is, I do not know what will happen. Still, this shot at returning America to greatness is a once-in-a-generation opportunity. And, don't say it," I interjected before Verria could state the obvious, "I know I sound idealistic. Still, this is a risk worth taking and I think a lot of people will agree with me."

"I'll support you whatever happens, but I'd suspect that creditors will try to create obstacles," she said.

"Facilitating change is more effective than trying to prevent it," I said, reciting words from Agile Manifesto,[116] organizational anarchists effecting change through software programming. "We need to trust in our ability to respond to unpredictable events. That is more important than trusting in our ability to plan for disaster."[117]

"Telling everyone to not pay their unaffordable debts is not going to be too popular with the elite," she said, sounding worried, as we navigated a section obstructed with some large boulders.

"I'll be clogging up the straw which many in the 1% use to slurp up the wealth of the 99%," I said. "They may get upset, but this is for

---

116 Martin Fowler and Jim Highsmith. "The Agile Manifesto", *Drdobbs.com*, August 1, 2001. http://www.drdobbs.com/open-source/the-agile-manifesto/184414755

117 Idib.

their own good. The American people are not a bottomless soda that the elite can slurp forever. Debt Cleanse will be a timeout, so we can take a break, allow the masses to heal and chart a better course for everybody."

LIVE DEBT-FREE

"How are people going to live without credit?" asked my wife as we continued our hike in Topanga. "I mean most people do not have the cash on hand to buy a new house. They usually get loans, which can take years to pay off."

"Exactly, they can take years because, when you finance, you get the worst prices," I said. "If you pay cash, you can buy a used fixer upper house, car, or whatever for cheap and add value. Create wealth instead of forfeiting a lifetime of wealth."

"But not everyone wants to fix stuff up," she said.

"If needed, they can hire someone to fix it up. If an investor buys a house for $40,000 and then does $20,000 in repairs, they can flip it for $100,000. The reason they can do that is the end buyer, the one paying the $100,000, is looking at their monthly payments saying, 'I can afford this if I commit 30% of my wages for 30 or 40 years, much of my adult life.' That makes no sense," I said.

"But where is the person going to get the $40,000 to start with?" she asked.

"They save it. Let's say a family is bringing in $4,208, [the median U.S. Household income] every month and they stop paying all their debts. Some they use to settle their debts, and the other money is saved to buy stuff for cash."

"But, what if they want a shiny new house with everything already fixed up?" she asked.

"Well, that's the mentality that needs to change," I said. "Patience, focus, and hard work. Taking on debt is an expensive shortcut. Look forward long-term, do the work and renovate a clunker into your dream home. The journey can be fun. Defer gratification— allow life to get greater later."

"So, what about a ride? Most people don't know how to fix up cars," she said as we reached the top.

"Look on craigslist and buy a running used car for the same as a down payment on a new car," I said. "Or save money to buy a new car. Buying used is not the focus; the goal is to live without taking on debt. Without debt, life will be more fulfilling. People will be amazed at the extra cash they have, and the dissipation of stress."

"Dissipation? Just say they will have less stress. Why do you use ten dollar words when a one dollar word would do?" she said as we descended. "Stick to cheaper words. Your big words sound like they need to be financed."

YOUR MAGIC BULLET

This is your battle. You are your magic bullet. It's hard to say exactly what is going to happen with your particular set of debts and circumstances. The uncertainty is what made me grind my teeth at night when I had unaffordable debts. However, you have this book to provide insight into what to expect. Your journey may be difficult at times and only you can muster the resolve to endure and succeed. Others may help, but no one can do this for you.

Share the magnitude of your debt with friends and family, the challenges you are facing as a result, and ask their support to help you get through your Debt Cleanse. Expect to be uncomfortable. Some may disagree with you about not paying your bills. That is fine. You are not asking for their agreement, just their support and strength. You may be in unfamiliar territory, but take your journey one day at a time. We will all be here to support each other and get you through this.

The best thing you can do for your unaffordable debts is to stop paying them and spread the word to your friends and family about the negative health, social, and economic problems caused by debt. Pay cash instead of credit, buy used to add value, and celebrate your new and fulfilling debt-free lives. Our country needs a fresh start so that all our citizenry are empowered to prosper. The past cannot be corrected, but the future can.

Imagine your life without debt.

CHAPTER 15

ACTION TOOLS

You will find over 900 deficiencies, document requests, interrogatories, requests for admissions, deposition questions, and letter templates in this section. This is by no means an all-inclusive list. I recommend that you visit debtcleanse.com to review additional weapons in the perpetually updated toolboxes. Based on the specifics of your cases, you and your attorney are likely to come up with more. We welcome you to contribute these to debtcleanse.com to help others.

ACTION TOOLS A

134 DEFICIENCIES

Here are 134 deficiencies, most of which are loosely categorized and common to most debt types. In addition, there are some that are specific to certain debt types. These creditor flaws are the crux of Debt Cleanse and generate the leverage that can empower you to settle your debts at significant discounts.

DOCUMENTATION ISSUES

1. Original promissory note, or similar evidence of the debt, is lost or missing.

2. Personal guarantee document is missing.

3. Allonges, endorsements, and/or assignments are lost or missing.

4. Security instrument is missing and/or, if applicable, never filed or recorded.

5. Your signature or a guarantor's signature is missing on the promissory note or security agreement.

6. Allonges, endorsements, assignments, affidavits, and other documents are not signed, incorrectly signed, signed by persons without the proper capacity or authority to sign, signed by someone other than the signor (for instance, some mortgage servicer employee named Joe signed "Linda Green"), or without verifying the contents of the document.

7. Creditor has no signed contract.

8. Contract does not name the correct original creditor.

NOTARY DEFECTS

9. The date of the notary acknowledgement does not match the date of signing.

10. The notary acknowledgment is not completely filled out and is therefore defective.

11. The notary name is not in seal or printed out and therefore notary is defective.

12. The signer name in the acknowledgment does not match the signer name.

13. The notary did not actually witness the signer signing.

ORIGINATION BLOOPERS

14. The loan was the result of fraud and an ongoing pattern or practice of deceptive conduct, such as advertising and/or marketing that encouraged debtor to take on a loan that the creditor knew, or should have known, was unaffordable for the borrower and likely to result in default.

15. Originator or their salesperson misrepresented borrower income or other qualifications on credit application.

16. Originator and lender sold borrower on interest rate higher than they qualified for.

17. Originator steered borrower to lender based on kickbacks or other incentives, rather than what financing option was best for borrower.

18. An extended warranty was financed with the product and provided limited and unnecessary coverage (often duplicating coverage provided by manufacturer), and was provided at an unconscionable cost and mark-up.

19. The extended warranty's cost and coverage limitations were not disclosed to the consumer.

20. Consumer was not advised that the extended warranty was optional.

21. Originator and salesperson did not possess required licenses to sell insurance products, including extended warranties.

22. Originator did not advise borrower as to the cost of add-on products and that these were optional.

23. There was inadequate disclosure of financing terms to the consumer.

24. If borrower is a racial or ethnic minority or a female: originator and salesperson disproportionately upsold high interest rates and overpriced add-on products to minority consumers more than white or male consumers.

25. Value of goods or services financed was misrepresented.

26. Loan was not originated in compliance with all federal and state laws, regulations and other laws.

27. All appropriate disclosures of terms, costs, commissions, rebates, kickbacks, and fees were not properly disclosed at the inception of loan.

28. Originator sold over-priced and almost worthless identity theft, credit monitoring and insurance products which were not disclosed, were not presented as optional, and/or contributed to making the debt unaffordable.

29. Dealer misrepresented the condition of the product purchased.

30. Dealer breached implied warranty.

31. Lender did not immediately provide copies of agreements at time of execution.

32. Lender utilized and paid illegal compensation to unlicensed third parties, such as a lead generation firm.

33. Advertising by lender and/or third parties was false and deceptive and/or lacked proper disclosures.

ACCOUNTING BOO-BOOS

34. The amount allegedly due is not be evidenced by a life of loan payment history.

35. Charges and fees assessed to account were paid to affiliates of lender or servicer, or to third parties which shared a portion of the fee with the lender or servicer through a revenue-sharing agreement (also known as "kickback").

36. Payments made on the loan were not properly credited.

37. The interest rate and/or fees charged to the account are inconsistent with the terms of the promissory note and/or are improperly calculated.

38. Collection costs, charges, and/or fees cannot be justified and/or are excessive, usurious, not authorized in the note, and/or unlawful.

39. Some or all of the charges allegedly due are incorrect.

40. The debt holder cannot provide detailed back up documentation for charges or fees assessed to account.

41. Loan has not properly been credited, debited, adjusted, amortized, and charged correctly.

42. Interest and principal have not been properly calculated and applied to loan.

43. Principal balance has not been properly calculated and accounted for.

44. Late charges were improperly assessed.

45. Late charges assessed were excessive in relation to the purported expenses and damages incurred for any payment that was late.

46. Interest was charged on late fees.

47. Failure to timely and accurately apply payments made by borrowers and failing to maintain accurate account statements.

48. Unauthorized fees for default-related services were charged to account.

COLLECTION BLUNDERS

49. Notices required in the promissory note were not furnished, or were not furnished in the timeframe specified in the promissory note.

50. Debt holder or collector reported inaccurate creditor information to a credit bureau.

51. Debt holder or collector impersonated law enforcement and threatened to have debtor arrested, directly garnish a person's wages, or seize their property when such action is not actually planned.

52. Debt holder or collector failed to validate debt in writing when requested.

53. Debt holder or collector continued to call a place of employment when instructed not to do so.

54. Debt holder or collector ignored cease contact notices to stop telephoning and communicate only via mail.

55. Debt holder or collector verbally abused (i.e. called you names), used obscene language, threatened, and/or harassed debtor.

56. Each servicer and sub-servicer of loan has not serviced loan in accordance with the terms of the promissory note and, if applicable, security agreement.

57. Property inspectors, repo men, and other agents made contact to collect the purported debt and were not properly licensed to do so.

58. Debt holder and/or collector provided false or misleading information in response to complaints.

59. Debt holder and/or collector executed inaccurate affidavits and failed to properly validate document execution processes.

60. Debt holder and/or collector failed to properly maintain books and records.

61. Debt holder and/or collector called at unreasonable hours (i.e., in the middle of the night).

62. Debt holder and/or collector repeatedly or continuously called with the intent to annoy, abuse, or harass.

63. Debt holder and/or collector made contact with debtor despite being advised that debtor was represented by an attorney.

64. Debt holder and/or collector made false, deceptive, or misleading representations.

65. Debt holder and/or collector misrepresented debtor's rights.

66. Debt holder and/or collector contacted family members, friends, or co-workers about debt.

67. Debt holder and/or collector used deceptive means to collect information about the debtor.

68. Debt holder and/or collector failed to conform to accepted standards of care and code of conduct as required by their state and/or federal license.

69. Debt holder and/or collector failed to exercise the degree of

care which a reasonable and prudent lender and/or servicer would use under the same or similar circumstances.

70. Debt holder and/or collector breached duty to act as a reasonable and prudent lender and/or servicer would under the same or similar circumstances.

71. Debt holder and/or collector breached this duty of care.

72. Debt holder and/or collector engaged in deceptive or unfair debt collection and billing practices.

73. Legal notices and letters were backdated in order to accelerate the collection legal process.

74. Lender and lender's bank originated, or attempted to originate, unauthorized debits from debtor's bank account.

TRANSFER GAFFES

75. Any sale or transfer of loan was not conducted in accordance with proper laws and was not a true sale of the note.

76. The claimed holder in due course of promissory note and, if applicable, security instrument is not holding such note in compliance with State and Federal laws and is not entitled to the benefits of payments.

LACK OF STANDING

77. Plaintiff in lawsuit was not the owner of the debt when the lawsuit was filed.

LICENSING, REGISTRATION... EVEN EXISTENCE

78. Dealer or originator was not registered to do business in your state at the time debt was originated.

79. Debt holder and/or collection agency was not registered to do business during the time they held the debt, and did not possess necessary state licenses to do so.

80. Lender, or lender's branch, was not properly licensed in debtor's state.

81. Collection agency or loan servicer was not registered to do business during the time they held the debt, and did not possess necessary state licenses to do so.

82. Lender does not exist.

STATUTE OF LIMITATIONS

83. Debt holder is collecting, suing on, or threatening to sue on debts past the applicable statute of limitations.

84. Debt holder issued a 1099, which cancelled the debt.

LEGAL PLEADINGS

85. Legal pleadings contain inconsistencies and other errors.

86. Collateral is improperly described in lawsuit and thus any taking is void.

87. Affidavit is not based on a review of the creditor's books and records.

MORTGAGE ORIGINATION

88. Mortgage was not originated in compliance with Real Estate Settlement Procedures Act.

89. HUD1 or HUD1A was not completed according to Appendix A to Regulation X, most often for omitting the name of the ultimate recipient of a settlement service or for not disclosing charges paid outside of closing.

90. Applicant's ethnicity or race was not indicated on applications for secured loans to purchase or refinance a principal dwelling.

91. Originator failed to complete special flood hazard determination forms (SFHD) prior to loan consummation, completed SFHD incorrectly, or failed to retain SFHD.

92. Originator failed to ensure that adequate property and/or flood (if property is in an area at risk of flooding) insurance was in place prior to loan closing and/or maintained throughout the life of the loan.

93. Originator failed to provide the good faith estimate within three days of receiving the application.

94. Originator failed to include the names and contact information of required settlement service providers on the good faith estimate.

95. Originator failed to comply with Home Ownership and Equity Protection Act of 1994, which applies to high cost, also known as Section 32, mortgages. First mortgages on which the annual percentage rate exceeds the rates of Treasury securities by more than 10 points, or on which the total fees and points exceed 8% of the loan amount, are subject to additional disclosures, and a ban on abusive features such as balloon payments and negative amortization.

MORTGAGE FORECLOSURE

96. Notice of Sale or Transfer of Mortgage, commonly known as a "TILA notice," was not provided.

97. Force-placed insurance was imposed when servicer knew, or should have known, that borrower already had adequate home-insurance coverage.

98. Servicer and/or lender did not provide accurate information about loan modifications and other loss mitigation services.

99. Servicer and/or lender failed to properly process borrower's application and calculate eligibility for loan modification.

100. Servicer and/or lender provided false or misleading reasons for denying loan modifications.

101. Servicer and/or lender failed to honor previously agreed upon trial modification with prior servicer.

102. Servicer and/or lender deceptively sought to collect payments under the mortgage's original unmodified terms after borrower had already begun a loan modification with the prior servicer.

103. Servicer and/or lender provided false or misleading information to borrower about the status of foreclosure proceedings where the borrower was in good faith actively pursuing a loss mitigation alternative also offered by servicer and/or lender.

104. Servicer and/or lender failed to confirm legally that it had the right to foreclose before initiating foreclosure proceeding.

105. Servicer and/or lender failed to ensure that its statements to the court in foreclosure proceedings were correct.

106. Servicer and/or lender pursued foreclosure even while modification application was pending.

107. Servicer and/or lender failed to maintain records confirming that it is not pursuing foreclosure of service member on active duty.

108. Seller, real estate agent, appraiser, and/or mortgage broker misrepresented the value of the property to borrower in order to maximize commission and profits, leaving borrower with a home worth less than the mortgage debt.

109. Qualified Written Request was not responded to, or was responded to incompletely or in an untimely manner.

110. Servicer has demonstrated a pattern of noncompliance with Real Estate Settlement Procedures Act by not responding to Qualified Written Request despite repeated attempts (initial request and two reminder letters).

111. Lender does not have rights to any outstanding insurance proceeds or additional collateral in the event lender bid full indebtedness at foreclosure sale.

POST-FORECLOSURE SALE EVICTION/EJECTMENT

112. Lender lacks standing, as deed was not recorded into lender name when eviction case filed.

113. Cash for keys offers were an attempt to collect a debt by misrepresentation in order to induce borrower to give up possession of collateral.

114. Cash for keys offers were an attempt to collect a debt by an unlicensed debt collector.

115. Despite requests, repairs were not completed, were not fully completed, or were completed in an untimely and/or un-workmanlike manner.

VEHICLE REPOSSESSION

116. GPS tracker and disabler device was installed on vehicle without disclosure at purchase.

117. Dealer is attempting to repossess car in order to churn inventory and resell multiple times.

118. Vehicle was wrongfully repossessed due to a breach of the peace or facilitation by a police officer.

119. After repossession, lender did not provide written notice to redeem the vehicle, including the payoff amount necessary to redeem the car. This is required in most states.

120. After repossession, vehicle was not sold in a commercially reasonable manner. Many repossessed vehicles are sold at "dealer only" auto auctions, which routinely bring far less money than a traditional sale and may not qualify as commercially reasonable. As a result, the deficiency amount claimed is excessive.

121. The creditor did not apply the proceeds of the sale to the balance of the account. Any sale proceeds must be applied towards the debt.

122. Lender did not provide an accounting of any surplus or deficiency on the loan.

STUDENT LOANS

123. Schools and lenders knew, or should have known, based on statistics which they compiled and/or which they were aware of, that advertised placement rates were misleading and fraudulent.

BUSINESS LOANS

124. Franchisor and/or lender knew, or should have known, based on statistics which they compiled and/or which they were aware of, that advertised forecast projections of profitable operation rates were misleading and fraudulent.

125. If loan was guaranteed through the Small Business Administration, correspondence and notices were deficient and missing required disclosures.

MEDICAL BILLS

126. Patient should have been provided free or discounted services due to income level and/or insurance coverage status.

127. The services that were not requested and/or agreed to and were not medically necessary.

128. Representatives led patient to believe that there would be no charge for some or all of the services purportedly provided.

129. The charges are excessive and greatly exceed the amounts accepted for the majority of patients.

130. The charges violate the agreement between the medical provider and insurance company, which provides that provider was to accept insurance reimbursement solely.

131. The charges were not timely or properly submitted to health insurance company/Medicare/Medicaid/No-Fault Insurance and/or Workers' Compensation.

132. Medical billing is often complicated and insurers frequently and arbitrarily set tight deadlines for claims to be submitted. Claims billed to insurers were inadequate and/or late, presenting opportunities for insurers to deny claims due to no fault of patient. Additionally, despite request, patient was not provided with:

   a. A full copy of Uniform Bill including all DRG/ICP/CPT codes for diagnosis and treatment claimed to have been rendered by provider.

   b. A breakdown of reimbursement rates for Medicare/Medicaid/and all third-party payors for the DRG/ICP/CPT codes for patient's treatment evidencing the customary rates paid for similar services so that the reasonable rates for the allegedly provided services may be determined.

   c. A copy of any and all Financial Responsibility Agreement allegedly signed by patient.

d. Written verification of the medical necessity for each medical procedure, test, medication, etc. for which patient is being charged.

PAYDAY LOANS

133. Lender violated restrictions on fees and interest rates.

134. Lender engaged in an unfair and deceptive practice by not restricting their payday lending to satisfying customer's short-term needs.

ACTION TOOLS B

140 DOCUMENT REQUESTS

DOCUMENTATION ISSUES

1. Produce the original [promissory note, personal guarantee document, endorsement, assignment, and/or security instrument] or similar document evidencing the debt.

2. Produce evidence that the security instrument was filed or recorded.

3. Produce evidence that all parties properly executed the promissory note or security agreement.

4. Produce evidence that the parties who signed the promissory note or security agreement had the proper capacity and authority to sign.

5. Provide evidence that all [allonges, endorsements, assignments, affidavits, and/or other documents] are correctly signed by a person with property authority and capacity to do so.

6. Provide the original contract.

NOTARY DEFECTS

7. Provide the full notary acknowledgement.

8. Provide evidence that the notary actually witnessed the signer signing.

ORIGINATION BLOOPERS

9. Please provide all marketing materials produced during the time period of _____ to _____.

10. Please provide any and all materials used to assist potential customers in determining the amount of debt that they could afford.

11. Please provide any and all training materials provided to your staff during the time period of _____ to _____.

12. Please provide any and all sales and marketing scripts, training materials, and employee memos/materials available during the period of _____ to _____.

13. Produce copies of all consumer complaints (regulatory or legal) against the lender for fraud, deception, or predatory lending.

14. Provide a full list of consumers who made complaints to

the lender's customer service department for the period of
_____ through _____.

15. Provide a list of docket numbers and location of filing for all lawsuits filed against the sales person or originator for the period of _____ through _____.

16. Provide a list of docket numbers and location of filing for all lawsuits filed against the lender during the period of _____ through _____.

17. Please provide the original credit application and supporting documentation provided by the consumer.

18. Please provide the internal documentation used to qualify the consumer.

19. Please provide any documents showing the consumer's income as reported by the originator or salesperson to potential lenders.

20. Provide all documents showing the interest rate or rates that the consumer qualified for during the period of _____ to _____.

21. Provide any and all documents, including internal and external communications between the originator or salesperson and all lenders regarding the consumer.

22. Provide full documentation of the details of any and all warranties or extended warranties financed with consumer's loan product.

23. Provide all documents showing that the details of the extended warranty were provided to the consumer.

24. Provide all documents showing that the cost and coverage limitations were provided to the consumer.

25. Provide all documents showing that the consumer was advised that extended warranties are optional only.

26. Provide the documentation to show that the originator or salesperson in this case was properly licensed to sell insurance products, including extended warranties during the period of _____ to _____.

27. Provide all documents that show that the originator provided the consumer full details about add on products and extended warranties including costs and a disclosure that such products were optional.

28. Provide the documents showing the financing terms.

29. Provide documentary evidence that the financing terms were disclosed to the consumer.

30. Provide all internal documents, reports and data that show the demographic makeup of the customers of the dealer or salesperson.

31. Provide documents, reports and data showing the average interest rate of all female customers during the period of _____ through _____. Provide the same for all male customers during the same period.

32. Provide documents, reports and data showing the average interest rate of all customers who were racial or ethnic minorities during the period of _____ through _____. Provide the same for all white customers during the same period.

33. Provide the home appraisal documents provided to all potential lenders for the consumer.

34. Please produce the documents disclosing the terms, costs, commissions, rebates, kickbacks, and fees that were provided to the consumer at the inception of the loan.

35. Produce documentation for all identity theft, credit monitoring, and insurance products offered by the originator or salesperson during the period of _____ through _____.

36. Produce all documents showing any and all identity theft, credit monitoring, and insurance products purchased by the consumer.

37. Produce all documents provided to the consumer at the time the loan agreement in this case was executed.

38. Produce all documents showing communications, relationships with or payments to third parties such as lead generation firms.

39. Produce reports showing all payments made to lead generation firms from the period of _____ through _____.

40. Provide copies of all advertising materials, including online advertising and email solicitations used during the period of _____ through _____.

ACCOUNTING BOO-BOOS

41. Provide a full payment history for the entire life of the loan.

42. Provide an accounting of any and all fees and charges assessed to the consumer's account that were paid to affiliates of the lender or servicer.

43. Provide an accounting of any and all fees and charges assessed to the consumer's account that were paid to any third-party, including a description of each charge and/or payment to a third-party.

44. Provide all documents that show how the consumer's account was credited for payments made on the account.

45. Provide all documents that show or describe the method utilized by the lender and/or loan servicer to credit payments made to a consumer's account.

46. Provide all documents showing the interest rate charged to the consumer's account.

47. Provide an accounting of how the interest charges for the consumer's account were calculated.

48. Produce an accounting of all collection costs, charges, and fees assessed to the consumer's account along with a full description of the date and reason for each charge.

49. Produce all documents that support any and all fees and charges assessed to the consumer's account.

50. Produce all documents that show the full payment, credit, debit, adjustment, and amortization history of the consumer's account, including a full description of the date and reason for each item.

51. Produce all documents that show how the interest and principal have been calculated and applied to the consumer's account, including a full description of the date and reason for each item.

52. Provide an accounting for all late charges assessed to the consumer's account, including a date and full description of the reason for the charge for each item.

53. Provide an accounting for all payments made by the consumer, including a full description of the date the payment was made, the date on which the account was credited with the payment, and how each payment was applied to the consumer's account.

54. Produce all documentation showing any and all default-related services that were charged to the account, including a full description of the date and reason for each item.

COLLECTION BLUNDERS

55. Provide any and all collection notices that were sent to the consumer.

56. Provide documents showing the dates on which any and all collections notices were sent.

57. Provide any and all reports made to any credit reporting agency with regard to the consumer in this case.

58. Provide all communications sent to the consumer in this case.

59. Provide transcripts of any and all phone calls made to the consumer by a collection agency or the lender's collection department.

60. Produce any and all documents, including correspondence and electronic documents related in any way to validation of the debt.

61. Provide a listing of all telephone numbers the lender or collection agency called for this consumer.

62. Provide any and all cease and desist letters or other communications that the consumer sent to the lender's collection department or the collection agency.

63. Provide a complete listing of all servicers or sub-servicers of the consumer's account with their full business address and a telephone number.

64. Provide documents showing that the collection agency in this case is properly licensed.

65. Produce any and all affidavits used by the debt holder or collection agency in relation to the loan in question.

66. Provide all records from the collection agency with regard to the consumer's account.

67. Provide a listing of all calls made to the consumer listing the date and time of the call and a brief description of the call.

68. Provide a listing of all individuals contacted via telephone as part of the collection efforts in this case.

69. Provide all documents or communications you provided to the consumer advising them of their rights.

70. Provide all training materials the collection agency used to train its employees from the period of _____ through _____.

71. Provide a listing of all mailings sent to the consumer including the date upon which the mailing was generated and the date when the mailing was sent to the consumer.

72. Provide documentation to show that the consumer expressly authorized any and all ACH debits taken from their account by the lender or collection agency.

TRANSFER GAFFES
73. Provide all documents related to each and every sale or transfer of the consumer's loan.

LACK OF STANDING
74. Provide all documents that indicate that the Plaintiff in this case was the owner of the debt at the time the lawsuit was filed.

LICENSING, REGISTRATION...EVEN EXISTENCE
75. Provide documentary evidence that the dealer or originator was registered to do business in the state of _____.

76. Provide all registration and licensure documents for the lender in the state of _____.

77. Provide evidence that the branch office dealing with the consumer's account is properly registered in _____.

78. Provide all licensure and/or registration documents for the collection agency.

79. Provide all licensure and/or registration documents for the loan servicer.

80. Provide all business formation and/or incorporation documents for the [dealer, originator, lender, servicer, or collection agency].

STATUTE OF LIMITATIONS

81. Provide all evidence to support the claim or assertion that the debt in this case is not past the applicable statute of limitations.

82. Provide any 1099s that were issued, even if issued in error, with regard to the consumer in this case.

LEGAL PLEADINGS

83. Provide a copy of all legal pleadings in this case.

84. Provide all documents describing the collateral in this case.

85. Provide any and all affidavits in this case and the supporting documentation for the affidavits.

MORTGAGE

86. Provide all documents associated with the origination of this mortgage.

87. Provide the HUD1 or HUD1A form for this loan.

88. Provide the portion of the mortgage application that indicates the applicant's ethnicity or race.

89. Provide the completed SFHD forms.

90. Provide all documents related to determining the amount and type of property and/or flood insurance that was needed for this loan.

91. Provide documentation to show the actual amount of insurance in place at the time of closing.

92. Provide documentation showing that a good faith estimate was provided to the consumer within three days of the consumer's application.

93. Provide documentation showing where the required settlement providers' contact information was provided to the consumer on the estimate.

94. Provide all disclosures that were provided to the consumer with regard to high cost mortgages.

MORTGAGE FORECLOSURE

95. Provide the notice of sale or transfer of mortgage in this case.

96. Provide your policy regarding force-placed insurance.

97. Provide any communications with the consumer regarding force-placed insurance.

98. Provide any communications and/or information provided to the consumer regarding loan modifications.

99. Provide full documentation of each loan modification or loss mitigation program in place on or about _____.

100. Provide all documents related to the consumer's application for a loan modification.

101. Provide all documents related to the processing of the loan modification application.

102. Provide all documentation regarding the denial of the consumer's loan modification.

103. Provide all documents regarding any trial modifications the consumer had with a previous lender.

104. Provide all payment documentation that shows payments made under a loan modification.

105. Provide all communications to the consumer regarding foreclosure.

106. Provide all documents regarding the foreclosure proceedings.

107. Provide all documents showing that the consumer was a service member on active duty.

108. Provide documentation showing how the value of the property was calculated.

109. Provide a record of all Qualified Written Requests (QWRs) received on the consumer's behalf and all responses, by the lender, including the documents provided with the response.

POST-FORECLOSURE SALE EVICTION/EJECTMENT

110. Provide a copy of the deed recorded into the lender name at the time the eviction case was filed.

111. Provide all communications to the consumer regarding the sale/eviction/ejectment proceedings.

112. Provide the name of the debt collector and full documentation of the collector's licensure.

113. Provide any and all documents or communication regarding repairs at the property in question.

VEHICLE REPOSSESSION

114. Provide all documentation that was provided to the consumer regarding the use of a GPS tracker and disabler device.

115. Provide a full Carfax or AutoCheck report for the vehicle in question.

116. Provide any documentation of the repossession.

117. Provide any and all police reports filed with regard to the repossession.

118. Provide the full written notice provided to the consumer with instructions on how to regain possession of their vehicle.

119. Provide all documents relating to the sale of the repossessed vehicle following repossession.

120. Provide a full accounting of the consumer's account, specifically documentation showing how the proceeds of the repossession were applied to the consumer's account.

121. Provide any and all documents and correspondence to the consumer regarding the repossession.

STUDENT LOANS

122. Provide any and all documentation available to the institution on or about _____ that showed placement rates for graduates.

123. Provide all marketing, advertising, promotional, and admissions materials that list a placement rate for graduates or provide any information regarding job placement or salary of graduates.

BUSINESS LOANS

124. Provide all documents showing how business projections were forecasted in this case.

125. Provide all documentation submitted with the loan application.

126. Provide all communications between the lender and the consumer regarding business valuation and projections.

127. Provide documentation to show how the loan amount was calculated in this case.

128. Provide all correspondences and notices provided to the consumer pursuant to a guarantee by the Small Business Administration.

MEDICAL BILLS

129. Provide documentation of the consumer's income.

130. Provide documentation of the services provided to the consumer and the cost of each service.

131. Provide the full bill issued to the consumer.

132. Provide evidence of any insurance coverage at the time of service.

133. Provide a full accounting of the consumer's account including billed charges, insurance payments and consumer payments.

134. Provide documentation of the medical necessity of the services provided.

135. Provide all disclosures regarding cost of services that were given to the consumer.

136. Provide the agreement between the consumer's insurance company and the medical provider.

137. Provide all documentation submitted to the insurance company for payment.

PAYDAY LOANS

138. Provide documentation of the fees and interest rates for the consumer's loan.

139. Provide the loan agreement for this consumer.

140. Provide documentation showing how the loan amount for the consumer was calculated.

ACTION TOOLS C

208 INTERROGATORIES

DOCUMENTATION ISSUES

1. Please identify any person(s) known or believed by anyone at [debt holder name] who has physical possession of the [promissory note, personal guarantee document, endorsement, assignment, and/or security instrument] or other document evidencing the debt.

2. Please state the date and location where the security instrument was filed or recorded.

3. Provide the name of any and all parties who signed the allonges, endorsements, assignments, or affidavits and provide an explanation as to how the signing parties have the proper capacity or authority to do so.

4. Does the creditor have a signed contract? If so, please state the last known location of the signed contract including full address and a designated contact person.

5. Does the contract name the correct original creditor? If yes, please state the last known location of the contract including a full address and designated contact person.

NOTARY DEFECTS

6. Does the date of the notary acknowledgement match the date of signing?

7. If yes, please provide documentary evidence.

8. Is the notary acknowledgement completely filled out?

9. If yes, please provide documentary evidence.

10. Does the notary's name appear in the notary seal?

11. If yes, please provide documentary evidence.

12. Is the notary's name properly printed out?

13. If yes, please provide documentary evidence.

14. Does the signer name in the acknowledgement match the signer name?

15. If yes, please provide documentary evidence.

16. Did the notary actually witness the signer signing?

17. Please provide the name, address, and telephone number of all individuals who were present at the time the documents were signed and notarized.

18. Please provide the full name, address, and telephone number of the notary who notarized the documents.

ORIGINATION BLOOPERS

19. Has the lender been accused of fraud, deception, or predatory lending?

20. If yes, please list all regulatory complaints, consumer complaints, or lawsuits filed by consumers against the lender for fraud, deception, or predatory lending. Provide the full name of the consumer(s) filing the complaint or report, the agency or court in which the complaint or report was filed and any other identifying details of the complaint or report such as reference numbers, docket numbers, or identification numbers.

21. Provide a listing of all of the locations where the Defendants advertised, including online advertising, during the period of _____ through _____. List the type of advertisement and the location.

22. What was the actual income [or other qualifying factor] of the consumer(s) at the time of application?

23. What was the income [or other qualifying factor] provided to potential lenders for the consumer at the time of application?

24. What was the lowest interest rate the consumer qualified for

at any time during the period of _____ through _____ ?

25. What was the actual interest rate of the consumer's loan at the time of closing?

26. List all companies or lenders that the sales person or dealer received kickbacks from for the period of _____ through _____ .

27. Did the sales person or originator receive a kickback for the consumer's loan?

28. Provide a list of all extended warranties offered to the consumer.

29. Provide a list of all extended warranties purchased and/or financed by the consumer.

30. Provide a full list of terms, conditions and coverage of any and all extended warranties purchased by the consumer.

31. Were the cost and coverage limitations of all extended warranties purchased by the consumer fully disclosed prior to purchase? If yes, please provide the date of the disclosure and describe the manner in which the disclosure was made to the consumer.

32. Was the consumer advised that the extended warranty was optional? If yes, provide the date of the disclosure and describe the manner in which the disclosure was made to the consumer.

33. Did the salesperson or dealer possess the required licenses to

sell insurance products, including extended warranties? If yes, list the name of the salesperson or originator licensed to sell such products, the state in which they are licensed and their full license number.

34. Did the consumer purchase any add-on products? If yes, provide a full list of all add-on products purchased by the consumer.

35. Was the consumer advised of the cost of all add-on products purchased? If yes, provide the date of the disclosure and describe the manner in which the disclosure was made.

36. Was the consumer advised that all add-on products were optional? If yes, provide the date of the disclosure and describe the manner in which the disclosure was made.

37. Were the financing terms disclosed to the consumer? If yes, provide the date of the disclosure, a listing of all terms provided during the disclosure, and a full description of the manner in which the disclosure was made.

38. Was the consumer a racial or ethnic minority, or female?

39. Please provide the percentage of customers to which the salesperson or originator sold add-on products to from the period of _____ through _____.

40. Please provide the percentage of the customers to which the salesperson or originator sold add-on products who were a racial or ethnic minority during that period. Provide the same data for customers who were white; female; and male.

41. Please provide the average interest rate of the sales-person or dealer's customers from a period of _____ through _____.

42. Please provide the average interest rate of the salesperson or originator's customers who were racial or ethnic minorities during that period. Provide the same data for white customers.

43. Please provide the average interest rate of the salesperson or originator's female customers during that period. Provide the same data for male customers.

44. Were all the terms, costs, commissions, rebates, kickbacks, and fees properly disclosed to the consumer? If yes, please provide the date of the disclosure of those items and a description of the manner in which the disclosure was made.

45. List all identity theft, credit monitoring, and insurance products sold by the salesperson or originator to any customer during the period of _____ through _____.

46. List all identity theft, credit monitoring, and insurance products sold to the consumer in this case. Provide a description of the product sold and the cost of each product sold.

47. Did the lender provide the consumer with copies of the loan agreements? If yes, please provide the date upon which the agreements were provided to the consumer and a description of manner in which the agreements were provided to the consumer.

48. Did the lender pay compensation to any third-party in

connection with the consumer's loan? If yes, list all third parties that were paid in connection with the consumer's loan and the service for which the third-party was paid.

49. Did the lender utilize any lead generation firm(s) during the period of _____ through _____? If yes, please provide a full list identifying each lead generation firm used and providing their most current address and telephone number.

ACCOUNTING BOO-BOOS

50. Can you explain how the amount due on the consumer's account was calculated?

51. What is the total amount due currently?

52. Were any charges or fees paid to affiliates of the lender or servicer with regard to consumer's account? If yes, please provide the full name and address of the affiliate paid, a listing of each payment made, and a full description of each payment, including the date and reason for the payment.

53. Were any charges or fees paid to any third-party with regard to the consumer's account? If yes, please provide the full name and address of the third-party, a listing of each payment made, and a full description of each payment, including the date and reason for the payment.

54. Describe the method used to credit payments to the consumer's account.

55. What was the interest rate charged on the consumer's account?

56. How was that interest rate calculated?

57. Were collection costs, charges, and/or fees assessed to the consumer's account? If yes, please state the amount of each fee and the date and reason for the charge.

58. Do you keep documentation to support the fees and charges assessed to accounts?

59. Do you have documentation to support the fees and charges assessed to the consumer's account? If yes, please provide the location, with address, of such documentation.

60. How do you calculate account credits?

61. How did you calculate account credits on the consumer's account?

62. What is the total amount of account credits on the consumer's account to date?

63. How do you calculate account debits?

64. How did you calculate account debits on the consumer's account?

65. What is the total amount of account debits on the consumer's account to date?

66. What is an account adjustment?

67. How do you calculate account adjustments?

68. How did you calculate adjustments on the consumer's account?

69. What is the total amount of account adjustments on the consumer's account to date?

70. How do you calculate amortization?

71. How did you calculate amortization on the consumer's account?

72. What is the total amount of amortization applied to the consumer's account to date?

73. How do you calculate interest and principal?

74. How was interest and principal calculated on the consumer's account?

75. How are interest and principal applied to accounts?

76. How was the interest and principal applied to the consumer's account?

77. Please explain how late charges are calculated and assessed.

78. Were late charges assessed to the consumer's account?

79. What is the total amount of late charges assessed to the consumer's account to date?

80. Was interest charged on late fees assessed to the consumer's account?

81. What is your policy for applying payments to a borrower's account?

82. How were payments applied to this consumer's account?

83. Do you charge fees for default related services? If yes, what are those fees and how are they calculated and assessed?

84. Was the consumer in this case charged default related fees? If yes, please list all such fees charged along with a date and description for the charge.

COLLECTION BLUNDERS

85. What notices were required in the consumer's promissory note?

86. What notices was the consumer sent?

87. When were those notices to be sent according to the promissory note?

88. What information did the lender report to the credit bureaus?

89. Did the collection agency ever hold itself out to be law enforcement?

90. Did the collection agency in this case ever threaten to garnish the consumer's wages or seize their property?

91. If yes, please explain what actions the collection agency told the consumer it was planning to take.

92. Did the consumer ever request a debt validation in this case?

93. Did the lender or servicer validate the debt?

94. How was the debt validated?

95. How many days after the request for validation was the response sent to the consumer?

96. Did the lender ever call the consumer's place of employment?

97. Did the consumer request that any person or entity in connection with this case stop calling his or her place of work?

98. How do servicers and sub-servicers generally ensure that they are following everything required by the promissory note?

99. What was the lender or collection agency's practice for maintaining records?

100. What were the collection agency's hours of operation?

101. What were the hours during which the collection agency made calls to consumers?

102. List all locations at which the consumer was contacted.

103. List all third parties, including full name and contact information, that were contacted with regard to the consumer.

104. Was the consumer's interest rate ever changed during the collection process?

TRANSFER GAFFES

105. How many times was the consumer's loan sold or transferred?

106. Provide a complete list of each entity the loan was transferred to and the date of transfer.

LACK OF STANDING

107. Who was the loan holder at the time this lawsuit was filed?

108. On what basis is _____ the legal owner of the debt in this case?

LICENSING, REGISTRATION...EVEN EXISTENCE

109. What states was the lender or originator licensed to do business in on _____.

110. What states was the [debt holder/collection agency] licensed to do business in on _____?

111. Which of the lender's branch offices was handling the consumer's account?

112. What licenses and/or registrations did the branch office have at the time?

STATUTE OF LIMITATIONS

113. What is the applicable statute of limitations for a debt in this state?

114. What is the date of the consumer's first default in this case?

115. What is the date this action was filed?

116. What is the date upon which the consumer was properly served with this lawsuit?

117. Where any 1099s ever issued to the consumer with regard to this account?

118. Please describe when each 1099 was issued and the reason for its issuance.

LEGAL PLEADINGS

119. How was the description of the collateral formed in this case?

120. What was relied upon in describing the collateral?

121. Provide a list of all affidavits in this case and their purpose.

122. Indicate what information and documents were relied upon in forming each individual affidavit.

MORTGAGE ORIGINATION

123. How do you ensure compliance with RESPA?

124. Explain how and why the consumer's application fully complies with RESPA.

125. What is your policy regarding property and flood insurance?

126. How much property and/or flood insurance was the consumer determined to need?

127. What amount of property and/or flood insurance did the consumer have at the time of closing?

128. What amount of property and/or flood insurance was maintained throughout the life of the loan?

129. What is your policy regarding the timeframe for a good faith estimate?

130. How was that policy applied with regard to this consumer in this case?

131. What is your policy on high cost mortgages?

132. How do you ensure that your policy is complied with?

133. How was that policy applied to this particular consumer?

134. How do you insure that mortgages are issued in compliance with the Real Estate Settlement Procedures Act (RESPA)?

135. Was the mortgage in this case checked for compliance with RESPA?

136. How was this mortgage checked for compliance with RESPA?

137. How was it determined that this mortgage complied with RESPA?

138. What is your policy regarding SFHD forms?

139. How do you determine when a SFHD form is needed?

140. Was there a SFHD form for this loan?

141. How was the amount of property and/or flood insurance determined?

142. How was the amount of property and/or flood insurance determined in this case?

143. Did the consumer have that amount of insurance at the time of closing?

144. Did the consumer maintain that amount of insurance?

145. What was the submission date of the consumer's application?

146. What was the date of the good faith estimate?

147. Is this mortgage a high cost mortgage?

MORTGAGE FORECLOSURE

148. Describe why force-placed insurance was required in this case.

149. What loss mitigation and/or loan modification information was provided to the consumer?

150. Describe, in detail, the details, terms, and conditions of each loan modification or loss mitigation program in place on or about _____.

151. How was eligibility for loan modification determined in this case?

152. Why was the consumer's application denied?

153. Did the consumer have a previous loan modification with a prior servicer at any time?

154. If yes, please list all previous loan modifications, the servicer and the date of each.

155. How did the lender comply with the terms of loan modifications with the prior servicer?

156. What notices and/or information did the lender provide to the consumer regarding how the new lender would handle their previous loan modification?

157. What was the date foreclosure was initiated?

158. Provide the dates for any and all loan modification applications the consumer made.

159. Describe how the lender had the right to foreclose on the consumer's property.

160. What is the lender's policy regarding service members on active duty?

161. How does the lender ensure that this policy is followed?

162. How many QWRs did the consumer make in this case?

163. What is the date for each QWR?

164. What is the corresponding response date for each QWR?

165. Did the lender ever make a claim for any outstanding insurance proceeds or additional collateral in this case?

166. If yes, please describe in detail all such claims made and the legal justification for each.

POST-FORECLOSURES SALE EVICTION/EJECTMENT

167. When was the deed recorded into the lender's name?

168. When was the eviction case filed?

169. Describe any repairs requested by the consumer.

170. List the date of each request and how and when each request was fulfilled.

VEHICLE REPOSSESSION

171. Does the lender utilize GPS tracker and disabler devices?

172. How does the lender disclose this to consumers?

173. Was the consumer in this case notified of the use of a GPS tracker and disabler device?

174. How was the consumer notified?

175. How many times has the vehicle in question been sold, both prior to and following the repossession?

176. Describe how the vehicle was repossessed.

177. When was the vehicle repossessed?

178. What time of day was the vehicle repossessed?

179. From where was the vehicle repossessed?

180. When did you provide the consumer with written notice to redeem the vehicle?

181. How was the vehicle sold following the repossession?

182. What was the final sale price of the vehicle when it was sold following the repossession?

183. How did you apply the proceeds of the sale to the consumer's account?

184. How did you notify the consumer of the status of his or her account following the sale of the vehicle?

STUDENT LOANS

185. How did you calculate the job placement rate for your graduates?

186. What was your placement rate based upon?

187. How did you advertise this information to potential students?

BUSINESS LOANS

188. How did the lender evaluate the forecast projections of the profitable operation rates?

189. What was the projection for profitable operation rates at the time the loan was issued?

190. Was the loan guaranteed through the Small Business Administration?

191. What was the amount of the loan provided to the consumer?

MEDICAL BILLS

192. Was the patient eligible for free or discounted services at the time of treatment?

193. What qualifies someone for free or discounted services?

194. What information do you take from patients regarding income level?

195. What services were provided to the consumer in this case?

196. Were the services provided medically necessary?

197. Was there any reason for the patient to believe that there would be no charge for some or all of the services provided?

198. If no, explain why?

199. Explain the way in which the cost of the consumer's procedures were calculated.

200. Provide a listing of the cost for the consumer's procedures on the Medicare Fee Schedule, the Medicaid Fee Schedule, and per your agreement with three major commercial insurers at the time the services were provided.

201. Describe your claims submission process.

202. What was the date that the consumer's claims were submitted?

PAYDAY LOANS

203. What are the restrictions on fees and interest rates in the consumer's home state?

204. What were the fees and interest rates applied to the consumer's loan?

205. How were the fees and interest rates calculated?

206. How is the short-term of the need of the consumer determined?

207. What was the short-term need of this particular consumer?

208. What was the total amount of the consumer's loan?

ACTION TOOLS D

156 REQUESTS FOR ADMISSIONS

DOCUMENTATION ISSUES

1. Admit that [insert debt holder name] or any agent does not possess the original [promissory note, personal guarantee document, endorsement, assignment, and/or security instrument] or similar document evidencing the debt.

2. Admit that the security instrument was not properly filed and/or recorded.

3. Admit that the [promissory note, personal guarantee document, endorsement, assignment, and/or security instrument] are not signed.

4. Admit that the [promissory note, personal guarantee document, endorsement, assignment, and/or security instrument] was signed by a person without the proper capacity or authority to sign.

5. Admit that the [promissory note, personal guarantee document, endorsement, assignment, and/or security instrument] was signed using robo-signing.

6. Admit that the creditor does not have a signed contract.

7. Admit that the contract does not name the correct original creditor.

NOTARY DEFECTS

8. Admit that the date of the notary acknowledgment does not match the date of signing by the consumer.

9. Admit that the notary acknowledgement is incomplete.

10. Admit that the notary name is not in the seal or printed out.

11. Admit that the signer name in the acknowledgment does not match the signer name.

12. Admit that the notary did not actually witness the consumer signing the document.

13. Admit that the notary acknowledgement is defective.

ORIGINATION BLOOPERS

14. Admit that the loan was a result of fraud, deception and/or predatory lending.

15. Admit that the originator or salesperson misrepresented the borrower's income [or other qualifying factor] on the credit application.

16. Admit that the originator or salesperson sold the borrower on a higher interest rate than the borrower qualified for.

17. Admit that the originator steered the borrower to the lender based upon kickbacks or other incentives.

18. Admit that the originator received kickbacks or other incentives for steering the borrower to the lender in this case.

19. Admit that an extended warranty was financed in this case.

20. Admit that the extended warranty provided limited and unnecessary coverage.

21. Admit that the extended warranty was priced to exceed its value to the consumer.

22. Admit that the cost and terms of the extended warranty were not disclosed to the consumer.

23. Admit that the consumer was not advised that the extended warranty was optional.

24. Admit that the originator or salesperson in this case was not licensed to sell insurance products.

25. Admit that the originator or salesperson did not advise the consumer of the cost of all add-on products.

26. Admit that the originator or salesperson did not advise the consumer that all add-on products were optional.

27. Admit that the financing terms of the loan were not properly disclosed to the consumer.

28. Admit that the borrower was a racial or ethnic minority or female.

29. Admit that the originator or salesperson sold higher interest rate loans to racial and ethnic minorities and/or females than to other consumers during the period of _____ through _____.

30. Admit that the value of the goods and/or services financed were misrepresented.

31. Admit that the loan in this case was not originated in compliance with all applicable laws and regulations.

32. Admit that the originator or salesperson failed to properly disclose all terms, costs, commissions, rebates, kickbacks, and fees.

33. Admit that the originator or salesperson sold unnecessary identity theft, credit monitoring, and/or insurance products.

34. Admit that the originator or salesperson failed to disclose the cost of any identity theft, credit monitoring, and/or insurance products sold to the consumer.

35. Admit that the originator or salesperson failed to advise the consumer that any identity theft, credit monitoring, and/or insurance products were optional.

36. Admit that the originator or salesperson misrepresented the condition of the product purchased.

37. Admit that the originator or salesperson breached the implied warranty.

38. Admit that the lender failed to immediately provide copies of the agreements to the consumer at the time of execution.

39. Admit that the lender utilized and paid one or more unlicensed third-parties in connection to the consumer's loan.

40. Admit that the lender's advertising materials were false, deceptive, and/or lacked the required disclosures.

ACCOUNTING BOO-BOOS

41. Admit that the amount the lender is alleging is due is not evidenced by the payment history over the life of the loan.

42. Admit that charges and fees assessed to the account were paid to affiliates of the lender or servicer.

43. Admit that charges and fees assessed to the account were paid

to a third-party that shared a portion of the fee through a revenue sharing agreement.

44. Admit that payments made on the loan were not properly credited.

45. Admit that the interest rate charged to the account is inconsistent with the terms of the promissory note.

46. Admit that the interest rate charged to the account is improperly calculated.

47. Admit that fees charged to the account are inconsistent with the terms of the promissory note.

48. Admit that fees charged to the account are improperly calculated.

49. Admit that collection costs, charges, and/or fees applied to the account were not justified.

50. Admit that collection costs, charges, and/or fees applied to the account are excessive.

51. Admit that the note does not authorize collection costs, charges, and/or fees applied to the account.

52. Admit that the lender does not have proper documentation to support all of the charges and fees assessed to this account.

53. Admit that the loan account was not [credited, debited, adjusted, amortized, or charged] correctly.

54. Admit that the interest applied to the loan in this case was not properly calculated.

55. Admit that the principal amount in this case was not properly calculated.

56. Admit that late charges were assessed to the account improperly.

57. Admit that late charges assessed to the account are excessive when compared to the expenses and damages incurred for a late payment.

58. Admit that interest was charged on late fees.

59. Admit that the lender failed to accurately apply payments made by the consumer.

60. Admit that the lender failed to maintain accurate account statements for the consumer's account.

61. Admit that the consumer was charged unauthorized fees for default related services.

COLLECTION BLUNDERS

62. Admit that the collection notices in this case were not provided in accordance with the promissory note.

63. Admit that the lender or collection agency reported incorrect information to the credit bureau.

64. Admit that an employee or agent of the collection agency

impersonated law enforcement when communicating with the consumer.

65. Admit that the collection agency threatened to take actions against the consumer that were not actually planned.

66. Admit that the collection agency threatened to take actions against the consumer that were not allowed by law.

67. Admit that the collection agency failed to properly respond to the consumer's debt validation request.

68. Admit that the consumer instructed the collection agency to stop calling his or her place of employment.

69. Admit that the collection agency continued to make calls to the consumer's place of employment after the consumer requested that they stop.

70. Admit that the consumer requested that the collection agency stop communicating via telephone with the consumer.

71. Admit that the collection agency did not cease to call the consumer even after the consumer requested that all telephone contact stop.

72. Admit that the collection agency verbally abused the consumer.

73. Admit that the collection agency in this case was not properly licensed.

74. Admit that the collection agency knowingly provided false

and/or misleading information to the consumer during collection efforts.

75. Admit that the collection agency executed one or more inaccurate affidavits with regard to the consumer's account and the collection efforts in this case.

76. Admit that the collection agency called the consumer before 8:00AM.

77. Admit that the collection agency called the consumer after 9:00PM.

78. Admit that the collection agency called the consumer repeatedly to harass and annoy the consumer.

79. Admit that the collection agency contacted the consumer even after receiving notice that the consumer was represented by an attorney.

80. Admit that the collection agency contacted family members, friends, or co-workers about the consumer's debt.

81. Admit that the collection agency gave improper information to a family member, friend, or co-worker about the consumer's debt.

82. Admit that the collection agency called a family member, friend, or co-worker of the consumer more than once.

83. Admit that the collection agency used deceptive means to collect information about the consumer.

84. Admit that the collection agency engaged in deceptive collection and billing practices.

85. Admit that the collection agency engaged in unfair debt collection practices.

86. Admit that the collection agency backdated letters sent to the consumer.

87. Admit that the consumer's interest rate was raised during the collection process.

88. Admit that debits were taken from the consumer's bank account without authorization.

TRANSFER GAFFES

89. Admit that the sale or transfer of the loan in this case was not conducted in accordance with the law.

90. Admit that the sale of the loan in this case was not a true sale.

91. Admit that the loan holder on _____ was not holding the note in compliance with applicable laws.

92. Admit that the loan holder on _____ is not entitled to the benefit of payments.

LACK OF STANDING

93. Admit that the Plaintiff was not the legal owner of the debt at the time of filing.

LICENSING, REGISTRATION...EVEN EXISTENCE

94. Admit that the [dealer, originator, lender, holder, servicer, or collection agency] was not licensed to do business in _____ on or about _____.

95. Admit that the [dealer, originator, lender, holder, servicer, or collection agency] branch office that handled the consumer's account was not licensed to do business in _____ on or about _____.

96. Admit that the lender was not an actual, legitimate corporate entity.

STATUTE OF LIMITATIONS

97. Admit that the statute of limitations has expired for the consumer's debt.

98. Admit that this action is time barred by the applicable statute of limitations in the state of _____.

99. Admit that the consumer's first default was on _____.

100. Admit that this action was initiated on _____.

101. Admit that the consumer was properly served with this suit on _____.

102. Admit that the consumer was issued a 1099 cancelling this debt.

LEGAL PLEADINGS

103. Admit that the legal pleadings in this case [list the error, omission, or inconsistency].

104. Admit that the collateral in this case is not properly described.

105. Admit that [specify affidavit] is not based upon the information in the creditor's books and records.

MORTGAGE ORIGINATION

106. Admit that this mortgage was not originated in full compliance with RESPA.

107. Admit that the HUD1 or HUD1A was not completed as required by law.

108. Admit that the applicant's race or ethnicity was not properly indicated on the loan application.

109. Admit that the originator failed to complete a SFHD form prior to the consummation of the loan.

110. Admit that the loan originator failed to ensure that the consumer had adequate property and flood insurance at the time of closing.

111. Admit that the loan originator failed to ensure that the consumer maintained adequate property and flood insurance through the life of the loan.

112. Admit that the originator did not provide a good faith estimate within three days of the consumer's application.

113. Admit that the originator failed to include the names and contact information of the required settlement service providers on the good faith estimate.

114. Admit that the originator did not follow the law with regard to high cost mortgages.

MORTGAGE FORECLOSURE

115. Admit that the Notice of Sale or Transfer was not provided to the consumer.

116. Admit that force-placed insurance was improperly imposed upon the consumer in this case.

117. Admit that the lender failed to provide the consumer with accurate information about loan modifications and other loss mitigation services that may be available.

118. Admit that the lender failed to properly process the consumer's loan modification application.

119. Admit that the lender did not provide the consumer with the true reason for denial of his or her loan modification.

120. Admit that the lender failed to honor the trial loan modification with the consumer's prior loan servicer.

121. Admit that the servicer sought to collect payments under the unmodified terms after a loan modification had already begun with the prior servicer.

122. Admit that lender did not provide the consumer with accurate

and adequate information about the status of foreclosure proceedings during the time that the consumer was actively pursuing other loss mitigation options offered by the lender.

123. Admit that the lender did not have the right to foreclosure at the time foreclosure proceedings were initiated.

124. Admit that the lender pursued foreclosure while the consumer had a pending application for loan modification.

125. Admit that the servicer initiated foreclosure upon the consumer while the consumer was a service member on active duty.

126. Admit that the value of the property in this case was misrepresented.

127. Admit that the consumer sent a QWR to the lender.

128. Admit that the lender failed to provide a complete response to the consumer's QWR.

129. Admit that the lender consistently failed to provide any response to the consumer's QWR.

130. Admit that the lender made a claim for rights to outstanding insurance proceeds or additional collateral when the lender did not have the right to do so.

POST-FORECLOSURES SALE EVICTION/ EJECTMENT
131. Admit that the lender did not have standing at the time that the eviction case was filed.

132. Admit that the consumer was offered "cash for keys."

133. Admit that the debt collector used in this case was not properly licensed.

134. Admit that the consumer made proper and reasonable requests for repairs.

135. Admit that the consumer's proper and reasonable requests for repairs were not addressed adequately.

136. Admit that the repairs made were not complete or adequate.

VEHICLE REPOSSESSION

137. Admit that a GPS tracker and disabler device was used without disclosing this to the consumer at the time of purchase.

138. Admit that the repossession created a disturbance of the peace.

139. Admit that you did not provide the consumer a proper written notice to redeem following the repossession.

140. Admit that the vehicle was not sold in a commercially reasonable manner following the repossession.

141. Admit that the sale price following the repossession was significantly below fair market value.

142. Admit that the proceeds of the sale were not applied to the consumer's account.

143. Admit that the consumer was not provided with a full accounting of their account following the sale of the vehicle.

STUDENT LOANS

144. Admit that the institution and/or lender were negligent in advertising job placement and salary figures to potential students.

BUSINESS LOANS

145. Admit that the lender knew, or should have known, that the advertised forecast projections of profitable operation rates were misleading.

146. Admit that the lender was negligent in their calculations and statistical analysis regarding projections of profitable operation rates.

147. Admit the loan was guaranteed by the Small Business Administration and therefore required certain disclosures.

148. Admit that the lender did not provide the required notices for loans guaranteed by the Small Business Administration.

MEDICAL BILLS

149. Admit that the patient should have been provided free or reduced cost care due to his or her income level.

150. Admit that the consumer received services that were not medically necessary.

151. Admit that the patient received information that would cause him or her to believe that there would be no charge for some or all of the services performed.

152. Admit that the charges for the patient's services were excessive.

153. Admit that the charges were not in accordance with the contract between the provider and the consumer's medical insurance company.

154. Admit that the charges for the consumer's services were not billed in a timely manner.

PAYDAY LOANS

155. Admit that the lender violated the state restrictions on fees and interest rates.

156. Admit that the lender provided a loan to the consumer in an amount that exceeded the consumer's short term needs.

ACTION TOOLS E

252 DEPOSITION QUESTIONS

DOCUMENTATION ISSUES

1. Who currently has physical possession of the [promissory note, personal guarantee document, endorsement, assignment, and/ or security instrument] or other document evidencing the debt?

2. Are you able to produce the [promissory note, personal

guarantee document, endorsement, assignment, and/or security instrument] or other document evidencing the debt?

3. Please provide the address where the [promissory note, personal guarantee document, endorsement, assignment, and/or security instrument] or other document is physically located today.

4. What is the last known address where the [promissory note, personal guarantee document, endorsement, assignment, and/or security instrument] or other document was located?

5. The [promissory note, personal guarantee document, endorsement, assignment and/or security instrument] was originally requested by [insert debtor name] on or about [insert date], correct?

6. And to date, the original [promissory note, personal guarantee document, endorsement, assignment, and/or security instrument] has not been produced as a part of the discovery process?

7. Are you able to say, with certainty, that the [promissory note personal guarantee document, endorsement, assignment, and/or security instrument] can be produced within the next ten (10) days?

8. Can you provide evidence that the [promissory note, personal guarantee document, endorsement, assignment, and/or security instrument] was properly executed?

9. Who signed the [promissory note, personal guarantee document, endorsement, assignment and/or security instrument]?

10. Did the person who signed the [promissory note, personal guarantee document, endorsement, assignment, and/or security instrument] have the authority to do so?

11. What is the basis for the signor's authority to sign the [promissory note, personal guarantee document, endorsement, assignment, and/or security instrument]?

12. Was the security instrument filed and/or recorded?

13. Can you provide the date of filing and/or recording?

14. Can you provide the location of filing and/or recording?

15. Where is the document evidencing proper filing and/or recording located currently?

16. Are you able to obtain this document within the next ten (10) days?

17. Are you aware of whether or not robo-signing was ever used by your company?

18. Do you know if robo-signing was used for any document relating to this case or this consumer?

19. Do you know if a signed contract exists for this consumer?

20. Please provide the location of that signed contract?

21. Can you provide this document within the next ten (10) days?

22. What is the name of the creditor on the contract?

23. Is [creditor's name] listed on the contract?

24. Please explain why [creditor's name] is the correct original creditor.

NOTARY DEFECTS

25. What is the date of the notary acknowledgement?

26. What is the date the consumer signed the document?

27. Do those dates match?

28. Can you tell me what the requirements are for a notary acknowledgment to be correctly and completely filled out?

29. Is the notary acknowledgment completely filled out?

30. Can you tell me which of the required elements this notary acknowledgement has?

31. Is the notary name on the acknowledgment in the notary seal?

32. Is the notary name on the acknowledgment printed?

33. What is the signer name in the acknowledgment?

34. What is the name of the actual consumer in this case?

35. Does the name of the consumer match the name of the signer on the notarized documents?

36. Can you show me where on the documents that this information matches up?

37. Are you aware of whether or not the notary witnessed the consumer signing the documents?

38. How do you know this?

39. Are you aware of any other individual who may have witnessed the notary present at the time that the consumer signed the documents?

ORIGINATION BLOOPERS

40. Describe the advertising materials you used during the period of _____ through _____.

41. Describe the marketing materials you used during the period of _____ through _____.

42. Describe the internal training materials used during the period of _____ through _____.

43. What type of training was provided to originators and/or salespeople with regard to determining the amounts borrowers would be able to afford?

44. How was the amount a borrower was able to afford calculated or determined?

45. Can you walk us through an example of how you would determine the amount a consumer would be able to afford?

46. How did you calculate a consumer's income?

47. Did you receive any training on how to calculate a consumer's income?

48. What was the training?

49. Can you please provide an example of how you would determine a consumer's income?

50. Did you ever sell a consumer a loan at an interest rate that was higher than the lowest rate the consumer qualified for?

51. Is there any reason why a consumer may choose or be sold a loan at a higher interest rate than the lowest rate they qualified for?

52. What was the lowest rate the consumer in this case qualified for?

53. What was the actual interest rate of the consumer's loan in this case?

54. Why was the consumer sold a loan at a higher interest rate than the lowest rate they were qualified for?

55. Were there any kickbacks or incentives from the lender to the originator or salesperson for this loan?

56. What lenders did the originator or salesperson in this case have a relationship with that would provide for kickbacks or other incentives?

57. What would trigger a kickback or incentive from the lender to the originator or salesperson?

58. What kickbacks or incentives did the originator or salesperson receive from the lender during the period of _____ through _____?

59. Was an extended warranty financed with this loan?

60. What was the coverage of the extended warranty?

61. What coverage is typically necessary in an extended warranty?

62. Why would an extended warranty be needed at all?

63. What types of consumers need extended warranties?

64. What does an extended warranty do for a consumer?

65. Were all consumers offered extended warranties?

66. What was the consumer in this case told about the extended warranty?

67. Was the consumer provided with the cost of the extended warranty prior to purchase? If yes, by whom? When? How was this information given?

68. Was the consumer provided the coverage limitations of the extended warranty prior to purchase? If yes, by whom? When? How was this information given?

69. Was the consumer told that the extended warranty was optional? If yes, by whom? When? How was this information given?

70. Did the originator or salesperson in this case have a license to sell insurance products?

71. What were the active dates of the license?

72. Was the insurance license of the originator or salesperson ever suspended or revoked?

73. Did the salesperson or originator ever have any other type of disciplinary action taken against his or her insurance license?

74. Was the consumer sold any other add-on products in this case?

75. Was the consumer told of the cost of the other add-on products sold to him or her? If yes, by whom? When? How was this information provided?

76. Was the consumer told that the other add-on products were optional? If yes, by whom? When? How was this information provided?

77. Were the financing terms of the loan disclosed to the consumer? If yes, by whom? When? How was this information provided?

78. What was the fair market value of the goods or services financed?

79. What was the value of the goods or services provided to the consumer?

80. How was the value of the goods or services determined or calculated?

81. Is there a standard way in which the value of goods and services is calculated?

82. Did originator or salesperson receive training on how to determine the value of goods and services?

83. Can you describe any training provided on determining value?

84. Can you provide an example of how originator or salesperson would determine the value of a good or service?

85. Was the consumer advised of all terms, costs, commissions, rebates, kickbacks, and fees associated with this transaction? If yes, by whom? When? How was this information provided?

86. Were any identity theft, credit monitoring, or insurance products offered or sold to the consumer?

87. Please describe any and all identity theft, credit monitoring, or insurance products purchased by the consumer.

88. What was the condition of the property or product purchased?

89. What information was the consumer given about the condition of the property or product? Who provided the information? When? How was that information provided?

90. Was the consumer provided copies of the loan agreement at

the time of execution? If yes, by whom? When? How was this information provided?

91. Did the lender pay any compensation to an unlicensed party in connection with this loan?

92. Did the lender use lead generators?

93. What lead generators did the lender use?

94. Describe the advertising materials used by the lender during the period of _____ to _____.

95. Has the lender ever been accused of fraud, deception, or predatory lending by a consumer?

96. Has the lender ever been sued for fraud, deception, or predatory lending by a consumer?

97. Has the lender ever been reported to the government, state or federal, by a consumer for fraud, deception, or predatory lending?

98. Has the lender ever undergone an investigation of any kind by an outside entity for fraud, deception, or predatory lending?

99. Has the lender ever been sanctioned for fraud, deception, or predatory lending?

ACCOUNTING BOO-BOOS

100. What is the amount allegedly due in this case?

101. Can you describe how that amount was calculated?

102. Is there a payment history for the life of the loan?

103. Is the payment history documented?

104. How is the payment history documented and where is this documentation currently located?

105. Did the lender have any revenue sharing agreements with any third-party from _____ through _____?

106. Did the lender pay charges or fees associated with the consumers account to a third-party?

107. Was that payment made through a revenue sharing agreement?

108. If not, what is the explanation for the fees charged?

109. How were payments by the consumer credited to this loan?

110. What was the interest rate charged to the consumer?

111. What was the interest rate contained in the promissory note?

112. How was the consumer's interest rate calculated?

113. How are interest rates typically calculated?

114. Was the consumer charged collection costs?

115. What was the amount of the collection costs?

116. What specifically were the collection costs for?

117. How were the collection costs calculated?

118. What basis did the lender have for assessing the collection costs?

119. How was the amount of interest due calculated in this case?

120. What is the amount of interest that the lender is alleging is due?

121. How was the principal amount calculated?

122. What is the principal amount that the lender is alleging is due?

123. Were late charges assessed to the consumer's account?

124. How are late charges calculated?

125. How much money does a lender lose when a customer is late on a payment?

126. Was interest charged on the late fees for this account?

127. Please explain how the lender maintains accurate account statements.

128. Were default related fees charged to this account?

129. Were those fees authorized in any way?

130. What documentation do you have to indicate that the fees were authorized?

COLLECTION BLUNDERS

131. How were the collection notices required by the consumer's promissory note furnished to the consumer?

132. When were those notices sent to the consumer?

133. What information regarding the consumer's account was reported to any of the credit bureaus?

134. What is your process for validating debts?

135. How did you validate the debt in this case?

136. What was the timeline for the whole debt validation process?

137. When was the collection agency told to stop calling the consumer's place of employment?

138. When was the last call made to the consumer's place of employment?

139. How can that information be verified?

140. When was the collection agency told to cease all telephone contact with the consumer?

141. When was the last telephone call made to the consumer?

142. How can that information be verified?

143. Is the collection agency licensed in the state of _____?

144. What is the effective date of the collection agency's license in the state?

145. What affidavits were executed with regard to the consumer's account and the collection efforts?

146. Where was the information for the affidavits obtained?

147. Describe the collection agency's policies and procedures with regard to record keeping.

148. What is your policy when a consumer informs the collection agency that he or she is represented by an attorney?

149. What occurred when the consumer in this case advised the collection agency that he or she was represented by an attorney?

150. What is your policy regarding the number of times per day a consumer is called?

151. What is the maximum number of times a consumer should be called in a day?

152. What is the highest number of times the consumer in this case was called in a day?

153. What is your policy regarding contacting friends, family members, or co-workers?

154. How do you collect information about the consumers whose accounts are assigned to you for collection?

155. How are letters and/or written communications with consumers generated?

156. How are letters and/or written communications with consumers dated?

157. How are letters and/or written communications with consumers mailed?

158. From beginning to end, how long does it take from the time a letter is generated until it is mailed?

159. What is your policy for initiating ACH debits from a consumer's account?

160. How many times was this particular consumer's account debited?

161. How did you obtain authorization to debit the consumer's account?

TRANSFER GAFFES

162. How many times was this loan sold or transferred?

163. What is the process for selling or transferring a loan?

164. What process was followed in selling or transferring the consumer's loan in this case?

165. How were the laws applicable to the sale of loans followed in this case?

166. What makes the loan holder on _____ entitled to the benefit of payments?

LACK OF STANDING

167. How is the Plaintiff the legal owner of the debt in this case?

168. When was the debt sold to the Plaintiff?

169. What was the process followed in connection with the sale of this note?

LICENSING, REGISTRATION…EVEN EXISTENCE

170. What licenses or registrations does the [dealer, originator, lender, holder, servicer, or collection agency] hold in _____?

171. What licenses or registrations did the [dealer, originator, lender, holder, servicer, or collection agency] hold in _____ on or about _____?

172. When was the [dealer, originator, lender, holder, servicer, or collection agency] formed/incorporated and in what state?

STATUTE OF LIMITATIONS

173. What was the first date of default on the consumer's account?

174. When was this lawsuit filed?

175. When was the consumer served?

176. What is the applicable statute of limitations in your state?

177. Was a 1099 ever issued to the consumer?

178. When was the 1099 issued to the consumer?

LEGAL PLEADINGS
179. Please describe the collateral in this case.

180. How was the description of the collateral used in the legal pleadings formed?

181. What information do you typically rely upon in forming a legal description of collateral?

182. Are there any affidavits that are a part of the record in this case?

183. Please describe each affidavit.

184. What information was used to form [specify affidavit]?

MORTGAGE FORECLOSURE
185. Was force-placed insurance required in this case?

186. What was the basis for requiring force-placed insurance?

187. What is the lender's policy regarding force-placed insurance?

188. What information did you provide to the consumer about loan modifications or other loss mitigation services?

189. When was the consumer's application for a loan modification received?

190. When was processing complete?

191. Describe the process in which a loan modification application is processed.

192. What are reasons that a loan modification would be denied?

193. Why was the consumer's loan modification denied in this case?

194. Were consumers who were denied loan modifications also considered for other loss mitigation services at the time of their modification application?

195. How does the lender handle prior loan modifications with a prior loan servicer?

196. How did the lender handle the consumer's previous loan modification in this case?

197. What notification and information did the lender provide the consumer regarding the status of foreclosure proceedings?

198. Can you provide a list of dates upon which statuses were provided to the consumer?

199. How do you ensure that you have the legal right to foreclosure prior to initiating foreclosure proceedings?

200. How was the value of the consumer's property determined?

201. What is the lender's policy on Qualified Written Requests?

202. How do you handle QWRs from consumers?

203. How do you ensure that QWRs are properly responded to?

POST-FORECLOSURE SALE EVICTION/ EJECTMENT
204. What was the basis upon which you filed the eviction case?

205. Were any cash offers made to the consumer in exchange for vacating the property?

206. If yes, when and by whom?

207. Who was the debt collector used in this case?

208. Was the collector licensed in _____ on or about _____?

209. What repairs did the consumer request?

210. Of the repairs requested, which were made?

211. When were the requested repairs made?

212. Who made the repairs?

VEHICLE REPOSSESSION
213. How do you inform consumers that a GPS tracker and disabler device will be used to repossess their vehicle?

214. When is that disclosure made?

215. Does the consumer have to sign/initial/acknowledge that disclosure?

216. How many times has this vehicle been sold in total?

217. How many times have you sold this vehicle?

218. How many times has this vehicle been repossessed?

219. How do you ensure that repossession does not disturb the peace?

220. Describe your process for providing consumers with a notice to redeem following a repossession.

221. How was the notice to redeem provided to the consumer in this case?

222. When was the vehicle sold?

223. What forum was used to sell the vehicle?

224. Who purchased the vehicle?

225. What was the purchase price?

226. What was the fair market value of the vehicle at the time it was sold?

227. How were the proceeds of the sale applied to the consumer's account?

STUDENT LOANS

228. What was your advertised job placement rate for graduates on or about _____?

229. What was your advertised median salary for graduates on or about _____?

230. What was the average student loan debt at the time of graduation from a 4 year degree program at your institution on or about _____?

BUSINESS LOANS

231. How were the advertised forecast projections of profitable operation rates calculated and analyzed?

232. What was the amount loaned to the consumer?

233. How was that determined?

234. What notices did the lender provide to the consumer regarding this loan?

MEDICAL BILLS

235. When does your institution provide free or discounted services for someone?

236. What criteria are used to decide if someone is eligible for free or low cost services?

237. Is there any time when a patient would not be charged for services at all?

238. How would the patient be notified of that?

239. How do you ensure timely submission of claims?

PAYDAY LOANS

240. Explain the terms and conditions of the consumer's loan?

241. Are you licensed to lend in the state of _____?

242. What is the maximum loan amount for any consumer?

243. What was the amount of this particular consumer's loan?

244. What is the applicable state restriction on interest rates and fees for short term lending?

245. How did the lender comply with those restrictions?

246. What was the total interest rate applied to the consumer's loan?

247. In total, what is the amount the consumer would have paid to the lender over the life of this loan?

248. How long was the loan for?

249. How do you determine a consumer's ability to repay the short-term loans?

250. How do you determine an applicant's creditworthiness?

251. How do you assess the short-term needs of a consumer?

252. What is the average loan amount in your short term lending program?

ACTION TOOLS F

24 LETTERS TO SHUT DOWN CREDITORS

There are 18 letters included in the debt-specific chapters throughout this book. The following 6 letters are either utilized for multiple debt types or are so long that I put them in Action Tools. By adding in the 6 below, there's a total of 24 letters. Visit debtcleanse.com for fillable templates of every letter in this book as well as updates and any new letters that may become available. You will easily be able to add your information, print, and save copies. Although emails, texts, and other electronic communication have diminished the use of letters in American society, letters are a key component of Debt Cleanse. You are going to learn to love letters.

Tips:

1. Always keep a copy of what you mail.

2. Mail letters certified, return receipt requested.

LETTER A

*   *   *

DISPUTE & VALIDATION LETTER

Your Name
Your Address
Your City, State Zip

**VIA CERTIFIED MAIL/RETURN RECEIPT REQUESTED/
COPY RETAINED**

Date

Creditor/Debt Buyer/Collection Agency/Servicer Name
Address
City, State Zip

Re: Acct # _____

To Whom It May Concern:

I am sending this letter to you in response to a notice I received
from you on [date of letter]. Be advised, this is not a refusal to pay,
but a notice sent pursuant to the Fair Debt Collection Practices
Act, 15 USC 1692g Sec. 809 (b) that your claim is disputed and
validation is requested.

This is NOT a request for "verification" or proof of my mailing
address, but a request for VALIDATION made pursuant to the
above named Title and Section. I respectfully request that your
office provide me with competent evidence that I have any legal
obligation to pay you.

Please provide me with the following:

- What the money you say I owe is for;
- An explanation of how you calculated what you say I owe;
- Proof that the amount you are claiming is within the law;
- Copies of any papers that show I agreed to pay what you say
  I owe;
- Verification or a copy of any judgment if applicable;
- The identity of the original creditor;
- Proof that the Statute of Limitations has not expired on

this account;

- Proof that you are licensed to collect in my state; and
- Your license numbers and Registered Agent contact information.

I am sure you are aware if you are unable to provide these few basic facts, you are in violation of the FCRA and FDCPA, as well as potential state and local laws. In addition, if you have reported any information that has not been validated to any or all of the Credit Bureaus (Equifax, Experian, or TransUnion) you are in violation of both State and Federal Law. That being said, if you cannot provide this basic information, and continue to report this unverified, non-validated debt, I will pursue this legally for the following reasons:

- Defamation of Character
- Violating the Fair Credit Reporting Act
- Violating the Fair Debt Collection Practices Act
- Potential for additional claims as my lawyer sees fit

Please note that during the validation period you must refrain from taking any negative or detrimental action against me with any of the Credit Bureaus. Should any information that has not been validated be reported to the Credit Bureaus, I will take legal action including reporting this matter to the Consumer Financial Protection Bureau as well as the Office of Consumer Protection in all states where your company conducts business.

If you are unable to provide the proof I requested within thirty (30) days of receipt of this notice, all collection activity must cease and desist immediately and you must remove and/or continue not reporting this account from all reporting agencies, which is mandated under federal law. Failure to respond by your company will be considered an inability to validate the alleged debt. Failure to provide all items requested will also be considered as an inability to validate.

Furthermore, if you fail to respond or are in any way unable to validate the above referenced account, you are required, under the law to remove all items reported to any Credit Bureau. A copy of each deletion request must be forwarded to me immediately. If you fail to take such action in a timely manner, I will exercise my rights under the law and pursue the issue legally.

Until the above request for irrefutable evidence about this account is sent to me, please cease and desist all further, future attempts to collect on this debt. This includes no phone calls to my home phone number, no calls to my place of work, and no calls to my mobile phone. All further, future attempts to collect on this unverified debt by phone must cease and desist unless and until it is validated, which I do not believe will be the case. All communication from this point forward must be done via mail and sent to the address noted in this letter. You must also cease and desist any and all contact with any third-party regarding this account, regardless of the nature of the contact. I would also like to warn you and your company that I may, and likely will, use devices to track and/or record any further, future attempts by you or your company to contact me by phone. If you fail to comply, it will be considered harassment and I will pursue all remedies available to me under the law.

This is an attempt to correct your records, and any information obtained shall be used for that purpose.

Sincerely,

Your Signature
Your Name

*   *   *

LETTER B

*   *   *

NOTIFICATION THAT EMPLOYER RESTRICTS PERSONAL
CALLS TO WORKPLACE

Your Name
Your Address
Your City, State Zip

**VIA CERTIFIED MAIL/RETURN RECEIPT REQUESTED/
COPY RETAINED**

Date

Creditor Name
Address
City State Zip

RE: Account #_____

Please stop contacting me at my place of work regarding account

#_____

with _____(identify debt holder). My employer does not permit personal phone calls. Therefore, I will consider any more phone calls to my place of work to be harassment.

The Fair Debt Collection Practices Act requires that you honor my request. If you fail to immediately cease and desist all contact as requested I will pursue all remedies available under the law, including, but not limited to reporting this matter to the Federal Trade Commission and Consumer Financial Protection Bureau. This letter is not intended to acknowledge or agree that your claims about the above referenced account are true and correct, nor is it an acknowledgement that I owe any money. Thank you in advance for your anticipated cooperation.

Sincerely,

Your Signature
Your Name

*   *   *

LETTER C

*   *   *

CEASE CONTACT REQUEST

Your Name
Your Address
Your City, State Zip

VIA CERTIFIED MAIL/RETURN RECEIPT REQUESTED/ COPY RETAINED

Date

Lender/Servicer/Collection Agency
Address
City, State Zip

RE: Loan #_____

Please accept this letter as a formal request that you immediately cease and desist all contact with me or any third-party regarding the above referenced account or any other matter. This includes no phone calls to my home phone number, no calls to my place of work, and no calls to my mobile phone. All communication from this point forward must be done via mail and sent to the address noted in this letter. All other contact must cease and desist immediately, regardless of the nature of the contact. I would also like to warn you and your company that I may, and likely will, use devices to track and/or record any further, future attempts by you or your company to contact me by phone. If you fail to comply, it will be considered harassment and I will pursue all remedies available to me under the law.

This letter is not intended to acknowledge or agree that your claims about the above referenced account are true and correct, nor is it an acknowledgement that I owe any money. Thank you in advance for you anticipated cooperation.

Sincerely,

Your Signature
Your Name

*   *   *

LETTER D

This is based on a sample from Pennsylvania Legal Aid Network, with some edits and additions.

*   *   *

QUALIFIED WRITTEN REQUEST

Your Name
Your Address
Your City, State Zip

VIA CERTIFIED MAIL/RETURN RECEIPT REQUESTED/ COPY RETAINED

Date

Mortgage Company Name
Address
City, State Zip

RE: Loan #_____, Property Address:_____

RE: RESPA Qualified Written Request, Complaint, and Dispute of Debt and Validation of Debt Letter

Dear _____,

I am writing to you to request specific itemized information about the accounting and servicing of my mortgage and of my need for understanding and clarification of various charges, credits, debits, transactions, actions, payments, analyses, and records related to the servicing of my loan from its inception to the present date.

I am disputing the validity of the current debt you claim that I owe. To independently validate this debt, I need to conduct a complete exam, audit, review, and accounting of my mortgage loan from its inception until the present date. Upon receipt of this letter, please refrain from reporting any negative credit information to any credit reporting agencies until you respond to my requests.

I also request that you conduct your own investigation and audit of my account since its inception to "validate" the debt you claim I owe you is accurate to the penny. Please do not rely on previous servicers or originators assurances or indemnity agreements. Instead, conduct a full audit and investigation of my account.

I want to insure that I, or we, have not been the victims of predatory practices. To ensure this, I have authorized a thorough review, examination, accounting, and audit of my mortgage loan #_____ by predatory lending experts. This exam and audit will review my mortgage loan file from the date of my initial contact, application, and the origination of my loan to the present date written above.

As such, please treat this letter as a "Qualified Written Request" under the Real Estate Settlement Procedures Act, codified as Section 2605 (e) of Title 12 of the United States Code. As you know,

RESPA provides substantial penalties and fines for non-compliance or answers to my questions provided in this letter within specified time periods.

In order to conduct this examination and audit, I need to have full and immediate disclosure including copies of all pertinent information regarding my loan. The documents requested and answers to questions are needed by me, and/or my counsel, and the predatory lending experts retained to ensure:

- That my loan was originated in lawful compliance with all federal and state laws and regulations including, but not limited to RESPA, HOEPA and other laws.
- That any sale or transfer of my loan was conducted in accordance with proper laws and was a "true sale" of my note.
- That the claimed holder in due course of my promissory note and deed of trust is holding such note in compliance with State and Federal laws and is entitled to the benefits of my payments.
- That all appropriate disclosures of terms, costs, commissions, rebates, kickbacks, fees, etc. were properly disclosed to me at the inception of my loan.
- That each servicer and sub-servicer of my mortgage has serviced my mortgage in accordance with the terms of my mortgage, promissory note, and/or deed of trust.
- That each servicer and sub-servicer of my mortgage has serviced my mortgage in compliance with local, state, and federal statutes, laws, and regulations.
- That my loan has properly been credited, debited, adjusted, amortized, and charged correctly.
- That interest and principal have been properly calculated and applied to my loan.
- That my principal balance has been properly calculated and

accounted for.

- That no charges, fees, or expenses not obligated by me in any agreement have been charged, assessed to, or collected on my account.

In order to validate my debt and audit my account, I need copies of pertinent documents to be provided and answers in writing to various servicing questions to be sent to me and/or to my representative:

Representative's Name: _____

Address: _____

Phone:_____ Email:_____

For each record kept on computer or in any other electronic file or format, please provide a paper copy of "all" information in each field or record in each computer system, program, or database used by you that contains any information on my account.

As such, please send to me, at the address above, copies of the documents requested below as soon as possible. Please provide me copies of:

1. All data, information, notations, text, figures, and information contained in your mortgage servicing and accounting computer systems including, but not limited to Alltel's CPI system, any system by Alltel, or any other similar mortgage servicing software used by you, any servicers, or sub-servicer of my mortgage account from the inception of my loan to the date written above.

2. All descriptions and legends of all codes used in your mortgage

servicing and accounting system so that the examiners, auditors, and experts retained to audit and review my mortgage account may properly conduct their work.

3. All purchase and sale of mortgage agreements, sale or transfer of servicing rights or other similar agreement related to any assignment, purchase or sale of my mortgage loan or servicing rights by you, any broker, affiliate company, parent company, servicers, bank, government sponsored enterprise, sub-servicers, mortgage broker, mortgage banker or any holder of any right related to my mortgage, promissory note, and deed of trust from the inception of my loan to the present date.

4. All prospectuses related to the sale or transfer of my note, deed of trust, mortgage, and servicing rights or other similar agreement related to any assignment, purchase or sale of my mortgage loan or servicing rights by you, any broker, affiliate company, parent company, servicers, bank, government sponsored enterprise, sub-servicers, mortgage broker, mortgage banker or any holder of any right related to my mortgage, promissory note, and deed of trust from the inception of my loan to the present date.

5. All assignments, transfers, allonges, or other document evidencing a transfer, sale or assignment of my mortgage, deed of trust, promissory note or other document that secures payment by me to my obligation in this account from the inception of my loan to the present date.

6. All deeds in lieu, modifications to my mortgage, promissory note, or deed of trust from the inception of my loan to the present date.

7. The front and back of each and every cancelled check, money order, draft, debit or credit notice issued to any servicer of my account for payment of any monthly payment, other payment, escrow charge, fee, or expense on my account.

8. All escrow analyses conducted on my account from the inception of my loan until the date of this letter.

9. The front and back of each and every cancelled check, draft or debit notice issued for payment of closing costs, fees and expenses listed on my disclosure statement including, but not limited to, appraisal fees, inspection fees, title searches, title insurance fees, credit life insurance premiums, hazard insurance premiums, commissions, attorney fees, points, etc.

10. Front and back copies of all payment receipts, checks, money orders, drafts, automatic debits, and written evidence of payments made by me or by others on my account.

11. All letters, statements, and documents sent to me by your company;

12. All letters, statements, and documents sent to me by agents, attorneys, or representatives of your company.

13. All letters, statements, and documents sent to me by previous servicers, sub-servicers, or others in your loan file or in your control or possession or in the control or possession of any affiliate, parent company, agent, sub-servicer, servicer, attorney, or other representative of your company.

14. All letters, statements, and documents contained in my loan file

or imaged by you, any servicer, or sub-servicers of my mortgage from the inception of my loan to present date.

15. All electronic transfers, assignments, sales of my note, mortgage, deed of trust, or other security instrument.

16. All copies of property inspection reports, appraisals, BPOs, and reports done on my property.

17. All invoices for each charge such as inspection fees, BPOs, appraisal fees, attorney fees, insurance, taxes, assessments, or any expense that has been charged to my mortgage account from the inception of my loan to the present date.

18. All checks used to pay invoices for each charge such as inspection fees, BPOs, appraisal fees, attorney fees, insurance, taxes, assessments, or any expense that has been charged to my mortgage account from the inception of my loan to the present date.

19. All agreements, contracts, and understandings with vendors that have been paid for any charge on my account from the inception of my loan to the present date.

20. All loan servicing records, payment payoffs, payoff calculations, ARM audits, interest rate adjustments, payment records, transaction histories, loan histories, accounting records, ledgers, and documents that relate to the accounting of my loan from the inception of my loan until the present date.

21. All loan servicing "transaction" records, ledgers, registers, and similar items detailing how my loan has been serviced from the inception of my loan until the present date.

22. All loan applications, income documentation, credit reports, Good Faith Estimates, disclosures, and HUD 1 settlement statement, and other documentation which was compiled when my loan was originated.

In order to conduct the audit and review of my account, and to determine all proper amounts due, I need the following answers to questions concerning the servicing and accounting of my mortgage account from its inception to the present date. Accordingly, can you please provide me, in writing, the answers to the questions listed below.

LOAN ACCOUNTING & SERVICING SYSTEMS

1. Please identify for me each loan accounting and servicing system used by you and any sub-servicer or previous servicer from the inception of my loan to the present date.

2. For each loan accounting and servicing system identified by you and any sub-servicer or previous servicer from the inception of my loan to the present date, please provide the name and address of the company or party that designed and sold the system.

3. For each loan accounting and servicing system used by you and any sub-servicer or previous servicer from the inception of my loan to the present date, please provide the complete transaction code list for each system.

DEBITS & CREDITS

1. In a spreadsheet form or in letter form in a columnar format, please detail for me each and every credit on my account and the date such credit was posted to my account as well as the date any credit was received.

2. In a spreadsheet form or in letter form in a columnar format, please detail for me each and every debit on my account and the date such debit was posted to my account as well as the date any debit was received.

3. For each debit or credit listed, please provide me with the definition for each corresponding transaction code you utilize.

4. For each transaction code, please provide me with the master transaction code list used by you or previous servicers.

MORTGAGE & ASSIGNMENTS

1. Has each sale, transfer or assignment of my mortgage or promissory note or any other instrument I executed to secure my debt been recorded in the county property records in the county and state in which my property is located from the inception of my loan to the present date? Yes or No?

2. If no, why?

3. Have any sales, transfers or assignments of my mortgage or promissory note or any other instrument I executed to secure my debt been recorded in any electronic fashion such as Mortgage Electronic Registration System ("MERS") or other internal or external system from the inception of my loan to the present date? Yes or No?

4. If yes, please detail for me the names of each seller, purchaser, assignor, assignee or any holder in due course to any right or obligation of any note, mortgage, deed or security instrument I executed securing the obligation on my account that was not recorded in the county records where my property is located.

ATTORNEY FEES

For purposes of my questions below dealing with attorney fees, please consider the terms "attorney fees" and "legal fees" to be one in the same.

1. Have attorney fees ever been assessed to my account from the inception of my loan to the present date? Yes or No?

2. If yes, please detail each separate assessment of attorney fees to my account from the inception of my loan to the present date and the date of such assessment to my account.

3. Have attorney fees ever been charged to my account from the inception of my loan to the present date? Yes or No?

4. If yes, please detail each separate charge of attorney fees to my account from the inception of my loan to the present date and the date of such charge to my account.

5. Have attorney fees ever been collected from my account from the inception of my loan to the present date? Yes or No?

6. If yes, please detail each separate collection of attorney fees from my account from the inception of my loan to the present date and the date of such collection from my account.

7. Please provide for me the name and address of each attorney or law firm that has been paid any fees or expenses related to my account from the inception of my loan to the present date.

8. Please identify for me in writing the provision, paragraph, section, or sentence of any note, mortgage, deed of trust, or any agreement I signed authorizing the assessment or collection of attorney fees.

9. Please detail and list for me in writing each separate attorney fee assessed to my account and for which corresponding payment period or month such late fee was assessed from the inception of my loan to present date.

10. Please detail and list for me in writing each separate attorney fee collected from my account and for which corresponding payment period or month such late fee was collected from the inception of my loan to present date.

11. Please detail and list for me in writing any adjustments in attorney fees assessed, on what date such adjustment was made, and the reasons for such adjustment.

12. Please detail and list for me any adjustments in attorney fees collected, on what date such adjustments were made, and the reasons for such adjustments.

13. Has interest been charged on any attorney fee assessed or charged to my account? ___Yes or ____No?

14. Is interest allowed to be assessed or charged on attorney fees charged or assessed to my account? Yes or No?

15. How much in total attorney fees have been assessed to my account from the inception of my loan until present date? $_____

16. How much in total attorney fees have been collected on my account from the inception of my loan until present date? $_____

SUSPENSE/UNAPPLIED ACCOUNTS

For purposes of this section, please treat the term "suspense account" and "unapplied account" as one in the same.

1. Has there been any suspense or unapplied account transactions on my account from the inception of my loan until present date? Yes or No?

2. If yes, why? If no, please skip the questions in this section dealing with suspense and unapplied accounts.

3. In a spreadsheet or in letterform in a columnar format, please detail for me each and every transaction, both debits and credits, that has occurred on my account from the inception of my loan until present date.

LATE FEES

For purposes of my questions below dealing with late fees, please consider the terms "late fees" and "late charges" to be one in the same.

1. Have you reported the collection of late fees on my account as interest in any statement to me or to the IRS? Yes or No?

2. Has any previous servicer or sub-servicer of my mortgage reported the collection of late fees on my account as interest in any statement to me or to the IRS? Yes or No?

3. Do you consider the payment of late fees as liquidated damages to you for not receiving my payment on time? Yes or No?

4. Are late fees considered interest? Yes or No?

5. Please detail for me in writing what expenses and damages you incurred for any payment I made that was late.

6. Were any of these expenses or damages charged or assessed to my account in any other way? Yes or No?

7. If yes, please describe what expenses or charges were charged or assessed to my account.

8. Please describe for me in writing what expenses you or others undertook due to any payment I made that was late.

9. Please describe for me in writing what damages you or others undertook due to any payment I made that was late.

10. Please identify for me in writing the provision, paragraph, section or sentence of any note, mortgage, deed of trust or any agreement I signed authorizing the assessment or collection of late fees.

11. Please detail and list for me in writing each separate late fee assessed to my account and for which corresponding payment period or month such late fee was assessed from the inception of my loan to present date.

12. Please detail and list for me in writing each separate late fee collected from my account and for which corresponding payment period or month such late fee was collected from the inception of my loan to present date.

13. Please detail and list for me in writing any adjustments in late fees assessed, on what date such adjustment was made, and the reasons for such adjustment.

14. Please detail and list for me in writing any adjustments in late fees collected, on what date such adjustment was made, and the reasons for such adjustment.

15. Has interest been charged on any late fee assessed or charged to my account? Yes or No?

16. Is interest allowed to be assessed or charged on late fees charged or assessed to my account? Yes or No?

17. Have any late charges been assessed to my account? Yes or No?

18. If yes, how much in total late charges have been assessed to my account from the inception of my loan until present date? $_____

19. Please provide me with the exact months or payment dates you or other previous servicers of my account claim I have

been late with a payment from the inception of my loan to the present date.

20. Have late charges been collected on my account from the inception of my loan until present date? Yes or No?

21. If yes, how much in total late charges have been collected on my account from the inception of my loan until present date? $_____

PROPERTY INSPECTIONS

For purposes of this section "property inspection" and "inspection fee" refer to any inspection of my property by any source and any related fee or expense charged for such inspection.

1. Have any property inspections been conducted on my property from the inception of my loan until the present date? Yes or No?

2. If your answer is no, you can skip the rest of these questions in this section concerning property inspections.

3. If yes, please tell me the date of each property inspection conducted on my property that is the secured interest for my mortgage, deed, or note.

4. Please tell me the price charged for each property inspection.

5. Please tell me the date of each property inspection.

6. Please tell me the name and address of each company

and person who conducted each property inspection on my property.

7. Please tell me why property inspections were conducted on my property.

8. Please tell me how property inspections are beneficial to me.

9. Please tell me how property inspections are protective of my property.

10. Please explain to me your policy on property inspections.

11. Do you consider the payment of inspection fees as a cost of collection? Yes or No?

12. If yes, why?

13. Do you use property inspections to collect debts? Yes or No?

14. Have you used any portion of the property inspection process on my property to collect a debt or inform me of a debt, payment or obligation I owe? Yes or No?

15. If yes, please answer when and why?

16. Please identify for me in writing the provision, paragraph, section, or sentence of any note, mortgage, deed of trust, or any agreement I signed authorizing the assessment or collection of property inspection fees.

17. Have you labeled in any record or document sent to me a property inspection as a miscellaneous advance? Yes or No?

18. If yes, why?

19. Have you labeled in any record or document sent to me a property inspection as a legal fee or attorney fee? Yes or No?

20. If yes, why?

21. Please detail and list for me in writing each separate inspection fee assessed to my account and for which corresponding payment period or month such fee was assessed from the inception of my loan to present date.

22. Please detail and list for me in writing each separate inspection fee collected from my account and for which corresponding payment period or month such fee was collected from the inception of my loan to present date.

23. Please detail and list for me in writing any adjustments in inspection fees assessed and on what date such adjustment was made and the reasons for such adjustment.

24. Please detail and list for me in writing any adjustments in inspection fees collected, on what date such adjustment was made, and the reasons for such adjustment.

25. Has interest been charged on any inspection fees assessed or charged to my account? Yes or No?

26. If yes, when and how much was charged?

27. Is interest allowed to be assessed or charged on inspection fees charged or assessed to my account? Yes or No?

28. How much in total inspection fees have been assessed to my account from the inception of my loan until present date? $_____

29. How much in total inspection fees have been collected on my account from the inception of my loan until present date? $_____

BPO FEES

1. Have any BPOs [Broker's Price Opinions] been conducted on my property? Yes or No?

2. If yes, please tell me the date of each BPO conducted on my property that is the secured interest for my mortgage, deed, or note.

3. Please tell me the price of each BPO.

4. Please tell me who conducted each BPO.

5. Please tell me why BPOs were conducted on my property

6. Please tell me how BPOs are beneficial to me.

7. Please tell me how BPOs are protective of my property.

8. Please explain to me your policy on BPOs.

9. Have any BPO fees been assessed to my account? Yes or No?

10. If yes, how much in total BPO fees have been assessed to my account? $_____

11. Have any BPO fees been charged to my account? Yes or No?

12. If yes, how much in total BPO fees have been charged to my account? $_____

13. Please tell me specifically what clause, paragraph, and sentence in my note, mortgage, or deed of trust or any agreement I have executed allows you to assess, charge, or collect a BPO fee from me.

SERVICING RELATED QUESTIONS

For each of the following questions listed below, please provide me with a detailed explanation in writing that answers each question.

In addition, I need the following answers to questions concerning the servicing of my mortgage account from its inception to the present date. Accordingly, can you please provide me, in writing, the answers to the questions listed below:

1. Did the originator of my loan have any financing agreements or contracts with your company?

2. Did the originator of my loan have a warehouse loan agreement or contract with your company?

3. Did the originator of my loan receive any compensation, fee,

commission, payment, rebate, or other financial consideration from your company or any affiliate of your company for handling, processing, originating, or administering my loan? If yes, please describe and itemize each and every form of compensation, fee, commission, payment, rebate, or other financial consideration paid to the originator of my loan by your company or any affiliate.

4. Please identify for me where the originals of my entire loan file are currently located and how they are being stored, kept, and protected.

5. Where is the "original" promissory note I signed located? Please describe its physical location and anyone holding this note as a custodian or trustee if applicable.

6. Where is the "original" deed of trust or mortgage I signed located? Please describe its physical location and anyone holding as a custodian or trustee if applicable.

7. Since the inception of my loan, has there been any assignment of my promissory note or mortgage to any other party? If the answer is yes, please kindly identify the names and addresses of each and every individual, party, bank, trust, or entity that has received such assignment.

8. Since the inception of my loan, has there been any assignment of my deed of trust to any other party? If the answer is yes, would you kindly identify the names and addresses of each and every individual, party, bank, trust, or entity that has received such assignment.

9. Since the inception of my loan, has there been any sale or assignment of servicing rights to my mortgage loan to any other party? If the answer is yes, would you kindly identify the names and addresses of each and every individual, party, bank, trust, or entity that has received such assignment or sale.

10. Since the inception of my loan, has any sub-servicer serviced any portion of my mortgage loan? If the answer is yes, would you kindly identify the names and addresses of each and every individual, party, bank, trust or entity that has sub-serviced my mortgage loan.

11. Has my mortgage loan been made a part of any mortgage pool since the inception of my loan? If yes, please identify for me each and every loan mortgage pool that my mortgage has been a part of from the inception of my loan to the present date.

12. Has each and every assignment of my mortgage or promissory note been recorded in the county land records where the property associated with my mortgage loan is located? Yes or No?

13. Has there been any "electronic" assignment of my mortgage with MERS or any other computer mortgage registry service or computer program? If yes, please identify the name and address of each and every individual.

14. Have there been any "investors" who have participated in any mortgage-backed security, collateral mortgage obligation, or other mortgage security instrument that my mortgage loan has ever been a part of from the inception of my mortgage to the present date? If yes, please identify the name and address of each and every individual, entity, or organization.

15. Please identify for me the parties and their addresses to all sales contracts, servicing agreements, assignments, allonges, transfers, indemnification agreements, recourse agreements, and any agreement related to my loan from its inception to the current date written above.

16. Please provide me with copies of all sales contracts, servicing agreements, assignments, allonges, transfers, indemnification agreements, recourse agreements, and any agreement related to my loan from its inception to the current date written above.

Please provide me with a detailed answer to each of my questions and the documents I have requested within the required lawful time frame. Upon receipt of the documents and answers, an exam and audit will be conducted that may lead to a further document request and answers to questions under an additional QWR letter.

Copies of this Qualified Written Request, Validation of Debt, request for accounting and legal records, and Dispute of Debt letter are being sent to HUD, all relevant state and federal regulators, local predatory lending task forces, other consumer advocates, my congressman, and various class action law firms and lawyers referred to me.

It is my hope that you can answer my questions, document and validate my debt to the penny, and correct and make right any errors uncovered.

Sincerely,

Your Signature
Your Name

Co-Borrower Signature
Co-Borrower Name

Copies to:

Counseling Agency (if any)
Department of Banking in your state
U. S. Department of Housing & Urban Development
U.S. Congressperson in homeowner's district

*   *   *

LETTER E

*   *   *

REASONS FOR OBJECTION TO GARNISHMENT

Your Name
Your Address
Your City, State & Zip

**VIA CERTIFIED MAIL/RETURN RECEIPT REQUESTED/
COPY RETAINED**

Date

Lender
Address
City, State Zip

RE: Account number _____

I object to the collection of this debt amount by garnishment of my salary for the following reasons:

1. _____

2. _____

3. _____

4. _____

5. _____

6. _____

7. _____

8. _____

9. _____

10. _____

Sincerely,

Your Signature
Your Name

*   *   *

LETTER F

* * *

DOCUMENT REQUEST

Your Name
Address
City, State Zip

**VIA CERTIFIED MAIL/RETURN RECEIPT REQUESTED/
COPY RETAINED**

Date

Lender
Address
City, State Zip

RE: Loan Number: _____

I am writing to request the documentation described below in regards to the loan secured by my _____ (describe equipment or service financed). Please provide:

1. Promissory Note along with any allonges, endorsements, and assignments

2. Security Agreement

3. All loan disclosures

4. Loan application

5. Copies of any income verification documents which were obtained as part of the loan application process

6. Payment history for the life of loan

7. Breakdown of any collection costs and the basis therefore

8. Copies of all payments statements and other financial records

Please forward these documents to me at _____ _____(provide your mailing address).

Sincerely,

Your Signature
Your Name

Any Co-borrower's Signature
Any Co-borrower's Name

*   *   *

ABOUT THE AUTHOR

JORGE P. NEWBERY is a successful entrepreneur, distressed debt and real estate investor, endurance athlete, and author.

He turned around some of the country's most troubled housing complexes in amassing a portfolio of 4,000 apartments across the USA. However, a natural disaster triggered a financial collapse in which he lost everything and emerged over $26 million in debt. He never filed bankruptcy, instead developing strategies to gain leverage over his creditors and settle debts at huge discounts, or simply not pay them at all. He is a veteran of dozens of court battles, once fighting a creditor to the Missouri Court of Appeals, which found that "the entire debt was inadvertently extinguished" by sloppy legal work. The debt was over $5,800,000!

Today, Newbery helps others crushed by unaffordable debts rebuild their lives. He is founder and CEO of American Homeowner Preservation, a socially responsible hedge fund which purchases nonperforming mortgages from banks at big discounts, then shares the discounts with families to settle their mortgages at terms many borrowers find "too good to be true."

He is the author of the autobiographical *Burn Zones: Playing Life's Bad Hands* and *Debt Cleanse: How To Settle Your Unaffordable Debts For Pennies On The Dollar (And Not Pay Some At All)*. He regularly contributes to Huffington Post and other publications, plus speaks regularly on debt, investing, finance, and housing issues.

Newbery raced bicycles for a living from 1986 – 1990 as a Category 1. He competed in the 1988 Olympic Trials and was 4th in the Spenco 500, a nonstop 500-mile bike race televised on ESPN.

Find him on Twitter @JorgePNewbery

CPSIA information can be obtained
at www.ICGtesting.com
Printed in the USA
LVHW081514020420
652016LV00018B/1752